Multilingual Classrooms for Young Children in the UK

Full details of all the books in this series and of all our other publications can be found on http://www.multilingual-matters.com, or by writing to Multilingual Matters, St Nicholas House, 31-34 High Street, Bristol, BS1 2AW, UK.

Multilingual Classrooms for Young Children in the UK

Advancing Diversity through Technology and Research

Jieun Kiaer

MULTILINGUAL MATTERS
Bristol • Jackson

DOI https://doi.org/10.21832/KIAER4686
Library of Congress Cataloging in Publication Data
A catalog record for this book is available from the Library of Congress.
Names: Kiaer, Jieun, author.
Title: Multilingual Classrooms for Young Children in the UK: Advancing Diversity through Technology and Research/Jieun Kiaer.
Description: Bristol; Jackson: Multilingual Matters, [2025] | Includes bibliographical references and index. | Summary: "This book is a call to action for educators, policymakers and parents, combining practical strategies with research-based insights to support its readers in advocating for multilingual education. It will enable teachers to combine technological innovations and the linguistic resources of their communities to support and promote multilingualism"— Provided by publisher.
Identifiers: LCCN 2024029633 (print) | LCCN 2024029634 (ebook) | ISBN 9781800414686 (hardback) | ISBN 9781800414679 (paperback) | ISBN 9781800414709 (epub) | ISBN 9781800414693 (pdf)
Subjects: LCSH: Linguistic minorities—Education—Great Britain. | Multicultural education—Great Britain. | Multicultural education—Great Britain—Case studies. | Translanguaging (Linguistics)—Great Britain. | Multilingual education—Research—Great Britain. | Multicultural education—Effect of technological innovations on—Great Britain.
Classification: LCC LC3736.G6 K53 2025 (print) | LCC LC3736.G6 (ebook) | DDC 371.829/914041—dc23
LC record available at https://lccn.loc.gov/2024029633
LC ebook record available at https://lccn.loc.gov/2024029634

British Library Cataloguing in Publication Data
A catalogue entry for this book is available from the British Library.

ISBN-13: 978-1-80041-468-6 (hbk)
ISBN-13: 978-1-80041-467-9 (pbk)

Multilingual Matters
UK: St Nicholas House, 31-34 High Street, Bristol, BS1 2AW, UK.
USA: Ingram, Jackson, TN, USA.

Website: https://www.multilingual-matters.com
X: Multi_Ling_Mat
Facebook: https://www.facebook.com/multilingualmatters
Blog: https://www.channelviewpublications.wordpress.com

Copyright © 2025 Jieun Kiaer.

All rights reserved. No part of this work may be reproduced in any form or by any means without permission in writing from the publisher.

The policy of Multilingual Matters/Channel View Publications is to use papers that are natural, renewable and recyclable products, made from wood grown in sustainable forests. In the manufacturing process of our books, and to further support our policy, preference is given to printers that have FSC and PEFC Chain of Custody certification. The FSC and/or PEFC logos will appear on those books where full certification has been granted to the printer concerned.

Typeset by Deanta Global Publishing Services, Chennai, India

Contents

	Acknowledgement	vii
	Abbreviations	ix
	Introduction	1
1	The Big 'Why': Questions for UK Language Education	5
2	Challenges and Prospects in the UK's Language Education	20
3	Why Language Matters	46
4	Why Home and Community Language Matters	65
5	Psychology of Language Learning	81
6	Digital Innovation Matters	108
7	Collaboration Matters	127
8	Towards Translanguaging Pedagogy	139
	References	156
	Index	178

Acknowledgement

This book would not have been possible without the support and contributions of many individuals and organisations. I would like to extend my deepest gratitude to my colleagues, students and teachers for their unwavering support, encouragement and valuable insights throughout this journey.

I am grateful to Oxford's Policy Engagement Fellowship for supporting this project and facilitating our collaboration with the UK's Department for Education. This partnership has been instrumental in shaping the research and perspectives presented in this book.

Special thanks go to the Core University Programme for Korean Studies of the Ministry of Education of the Republic of Korea and the Korean Studies Promotion Service at the Academy of Korean Studies (AKS-2021-OLU-2250004). Their generous support has been crucial in advancing this work.

I would like to express my sincere appreciation to Amena Nebres, Taeyeon Yoon, Simon Barnes-Sadler and Hee-Seong Ahn from the Korean Education Centre, along with many who have supported the project.

Most importantly, heartfelt thanks to my children. Moving to Oxford and experiencing their school life were the inspiration behind this book. Witnessing their journey and the challenges they faced in a multilingual environment fuelled my desire to explore and write about the importance of nurturing multilingualism in young children.

Thank you Sarah and thank you Jessie.

Abbreviations

AI:	Artificial intelligence
CEFR:	Common European Framework of Reference
CLIL:	Content and language integrated learning
CPD:	Continuous professional development
CPTPP:	Comprehensive and Progressive Agreement for Trans-Pacific Partnership
EAL:	English as an additional language
EBacc:	English Baccalaureate
EDI:	Equity, diversity, and inclusion
EFL:	English as a foreign language
ELF:	English as a lingua franca
EMI:	English medium instruction
EO:	English-only
ESL:	English as a second language
ESOL:	English for speakers of other languages
FLA:	Foreign language anxiety
FLAME:	Future for languages as a medium for education
FLB:	Foreign language boredom
FLE:	Foreign language enjoyment
FLP:	Family language policy
GCSE:	General Certificate of Secondary Education
GDP:	Gross domestic product
GME:	Gaelic medium education
HHCL:	Home, Heritage and Community Languages
HL:	Home language
HMIE:	Her Majesty's Inspectorate of Education
IC:	Intercultural couple(s)
ICT:	Information and computer technology
ITT:	Initial teacher training
JACS:	Joint academic coding system
KFL:	Korean as a foreign language
L1:	First language
L2:	Second language/first additional language

L2MSS:	L2 motivational self system
L3:	Third language/second additional language
LEP:	Latin Excellence Programme
LLMs:	Large language models
LOTE:	Languages other than English
MEP:	Mandarin Excellence Programme
MFL:	Modern foreign languages
MNC:	Multinational corporation(s)
NCELP:	National Centre for Excellence for Language Pedagogy
NCTM:	National Council of Teachers of Mathematics
REUK:	Refugee Education UK
SES:	Socioeconomic status
SLA:	Second language acquisition
TA:	Teaching assistant
TAM:	Technology acceptance model
TBLL:	Task-based language learning
TOEFL:	Test of English as a Foreign Language
UCAS:	Universities and Colleges Admission Service
UCL IOE:	University College London Institute of Education
UNICEF:	United Nations Children's Fund
WoLLoW:	World of Languages and Languages of the World

Introduction

Has anyone been taught how to raise multilingual children in antenatal classes? We learn about caring for babies, but raising children to be multilingual is rarely discussed. Many parents might wish to raise their children with multiple languages but aren't sure if it's feasible, or they worry it could hinder their children's English skills. As a mother of two multilingual children, and as both a teacher and a researcher, this question has lingered in my mind for a long time. It was for this reason that I wrote this book.

Multilingual Classrooms for Young Children in the UK: Advancing Diversity through Technology and Research is written to underscore the significance of nurturing young children to become multilingual, enabling them to thrive not only in English but also in their heritage and community languages. By doing so, they can grow to contribute to the enrichment of the languages and cultures within the UK. The UK is a vivid example of diversity, with a rich tapestry of cultures, languages, and histories woven within its borders. However, despite this clear diversity, there remains a significant lack of appreciation for the benefits of multilingualism in the UK. This is particularly true for community and heritage languages that are non-Western European, even though these languages are among the main ones spoken across the country. In the increasingly interconnected world we inhabit today, diversity is not just a backdrop but a dynamic tapestry that enriches every facet of our lives.

This book is crafted for a wide-ranging audience, including educators, academics, policymakers and parents, all of whom play a crucial role in shaping the linguistic landscape of the future. The advantages of raising multilingual children extend beyond personal growth; they benefit society at large by fostering a future where individuals can coexist harmoniously with people from diverse linguistic and cultural backgrounds. A lack of multilingual and multicultural understanding often leads to societal conflicts. When communities fail to appreciate or even recognise the linguistic and cultural backgrounds of their members, misunderstandings can proliferate, potentially escalating into broader social tensions. This friction not only diminishes the sense of community but can also lead to segregation along linguistic and cultural lines, thereby weakening the social fabric.

This book emphasises that fostering multilingual abilities and multicultural awareness from a young age is crucial in preventing such conflicts. By encouraging children to learn and appreciate multiple languages and cultures, we equip them with the tools necessary for empathy and cross-cultural communication. These skills are essential in our increasingly globalised world, where interactions among people from diverse backgrounds are commonplace. Moreover, multilingual and multicultural education helps in developing a more inclusive society. It prepares individuals to engage positively with the complexities of our world, promoting social cohesion and mutual respect. When people understand and value the perspectives and traditions of others, they are less likely to feel threatened and more likely to collaborate, creating a more peaceful and integrated community.

While the general public and various stakeholders might concur with this viewpoint, there remains a significant gap in common knowledge and understanding about this subject. This book aims to bridge that gap by providing compelling evidence of the benefits of multilingual upbringing. A prevalent myth suggests that multilingual children may experience delays in learning English. However, one of the core objectives of this book is to dispel this misconception with a wealth of evidence demonstrating that, contrary to slowing down English language acquisition, mastering multiple languages can actually enhance and enrich the ways they use English. The content of this book delves in-depth into status quo literature on the topic, but my intention is to supply the readers – be they parents, educators or policymakers – with compelling reasons why languages other than English are crucial for them. This approach not only informs but also equips our audience with the knowledge to appreciate and support multilingual growth among children. What I have outlined may sound a bit abstract, so I have condensed the information into an easily digestible video: https://www.youtube.com/watch?v=qg4J0cFaGVQ&ab_channel=kiaerjieun.

Once we acknowledge the value of creating multilingual classrooms for young children, the subsequent question arises: How can we effectively nurture multilingual growth? At this juncture, readers and key stakeholders often express concerns about resources, particularly regarding the availability and affordability of qualified teachers. This represents a significant and challenging obstacle. However, the landscape of education is changing, especially with advancements in digital technology.

The use of technology in education, while not a new concept, has been revolutionised by the emergence of large language models (hereafter, LLMs), which continue to transform our classrooms worldwide. However, the extent to which this is reshaping teaching and learning greatly varies; in the UK, for instance, there is still ample room to incorporate

Figure 0.1 'Why should we teach our children languages other than English'

new technologies in our classrooms. Despite this progress, there is a notable reluctance among some stakeholders in the UK to integrate these technologies, a sentiment not widely shared globally. For example, many Asian countries have already proactively adopted artificial intelligence (hereafter, AI) technologies in language learning classrooms, showcasing a forward-thinking approach. Reflecting on a quote from Sun Tzu, 'If you know the enemy and know yourself, you need not fear the result of a hundred battles', we see the importance of understanding and mastering AI tools. AI and new technologies are not adversaries but tools that, when understood, can greatly enhance our educational practices.

It is imperative for stakeholders and readers to shift their viewpoints and proactively engage with AI and technological innovations for the benefit of our children. This change is already underway in many regions outside the UK, where embracing technology is considered essential and a vital component of modern education.

This book includes insights from a project conducted with the UK's Department for Education, which revealed that UK children are highly motivated and interested in learning languages, a trend that became more pronounced during the COVID-19 lockdown. This enthusiasm contradicts the common misconception that UK children are disinterested in language learning due to the predominance of English. Our findings suggest that language education must be culturally relevant and deeply integrated with students' lived experiences to be effective. Traditional, grammar-focused methods often fail to engage young learners because they lack real-life applicability, potentially causing a loss of interest.

To address this issue, educational strategies must evolve towards more culture-driven approaches. Stakeholders are encouraged to harness the rich cultural diversity within communities, along with advancements in AI, to innovate classroom practices. By making language learning both educational and enjoyable, this approach intends to transform the way languages are taught and embraced in educational settings.

This book aims to provide a comprehensive exploration of the multifaceted benefits and strategies associated with fostering multilingualism. We delve into the cognitive, social and cultural advantages of acquiring multiple languages, emphasising how multilingualism not only enhances cognitive flexibility and problem-solving skills but also fosters a deeper appreciation of the world's diverse cultures, promoting empathy and open-mindedness. The book offers practical strategies for educators and parents, outlining actionable steps to create nurturing environments that promote both language learning and cultural appreciation. These range from curriculum design to everyday home-based language practices, providing a roadmap for encouraging children to embrace and master new languages.

Furthermore, the book promotes collaboration across various stakeholders, highlighting the crucial role of synergy among educators, parents and policymakers. It advocates for a unified approach where all parties actively support multilingual and multicultural education, thereby enriching the educational landscape. By merging research-based insights with practical advice, the book equips individuals and institutions with the tools necessary to unlock the immense potential of multilingual and multicultural competence in children. In doing so, it aims not only enhance individual abilities but also to contribute to building a more cohesive, understanding and inclusive society.

In summary, while UK children are keen on learning new languages, there is a clear need to enhance teaching methods to make them more fun and culturally engaging, utilising the resources of diverse communities and AI to achieve this goal. This book provides practical tips in each chapter, focusing particularly on debunking the prevalent myths about language learning and multilingualism in schools, homes and across broader UK society. Additionally, the book presents a long-term vision for stakeholders. By clarifying these misconceptions and offering strategic insights, we hope to inspire a more informed and proactive approach to fostering multilingual capabilities across various educational and social settings.

1 The Big 'Why': Questions for UK Language Education

Practical tips:
- **Learn about culture through language:** Integrate cultural experiences with language learning. Use food, music or traditional crafts to introduce vocabulary and spark curiosity about different cultures.
- **Accommodate different learning styles:** Create flexible lesson plans that cater to visual, aural, kinaesthetic, verbal, logical, social and solitary learning styles. This can be achieved by incorporating a variety of teaching methods and materials to engage students with different learning preferences.
- **Make it fun:** Design lessons that incorporate games, role-playing or technology to keep students engaged.

Multilingualism: A National Asset

Lord Dearing's 2006 observation regarding the UK's untapped national asset of multilingualism still holds true in 2023 (Taylor, 2013). While the UK boasts a wealth of multilingual individuals, the dominance of the English language, often rooted in the 'English-is-enough' concept, tends to overshadow linguistic diversity. Consequently, many children end up losing their heritage languages rather than nurturing them. It is a poignant reality that even in a city as diverse as London, where over 300 languages are spoken, these languages and the rich cultures they embody struggle to thrive in the lives of its inhabitants (Greater London Authority, n.d.). In London, a city where linguistic diversity is unparalleled, the potential for cultural exchange and enrichment is vast. However, it is evident that these languages and the vibrant cultures they encapsulate often lack the opportunities they deserve to flourish within individuals and society as a whole. Paradoxically, despite being one of the world's most multilingual cities, London's remarkable linguistic diversity remains one of its lesser-celebrated aspects. Of course, this situation does not apply to London alone – it is pertinent to the bigger picture of the UK in general.

It is vital to tackle the deep-rooted social norm of 'English-is-enough', as it can lead to significant linguistic and cultural deficits, potentially causing distress at both individual and societal levels within multilingual and multicultural communities. This book underscores the importance of fostering a balanced and harmonious language teaching and learning environment, catering not only to monolingual children but also to multilingual children who are, in fact, immersed in multilingual and multicultural environments in their daily lives. For instance, consider a boy growing up in the London Borough of Tower Hamlets. While his parents primarily speak English, his friends and neighbours converse in languages like Bengali. Thus, he too experiences a multilingual upbringing.

This book aims to answer the questions that form the foundation for our discussion on creating multilingual classrooms. Before we delve into the 'how', it is crucial to address the 'why' with thoughtful consideration. Here, we present questions that lie at the core of language education:

(1) Why did enrolments in the General Certificate of Secondary Education (GCSE) French and German nearly halve between 1996 and 2021? Does this mean that British youth do not have an interest in languages anymore?
(2) Why should individuals opt to study another language, particularly in a world where English often takes precedence as the dominant language? Is foreign language learning really necessary?
(3) Why is it necessary to study another language when fluency may not be readily attainable?
(4) Why do learners tend to lean towards European languages over other widely spoken languages in the UK?
(5) Why is language learning less prevalent in socially deprived areas?

These questions will serve as our compass as we navigate the intricate landscape of multilingual education, offering a balanced and engaging perspective on these critical issues.

A Diverse and Changing Linguistic Landscape

Lord Dearing stated that the UK's multilingualism is a national asset upon which we are not yet fully capitalising (Dearing & King, 2006). Unless we change our attitude towards other languages, particularly non-European languages, we will never achieve this goal. The genesis of this project traces back to 2016 when my two daughters enroled in a small, local primary school in Oxfordshire. Although humble in size, the school was a melting pot of diverse populations and languages. I quickly learned that the students came from over 50 different language backgrounds, which was not only enlightening but also somewhat startling.

An incident that underscored the profound but perhaps overlooked complexity of this diversity involved a school visit I conducted as a director of outreach. In an effort to celebrate Asian languages, I was confronted with a startling misconception: numerous students, including those with Indian heritage, believed the singular language spoken in India was 'Indian'. This revelation, layered with shock and unexpected learning, hinted at the underlying challenges permeating multilingual classrooms in Britain, echoing the sentiments expressed by Lord Dearing. This raises critical reflections on multilingualism and its place within academic, educational and public discourses. This book explores an essential question: in a world where English serves as the lingua franca, why is there a need to advocate for linguistic diversity and the learning of other languages?

While it is widely acknowledged that multilingualism and exposure to other cultures and languages from an early age are beneficial, there is a glaring mismatch between this belief and language in practice. Crucially, those in the education sector, particularly teachers and policymakers, are unable to explain why these discrepancies exist. At present, there is a lack of much-needed evidence-based discussion properly communicated to relevant parties on the importance of other languages during a time when English is the lingua franca. As a result, we witness little to no motivation to expand one's linguistic repertoire, and instead promote the formation of a society filled with Anglophone monolinguals. As a linguist, I believe that the problems we face in the realm of language learning in the UK boil down to a failure to give strong reasons for the importance and benefits of multilingualism. Looking at the British Academy and University Council of Modern Languages' (2022) joint report, it seems that the cause of the overall decline in the number of university students studying modern languages is more than a simple case of 'British students do not care about other languages'. We should investigate *why* they do not seem to care and what we can we do about it.

Indeed, the root of the problems seems to lie in how we have implemented language education and policies. We acknowledge the value and importance of teaching English as a foreign language (hereafter, EFL) to a high standard, even giving it high priority due to the revenue it brings to the sector, but the dialogue is heavily imbalanced and other languages are marginalised. In comparing the UK 2021 census data on the main languages spoken by residents and our current language education provision (Collen, 2023; Waddington, 2022), we find a deep-rooted Eurocentrism in which Western European languages receive more attention, funding and care than non-Western European languages. Yet even then, the standard of EFL teaching in the UK remains superior, leading us to ask the following: Given the success of EFL teaching in the UK, why do we not use the same methodology for other languages? Despite our cultural and linguistic diversity, far too many languages remain disproportionately under-represented in formal public education.

We must rethink how we view and tend to the overall landscape of multilingualism in the classroom. To do this, I spotlight linguistic evidence that shows why it is good for pupils to learn other languages in a variety of domains, such as the cognitive, psychological and social benefits of multilingualism, which can nurture not just individuals but also society as a whole. However, rather than tackling questions of methodology first, I propose that solutions will arise when we better understand why we need to invest in new languages and communicate the rich research to relevant people.

Rethinking multilingualism is particularly important in a post-Brexit era. Before continuing, I want to stress that my proposal does not involve the complete replacement of Western European languages, such as French, German and Spanish, with other languages. Rather, I intend to highlight the need to improve the balance of language education provision. It is a linguistic injustice for European children to have ample opportunities to learn their home language, while the large UK Asian population, for instance, does not. Following Brexit, it is prime time for us to change our foreign language education, which has been far too Eurocentric and exclusive, reflected even in the terminology we use. While we often use the term 'international' or 'global' to describe our conferences, we may question to what extent they are truly international and global. More often than not, such international conferences betray a bias for the Global North, leaving the Global South under-represented. The use of the term 'modern foreign languages' (hereafter, MFLs) is also problematic, considering that language education provision is highly Eurocentric even though modern languages are not merely European languages. It is time we proportionately teach the languages of the population.

The advent of the LLM in 2022 has also changed the linguistic landscape. While we have been using platforms like Google Translate for several years now, the LLM incorporates more pragmatic factors and AI is now closer to human language than ever before. Indeed, AI will be with us and will continue to develop; it is a reality we cannot avoid. What this means is that we have been given an opportunity to use AI as an innovative and objective tool for language teaching and practice. A major hurdle often cited in foreign language education is a lack of resources, but we can rethink the puzzle by incorporating AI into our learning. Through AI and virtual immersion, we can make language learning more enjoyable and accessible, even reducing feelings of anxiety among students. Particularly for beginner and intermediate levels, bringing this digital element into the classroom can help younger generations become better engaged, given that a significant proportion of these generations have been using apps like Duolingo and LingoDeer to learn new languages. Indeed, the usage of technology and AI in such ways is not foreign to many of us, although they may be new to educators and teachers. We should embrace this novel possibility to its fullest extent to solve a long-standing dilemma in language education in the UK.

In addition, for new arrivals to the UK, language teaching and learning are vital in enabling their smooth integration into society. How we approach this is therefore important. The number of new arrivals is projected to increase (Hall *et al.*, 2023), and we must have the right attitude and policies to adequately cater to their languages and cultures; the last thing we should do is turn them into monolingual, monocultural English children, negatively impacting their self-esteem. Researchers, educators and policymakers should work together to create opportunities for these new arrivals to be proud of their linguistic and cultural backgrounds so that they can flourish in their given environment. This is essential and imperative to the development of UK society, allowing the assets and potential of new arrivals to shine. Multilingualism for these people means learning English while also embracing and treasuring their heritage, even enriching others' knowledge of the world and its languages.

Overall, awareness of other languages is important and enhances an individual's cultural repertoire for their own benefit as well as society's. Myths must be dispelled, and we need to convey the facts to relevant parties so that positive change can be enacted.

Reinterpreting a Drop in MFL Uptake

First, let us tackle the why – Why did enrolments in GCSE French and German nearly halve between 1996 and 2021? Turning our attention to Figure 1.1, we observe a pronounced decline: enrolments in GCSE French and German decreased by nearly half from 1996 to 2021. This data raised a pressing inquiry that prompted the foundation of this study. Is it possible that this trend mirrors a waning interest in language studies among British students? One might think that the introduction of the Eurostar in 1994, an international high-speed rail service in Western Europe connecting Belgium, France, Germany, the Netherlands and the UK to foster greater travel and cross-border interactions between the UK and France, would bolster interest. However, the exact reasons for this decline in GCSE enrolments in French and German remain elusive. It is worth emphasising that finding answers to this phenomenon is a complex endeavour, as it is shaped by multiple facets and intricacies. For instance, in Figure 1.1, we observe that enrolment in Spanish has increased. Thus, the decline in French and German may be attributed to the rise in other modern languages. However, this does not fully capture the situation. Overall, GCSE enrolments in languages have decreased significantly year by year.

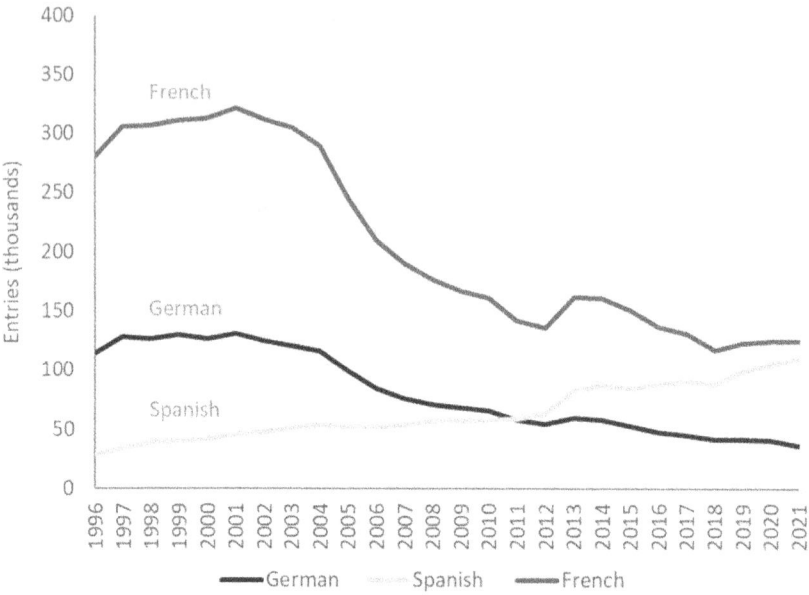

Figure 1.1 Number of pupils taking GCSEs in MFL, 1996-2021 (Gov.uk, 2022; Long & Danechi, 2022)

According to the British Academy's SHAPE Indicators initiative, the landscape of language learning in UK secondary education is shifting towards greater diversity. Languages such as Spanish, Arabic, Urdu and Chinese are witnessing increased popularity in England, Wales and Northern Ireland, especially at the GCSE level (Forsdick, 2023). Specifically, Spanish entries have surged by 11.4% since 2022, and the category Other Modern Languages – including those mentioned – has seen growth of 9.5% (British Academy SHAPE Observatory, 2023a). However, the A-levels present a more mixed picture. While overall there were fewer language entries in the last academic year compared to 2022, subjects like Arabic and Chinese experienced modest gains (The British Academy, 2023). Spanish was also shown to be the most popular A-level language in schools across England (British Council, 2023a). In Scotland, the uptake of languages fluctuates between National 5s, Highers and Advanced Highers, but the enthusiasm for Chinese languages is undeniable. Since 2022, entries for Chinese languages at the National 5s level grew by 9.8%, Highers by 9.3% and Advanced Highers by a commendable 13.3% (British Academy SHAPE Observatory, 2023b). Although the trends point towards a diversified language learning environment, there is still ample room for growth and enhancement.

While the number of GCSE language enrolments has decreased, it is difficult to interpret this as a lack of interest in languages among young people. The increased interest in learning Arabic and Chinese within the

UK can be traced back to several interconnected factors that highlight the cultural relevance and practical necessity of these languages. Firstly, the integration of Chinese and Arabic into the UK educational curriculum is a strategic move aimed at fostering cultural connectivity and preparing students for a globalised world where intercultural understanding is crucial. This initiative not only acknowledges the growing economic and political influence of China and Arab nations but also anticipates the need for future generations to navigate and contribute to complex international dynamics effectively.

Additionally, the rise in heritage learners – children from families of Chinese and Arabic descent – underscores the role of cultural preservation as a driver for learning these languages. These learners are not just acquiring a language; they are maintaining and deepening ties to their ancestral cultures, which enriches the UK's multicultural landscape and contributes to the vibrancy of these languages within the country.

Moreover, the strategic importance of Chinese and Arabic due to the political and economic ascent of their respective regions cannot be overstated. As China and the Arab countries expand their global influence, proficiency in these languages becomes invaluable, not just for cultural liaisons but also for forging robust business and diplomatic ties. In fact, a British Council report predicts that Mandarin and Arabic will be among the top five foreign languages most important for the UK post-Brexit (Campbell-Cree, 2017). In response, both government bodies and educational institutions in the UK are bolstering efforts to promote these languages, equipping the workforce with essential skills for effective engagement on international platforms. Thus, the increased interest in Chinese and Arabic in the UK reflects their increased cultural relevance, the emphasis on heritage learning, and their growing importance in global economic and political arenas.

When looking at the uptake of specific languages, we should also note the growth of Spanish learners. The data shows a significant increase in the number of UK people visiting Spain, especially from 1996 onwards (Office for National Statistics, 2017). While it is challenging to pinpoint a single reason for this surge, there appears to be a correlation with the growing interest in the Spanish language. Furthermore, the growth and popularity of apps like Duolingo – particularly during and since the COVID-19 pandemic – reveals a clear enthusiasm for language learning across the UK (Blanco, 2020). It is not that British youth have suddenly lost all desire to learn languages, but rather the methods of language learning have changed and these need to be adequately addressed. Additionally, in a 2022 YouGov poll commissioned by the British Academy (2022), 22% of respondents claimed that their interest in modern languages had grown since the pandemic. Indeed, interest in language learning is not dead – nor is it 'dying' as many articles have often falsely claimed – but is very much alive. What is more, the revival of language learning is key to a 'culturally and linguistically rich future' (Forsdick, 2023), as will be discussed more in Chapter 3.

Rethinking Fluency

I often reflect on Lord Dearing's quote and wonder how we can turn it into a reality. Recently, I had a conversation with my friend Janette, who works as a cleaner. She is originally from Paraguay but has lived in Brazil, Spain, and now the UK for the past six years. Although her English may not sound completely fluent, she possesses the ability to converse in various languages, including Spanish, Portuguese and English. My daughter has been studying Spanish for the past four years, which delighted Janette. However, their conversations have to be brief given my daughter's limited proficiency. Another friend of mine, Matt, is a hairdresser who came from Goa. He relocated to the UK a decade ago and learned English fluently during his time here. Interestingly, his grandmother is fluent in Portuguese, and he can also communicate effectively in Portuguese. He speaks with his parents daily in Konkani, the official language of Goa, and understands Marathi and Hindi fairly well. The UK is filled with people like Janette and Matt – multilingual individuals who contribute to the rich linguistic and cultural tapestry of the country. Regrettably, their languages and cultures are often overlooked and underappreciated.

Training the UK's workforce and young students to achieve fluency in these languages may prove challenging. I am not sure whether my daughters' Spanish or Mandarin can reach the level of what we can call fluency. Nevertheless, it is entirely feasible and worthwhile to support newcomers like Janette and Matt and their children in preserving their linguistic and cultural heritage. Specifically, encouraging them to maintain their spoken languages could bring communities and generations together. When we start mobilising our dormant multilingual population, I think it is practical for our children to pick up languages that they learn in school with the investment of time to reach fluency. It is possible for us to help our children pick up their heritage, home and community languages early on and invest in them. Allowing them to reach oral fluency.

Interestingly, according to the US's Foreign Service Institute (n.d.), language proficiency timelines vary based on language categories. The categories are as follows:

(1) Category I Languages (24–30 weeks, 600–750 class hours): This category comprises languages similar to English, such as Danish, Dutch, French, Italian, Norwegian, Portuguese, Romanian, Spanish and Swedish. With two to three hours of class time per week, it typically takes about four to five years to attain fluency in these languages, like Spanish or French.

(2) Category II Languages (approximately 36 weeks, 900 class hours): Languages like German, Haitian Creole, Indonesian, Malay and Swahili fall under this category. Pupils studying these languages usually require around six to seven months of study to achieve fluency.
(3) Category III Languages (approximately 44 weeks, 1100 class hours): These are considered 'hard languages' with substantial linguistic and cultural differences from English. Examples include Albanian, Armenian, Bengali, Bulgarian, Czech, Farsi, Greek, Hebrew and Hindi. Achieving fluency in these 'hard languages' typically necessitates roughly eight to nine months of study.
(4) Category IV Languages (88 weeks, 2200 class hours): 'Super-hard languages', including Arabic, Chinese (both Cantonese and Mandarin), Japanese and Korean, pose exceptionally formidable challenges for native English speakers. Mastery of super-hard languages typically demands approximately 17–18 years of study, assuming two to three hours per week of class time.

Yet, what is important to note is that the timelines outlined are for those who have never studied the languages before. In reality, a significant proportion of the US population is multilingual (Dietrich & Hernandez, 2022) and do not have to learn languages *ab initio*. In the UK context, a British Council (2021a) provisional report on the Mandarin Excellence Programme (hereafter, MEP) showed that the programme produced excellent results in terms of nurturing students to become fluent Chinese speakers, but indicated that learners require a significant amount of time, approximately eight hours a week, to achieve fluency. It is uncertain whether other GCSE language students can dedicate the same amount of effort on a weekly basis. What is important to note from this report is that one needs some commitment to learn a new language. Compared to foreign students taking up English as a second or additional language, it is difficult to expect the same level of fluency from UK children who are native English speakers. English is the current lingua franca, and a plethora of reports explaining the benefits of having this language in one's linguistic inventory have been clearly conveyed to the public (Howson, 2013). Our expectations of fluency may need to shift towards including a notion of 'casual fluency', where children are not learning languages *ab initio* to become trade negotiators in a foreign language, but rather, are picking up languages to an adequate level of oral fluency from their multilingual surroundings.

For children, if they have been exposed to and have learned community languages, this does not apply to them. This group of children can learn much quicker, with continuity, and gradually reach a certain fluency level. It is essential to acknowledge that achieving fluency in a foreign language is a challenging and time-consuming endeavour. The extensive time commitment shown above could be discouraging for both pupils and teachers alike. Therefore, focusing solely on becoming fluent can lead to discouragement and easily demotivate learners. Language acquisition is a multifaceted process that encompasses communication, cultural understanding, and the ability to engage with others in a foreign language. While fluency is undoubtedly a valuable goal, it should not be the sole objective. Encouraging a broader perspective on language learning, where these additional aspects are also recognised and valued, can make the journey more enjoyable and motivating. By doing so, language learning becomes a holistic experience, offering numerous benefits beyond fluency, and learners are more likely to remain enthusiastic and dedicated throughout their language learning journey.

One of the purposes of this book is to highlight the effects and benefits of partial fluency. There has been notable research on the benefits of learning languages, such as performance in other subjects, cognitive development and outcomes, health (such as links to delays in the onset of dementia and helping stroke recovery) and well-being, to list a few. However, there are limitations with the current data. For example, little research is based on the benefits of learning just a few hours a week or reaching a non-fluent standard, while conflicts in research exist because some studies show a positive effect whereas others show little to none, and there are also methodological issues, so findings are less robust and generalisable. We therefore require strong links with academics and experts to ensure that we have the best evidence base to advise ministers and inform policymaking. Moving forward, academics can work with policy and analyst officials in several ways to achieve this, such as by sharing the latest research in an easily digestible format, notifying upcoming publications in advance and identifying ministerial interest.

There are plenty of areas of research interest, including the following secondary domains: How can we make studying languages more appealing to young learners? How does/can language learning link to other curriculum subjects for mutual benefit? What is the impact and role of technology on language learning in schools? However, we can highlight several primary research areas of interest for future work, in particular investigating in-depth the question: Which are the most beneficial languages to teach in English mainstream schools? There may very well be a new core MFL.

Against the Western European Language Bias: Embracing Diversity

The UK prides itself on its remarkable diversity, with a substantial portion of its population originating from Asian and non-Western European backgrounds. However, a glaring oversight becomes apparent when we examine the availability of language education in schools for these communities. When delving into the UK's demographics, we encounter a truly diverse landscape. The population includes native UK and British nationals, European Union nationals, further categorised into EU14, EU8, EU2 and other EU countries, as well as non-EU nationals. Additionally, there is a noteworthy presence from the 'rest of the world', which encompasses countries like India, Poland and Pakistan, ranking among the top non-British nationalities residing in the UK. India, in particular, emerged as the most common country of origin for migrants in the UK, followed closely by Poland and Pakistan. In the year ending June 2021, these three countries collectively accounted for a significant portion of the foreign-born population, constituting 9.2%, 7.4%, and 6.2%, respectively, of the total (Roskams, 2022). While dropping from its first-place position in 2018, Poland still maintains a high representation among foreign-born citizens living in the UK, with 696,000 individuals. It has since been overtaken by India, which currently accounts for 920,000 individuals.

However, despite this rich cultural tapestry and the prevalence of Asian and non-Western European communities, a glaring gap persists in the provision of language education in schools. This gap is particularly pronounced when it comes to Asian languages and languages from non-Western European regions, which are integral to the cultural and linguistic heritage of many UK residents. The inadequate teaching of these languages not only undervalues them as 'people's languages', but also represents a missed opportunity to fully embrace the multiculturalism that defines the UK's diverse population. Addressing this educational gap and expanding language provision to include the languages of these communities may not only promote cultural diversity and inclusivity, but also demonstrate the UK's commitment to recognising the importance of these languages within its evolving demographic landscape.

The striking disparity in language provision in the UK, where Asian and non-Western European languages are often overlooked, raises important questions about the country's historical legacy and potential language discrimination. It is worth considering whether this oversight resonates with the UK's colonial past. Historically, colonial powers often imposed their own languages and cultures on colonised regions, leading to the marginalisation and suppression of native languages. In the context of the UK, which has a significant colonial history, this historical legacy might be contributing to the limited emphasis on teaching languages from former colonies and non-Western European regions.

Additionally, this language disparity can be seen as a form of language discrimination. By not adequately supporting the teaching of Asian and non-Western European languages, the UK may inadvertently perpetuate linguistic inequalities within its diverse population. This discrimination can hinder the full integration and participation of these communities in society and the job market, as language proficiency is often crucial for these aspects of life.

Addressing this issue is not only a matter of recognising the cultural and historical significance of these languages but is also a step towards rectifying past injustices and promoting social inclusion. By embracing and preserving the languages of its diverse population, the UK can move towards a more equitable and inclusive future while acknowledging its colonial history and striving to rectify the inequalities it may have caused. Unless we change our attitudes towards languages, particularly non-European languages, we will never achieve this goal of capitalising on our multilingualism (see Chapters 2 and 4 for more).

A closer look: The case of Korean

In a world where South Korea has brought K-pop and K-dramas to the forefront, the Korean language could be the next global phenomenon. Korean is currently one of the fastest-growing languages globally, thanks to the 'Korean wave' or 'K-wave' phenomenon. It is the most studied foreign language in the Philippines and enjoys popularity in countries like Thailand, Indonesia and Pakistan. Surprisingly, it has even surpassed Chinese in language learning platforms like Duolingo, and it ranks second among Asian languages, just behind Japanese (Blanco, 2022).

Korean language classes in the United States and the UK have witnessed significant growth, outstripping other languages. The South Korean government actively promotes the Korean language through its cultural exports, and Korean language courses are now part of school curricula in countries such as Laos, Myanmar and Thailand. The King Sejong Institute has established numerous learning centres globally to teach Korean.

This surge in interest is due to not only the appeal of language but also the broader cultural influence of South Korea. The Korean wave has introduced South Korean culture worldwide, especially through K-pop and K-dramas. Students are drawn to learning Korean for various reasons, from cultural interest to job opportunities. In contrast, Chinese enrolments have plateaued in the United States due to changing perceptions. Still, the growth of Korean language classes over the past decade underscores the power of cultural inspiration in language learning and the interest in languages beyond the Western European realm.

Language Learning in Low Socioeconomic Regions

While some studies suggest that there is a correlation between lower socioeconomic status (hereafter, SES) and reduced emphasis on heritage language preservation (Florit *et al.*, 2021; Zhang, 2012), it is crucial to approach this topic with nuance and recognise that there are many exceptions and individual variations. The desire to preserve heritage languages is influenced by a complex interplay of cultural, economic and/or personal factors (Alsahafi, 2022; Brown, 2011; Hur *et al.*, 2021; Park & Sarkar, 2007; Stavans & Ashkenazi, 2022).

The relationship between SES and parents' willingness or ability to support their children in learning heritage languages can be complex and is influenced by various factors. While it is not universally true that lower SES always leads to less interest in heritage language preservation (Jia, 2008; Sun *et al.*, 2023; Tovar-García & Podmazin, 2018), there are trends and reasons that can help explain this relationship. Some factors to consider include the following:

Time and resources

Parents from lower SES backgrounds may have limited time and resources due to economic constraints (Melzi *et al.*, 2022). They may need to work multiple jobs or longer hours, leaving them with less time to engage in language teaching and cultural activities with their children (Wang *et al.*, 2023).

Access to language resources

Families with higher SES often have greater access to resources such as language classes, books and cultural events (Li, 1982; Portes & Schauffler, 1994). Lower SES families may have fewer opportunities for language enrichment outside the home.

Differences in supporting children's language development

Parents from higher SES backgrounds may be able to provide better linguistic input and experiences, contributing to overall greater and faster language development in their children as compared to parents from lower SES backgrounds (Fernald *et al.*, 2013; Luo *et al.*, 2021; Romeo *et al.*, 2022; Schwab & Lew-Williams, 2016). This suggests that higher SES families may be better equipped to create a linguistic environment that promotes the learning of heritage languages.

Language prioritisation and internalised stigmas about heritage languages

In some cases, parents from lower SES backgrounds may prioritise teaching their children the dominant language (the language of the country they live in) rather then heritage languages because they perceive the former as more essential for future success and integration. This is often due to the situation in which they internalise the societal belief that a lack of proficiency in the majority language causes people to be relegated to or be considered as belonging to a lower SES, and as a result, choose to emphasise teaching their children the majority language instead of the heritage language (Appel & Muysken, 2005; Zepeda & Rodriguez, 2014).

This prioritisation can sometimes come at the expense of heritage language learning.

Cultural identity

Cultural identity plays a significant role in heritage language preservation. Parents from higher SES backgrounds may place a stronger emphasis on preserving their cultural heritage through language, while lower SES parents may have different priorities or experiences related to cultural identity (Jia, 2008; Yao, 2020).

Community support

In some communities with lower SES, there may be less access to heritage language resources and community support for language preservation efforts (Ibrahim, 2021; Perkins et al., 2013).

It is important to note that these trends can vary widely depending on individual circumstances, cultural backgrounds and personal values. Many lower SES parents are deeply committed to preserving their heritage languages and cultures (Haft et al., 2022; Mak et al., 2023; Yao, 2020), and they find creative ways to instil these values in their children. For example, some families engage in informal language learning through everyday interactions at home, cooking traditional foods, or participating in cultural events within their communities. Additionally, community organisations and schools may offer programmes to support heritage language learning, which can help bridge gaps related to SES (see Chapters 2 and 4 for more).

Towards Innovation

In this era of AI, fundamental innovations are required. In the past, learning typically involved desks, teachers and classrooms. However, the landscape is evolving rapidly. Language learning, especially for the 'AI natives', may no longer follow the traditional classroom model. AI-assisted self-study is poised to become the new norm in the future, which will be discussed in more detail in Chapter 6. By better incorporating AI into our formal language pedagogy, we would also tackle the often-cited problem of a lack of teachers and insufficient resources; the resources are already there, and we need to innovate creatively and effectively. Young children and youths in the UK are already familiar with digital learning, such as app-based learning through Duolingo and LingoDeer, and better integrating this into schools would help make language learning more engaging in this digital era. To achieve this, we must diversify our approach to language learning, considering various methods, scopes and goals. Instead of solely focusing on fluency or written language, it would be more effective to emphasise oral components, cultural aspects and intercultural awareness. Perhaps we should consider implementing a general language subject that all students must take (see Chapter 6 for more). A general language teacher could assist students in learning their home languages through collaboration with their parents and community, providing them with due recognition and guiding them towards appropriate resources and AI teachers. This approach would also encourage them to engage in cultural activities of their choice alongside members of their heritage communities. For children who do not have access to heritage language and culture learning, they could be given the option to choose languages based on their preferences and interests.

2 Challenges and Prospects in the UK's Language Education

Practical tips:
- **Reflect the community:** Advocate for curriculum diversification to include languages spoken by significant portions of the UK population.
- **Modernise pedagogy:** Explore technology-based teaching methods or gamified learning approaches to cater to students who are comfortable with AI.
- **Create positive experiences:** Focus on including experiences that will inculcate positive attitudes and emotions towards both the target and home language within the classroom setting. This can be achieved through interactive and engaging activities that make language learning enjoyable.

Defining Multilingual

In today's globalised world characterised by rapid transnational flows of people from a myriad of linguistic and cultural backgrounds, being able to communicate in more than one language is increasingly becoming the norm for most of the world's population (Singh, 2013). This is underscored by the fact that the ability to communicate across languages and cultures is progressively being perceived as an essential 21st-century skill, fuelling a demand to acquire additional languages apart from one's native tongue (ICEF Monitor, 2013). While there are no concrete numbers for the bilingual and multilingual population worldwide, it is estimated that around 50–60% of language users globally are characterised as bilinguals or multilinguals (Grosjean, 2022). However, what does it mean to be multilingual? Does it just refer to being proficient in various language skills (such as reading, listening and writing) across multiple languages, or are there finer gradations in the notion of multilingualism?

Currently, no single widely accepted definition for the notion of multilingualism and multilinguals exists. While conventions may perceive bilingualism as being able to use two languages, and multilingualism as an ability to understand more than two languages, multilingualism has, for a long time, been conflated with bilingualism in research on language acquisition. In fact, various definitions for bilingualism and multilingualism refer to the use of two or more languages by language users (Cenoz *et al.*, 2003; Grosjean, 1992; Oksaar, 1983). However, Szubko-Sitarek (2015) argues that both concepts are not the same, citing various factors that complicate the formation of a precise definition for multilinguals, such as the variety of language combinations in a multilingual's repertoire and the sociolinguistic contexts in which they acquired their languages.

Does fluency or level of proficiency of the languages in one's linguistic repertoire play a role in determining whether a person can be considered multilingual? Marini and Fabbro (2007: 50) note that, while an early definition of bilingualism by Bloomfield (1933) highlights native-like proficiency as a main criterion, this might lead to assumptions that multilinguals necessarily have 'native-like control' of all their languages. They suggest that this is unlikely, as such a strict definition would exclude language users who are not as equally proficient in their other languages as their first language. It has become generally accepted that it is very uncommon for bilinguals to have the same level of fluency across both of their languages (Ellis, 2016). This suggests that if most bilinguals are unable to achieve equal proficiency in two languages alone, it is very unlikely that the average multilingual would be able to achieve this outcome across two or more languages. As such, excluding the average multilingual based on the strict criteria of 'nativeness' would produce a definition of multilinguals that does not accurately reflect the reality of multilingual language practices. Marini and Fabbro (2007: 51) therefore advocate for a more practical definition of multilingualism that simply describes the ability to 'command and use two or more linguistic systems', without considering proficiency levels and age of acquisition as a significant part of the definition. Skutnabb-Kangas and McCarty (2008) also purport that in contemporary times, having equal levels of high proficiency across languages in one's repertoire is no longer perceived as necessary to be considered multilingual. Cenoz (2013) additionally notes that multilinguals can be balanced (equally proficient in their languages) or unbalanced (having a range of proficiency levels across their languages), which suggests that multilingualism lies on a continuum and fluency should not be a core determining factor of what a multilingual person is.

Rather than viewing proficiency in their individual languages as a defining characteristic of multilinguals, perhaps a more appropriate and inclusive way of describing multilinguals could be in terms of how they draw upon linguistic resources from their various languages concurrently in a dynamic manner to communicate, or in short, how they translanguage. In line with this view, Kennedy (2023) argues that translanguaging is intrinsic to multilinguals. Translanguaging involves shuttling between languages in one's linguistic repertoire in a systematic, intentional manner to communicate meaning that targets different contexts (Li, 2018), and does not 'simply mean the mixing of two or more separate languages' arising from a lack of proficiency in a particular language (Cho & Song, 2022: 2). Furthermore, Creese and Blackledge (2010: 556) argue that no evidence exists to show that translanguaging negatively affects the proficiency of a multilingual's individual languages. Following this perspective, the significance of proficiency in individual languages for describing the language practices of multilinguals is backgrounded, as the focus shifts towards how multilinguals simultaneously integrate different features from their various languages, regardless of fluency. These languages belong in a single, combined system where each language is not a 'separate entity' in the linguistic repertoire of multilinguals, and during communication, multilinguals are not using multiple discrete languages, but rather, using language as a unitary complex, amalgamated entity that integrates features from the languages in their repertoire (Babino & Stewart, 2020: 79). This lack of separation between languages in the language practices of multilinguals therefore renders the focus on multilinguals' fluency in discrete languages less useful for understanding how they actually communicate.

Translanguaging Competence

I proposed the concept of 'translanguaging competence' in my book titled *Multimodal Communication in Young Multilingual Children: Learning Beyond Words* (Kiaer, 2023a). Translanguaging competence intends to capture and explain young multilingual children's ability to produce languages that require different linguistic and cultural adjustments. The dynamic, flexible and innovative use of multilingual children's semiotic resources leads to language that is highly context-specific, seeking to create social harmony and a more emotionally and culturally rich form of communication in each situation. Such competence permits one to adapt their language use according to the needs of their speech partner(s) and re-create or re-assemble semiotic resources to increase efficiency and empathy within the communication. Building upon Steven Pinker's concept of 'language instinct', Li (2018) proposed that the concept of 'translanguaging instinct' can explain multilingual individuals' flexible applications of linguistic features and cues from more than two languages in their interactions. While 'translanguaging instinct' is close to the term 'translanguaging competence', I adopt the latter due to its connotation as an innate property of human language, following the conventions of Chomskyan linguistics. However, it is important to note that, though I use the term 'competence' for this reason, I assume that this competence is far from ideal monolingual speakers' ability in homogeneous environments initially proposed in the Chomskyan tradition. Rather, this competence is the knowledge that could function as (in the Chomskyan sense) competence and performance in diverse linguistic environments, which is both given and developed through linguistic experiences, social interaction and negotiation. Such competence is vital for multilingual speakers.

In particular, developing translanguaging competence is vital when the languages and cultures of a multilingual family share less common ground. For example, in my own family, Sarah, Jessie and I comfortably switch between Korean and English. However, this is not done without reason; we consider the topic, register and people with whom we are interacting. In Korean, contextual information is key. My children indeed find it difficult to make the correct pragmatic decisions when it comes to politeness in Korean – a truth that would be familiar to many other heritage language speakers. The main language that is used when I am with my children is Korean, but when my husband Ian is around, we use English too so that he is not left out. Translanguaging constitutes a lively, dynamic and thoughtful style of communication that makes fuller use of a multilingual's linguistic repertoire, including deftly switching between languages according to certain circumstances. When she was young and Jessie's English ability was not as developed, Sarah and I mediated whole family conversations to help involve Ian and Jessie in daily discourse. Jessie understood that she needed to make an effort to learn English, and even took time to practice English on her own. These are all efforts that the Kiaer family had to make to build up their translanguaging competence, and muddle through the ambiguous, unique blend of language that unites the family. The result has been that we have carved out a tailor-made method of daily discourse that works exclusively for our family and minimises any misunderstanding. Many other multilingual families could tell of a similar, although always unique, story with their own experiences of languages in the home. Translanguaging competence works symbiotically between and beyond the languages of a multilingual. It is not about being fully fluent in multiple languages, but rather it focuses on one's ability to develop abilities in the different functions served by different languages (Canagarajah, 2011).

It is, nonetheless, important to remember that the wider community also plays a crucial role in developing translanguaging competence; they gradually help to build up young children's translanguaging competence, moulding them to become translingual individuals. The more children engage in complex social interactions, the more they learn to appropriate different linguistic resources. When their given linguistic resources are limited, they can even creatively borrow resources from others, which results in more successful communication. This reminds me of a story involving my daughter, Jessie. When Jessie was eight years old, her closest friend was a Chinese–French-speaking girl called Eloise who could not speak English in the first few months. Jessie was in a French club for a few years. She knew some French words but could not speak French at a conversational level. However, two of her friends were bilinguals: Chloé was bilingual in French and English, while Penny was bilingual in Chinese and English. Jessie asked these two friends to help communicate with Eloise. Jessie's teacher used Google Translate in the classroom to talk to Eloise. Jessie communicated with Eloise mainly by using non-verbal gestures. By bringing her friends along and borrowing their languages, Jessie was able to bridge the communication gap between her and Eloise. Over time, Eloise was able to understand more English, which meant that Jessie could have a basic conversation with her in a common language. In our ever-globalising society, we cannot assume that everyone will be able to understand each other's languages without some help. Innovating methods such as those employed by Jessie are also a part of translanguaging competence that we need to live in such a linguistically diverse world.

Multilingualism for All

This book delves into the unique stories of multilingual children with complex backgrounds. These children, like Adam, who settled in the UK two years ago after being born in Afghanistan, represent a vibrant tapestry of diversity. Their lives and stories, as well as their identities, cannot be contained in English alone. Take Samir, who has Indian heritage and parents who speak both English and Urdu, which provides him with the opportunity to embrace both languages. Consider Mary, who, although born in a different country, upholds her Chinese heritage by celebrating cultural customs such as the Spring Festival, Mid-Autumn Festival, and Dragon Boat Festival. Now, let us look at Matt, who is unique in his own way. Matt's parents are English speaking, and he grows up in an environment where English is the primary language at home. However, his surroundings are different. He resides in a London borough where many of his neighbours speak Bengali. Despite living in an English-speaking household, he is exposed to linguistic and cultural diversity in his neighbourhood that enriches his life in unexpected ways. Finally, let us think of Karen. Like Matt, she has English heritage and is a monolingual herself. However, she likes anime and has started learning Japanese together with her friend as a result. As a K-pop fan too, she has started to learn Korean as well. These varied examples underscore the notion that all these children can and indeed have the potential to grow as multilingual individuals. Their lives, stories, and identities transcend the boundaries of a single language like English. It is my argument that all children in the UK, regardless of their linguistic backgrounds, have the potential to become multilingual. Drawing from the rich linguistic and cultural tapestry that surrounds them, this book explores how this diverse landscape of multilingualism can enrich the lives of children across the UK.

Refugee Children

British classrooms are increasingly multicultural; British-born children of mixed cultural heritage and refugee children alike straddle different cultural spheres and communicate through various linguistic traditions. The potential for cross-cultural communication in this situation is obvious, and this rich mix of global heritage in the classroom could be a real asset to the British education system. However, too often students' home cultures and experiences become secondary to the need to prioritise English. This is often particularly true for the children of refugee families, for whom there is an urgent need to adapt to the language and culture of the UK, while simultaneously dealing with the emotional and psychosocial consequences of being uprooted from their homes.

A large focus of this book has been on giving children of mixed cultural heritage the opportunity to value, share and celebrate their cultures and languages. However, it is important to remember that not everyone has the luxury of being able to 'celebrate' their cultural heritage and past life trajectory. Many refugees in the UK have experienced violence, family separation, and associated trauma both in their past and in the process of relocation to the UK. Having experienced such hardships, refugees are then thrust into a culture and community that may not only be vastly different from their own but may also be one that is lacking in knowledge of the refugees' cultural and linguistic background.

Being immersed in an entirely new culture and language is a challenging experience for anyone, and many take comfort in familiar cultural practices or conversations in their first language. In the context of those for whom aspects of their cultural identity are a reminder of traumatic events, such 'home comforts' may become painful reminders of past hurts. On top of this, some may also find that their culture is looked down upon, ignored, or misunderstood by British society at large. As a result, for many child refugees, the onus after their arrival in the UK is to pick up English as quickly as possible in order to be accepted into society. However, this is a great task for children who are already adapting to so many new things in their lives, particularly true for children who identify with cultural heritages that are largely under-represented in the UK.

Of course, English is a valuable and necessary skill for those growing up in the UK. According to the British Council, language classes can also constitute a helpful addition to the psychosocial support refugee children receive (Delaney, 2016). Classrooms can offer a safe space and a sense of structure, and when classes focus on dynamic and communicative styles of teaching rather than textbook learning, they can help children express their feelings. Clearly, encouraging refugee children to learn English is in their best interest.

However, despite their efforts to learn English and adapt to British life, difficulties in communicating and building friendships with other children may cause refugee children to feel excluded. Teachers who have not been trained to manage a multilingual classroom may also be frustrated by the language barrier. As a result, refugee children may feel extremely isolated from their classmates and new home. Such an educational environment puts stress on refugee children to adapt to a new language, culture and social setting while simultaneously managing the emotional and logistical consequences of their relocation. Furthermore, potential isolation from monolingual classmates may limit refugee children's access to one of the most effective forms of language learning: play.

It has been noted in various studies that learning through social communication, activities and playing with others is one of the fastest ways for children to become proficient in a language (De Wilde *et al.*, 2020; Willet, 1995). However, simply learning English from a textbook is not enough to encourage social communication with classmates from whom refugee children may already feel excluded. Therefore, while learning English is crucial, it is not a 'one-stop shop' for social inclusion and adaptation to British life and culture. Rather, successful communication with classmates and teachers that encourages social engagement is much more likely to benefit the children's language learning efforts in the long run, as well as their sense of inclusion.

In order to achieve this, instead of focusing on encouraging refugee children to seamlessly 'assimilate' to British culture and placing all the responsibility on them to catch up with their monolingual British classmates, we propose a move towards an 'integration'-orientated process that aims to celebrate cultural and linguistic differences and encourage cross-cultural and linguistic sharing. The goal of this is to pursue a process of full 'integration' whereby, rather than overlooking or downplaying differences, an individual's unique cultural and linguistic characteristics are instead valued and incorporated into the overarching norm – a process that can only strengthen the group.

In this process, rather than expecting refugee children to do all the work to catch up to their monolingual British peers, a process of mutual acculturation can take place in which monolingual students learn from their multilingual classmates and vice versa. There are several benefits to offering such an inclusive educational system. Firstly, it would help refugee children feel more welcome and supported in their new environment. Next, it would offer an opportunity for them to teach their classmates about their culture and language, and through this, they will begin to communicate and build relationships with their classmates based on mutual sharing of language and culture. This will, in turn, help refugee children to build friendships and spend time socialising with monolingual English speakers, which enables them to learn English in the most effective way and simultaenously offers an opportunity for monolingual British children to take preliminary steps towards understanding other cultures on a more global scale.

Evidence of such efforts can already be seen in some UK schools; one example is St Mary's School in Horsforth, Leeds, where students and staff have made an effort to welcome Syrian refugees by producing bilingual signs and encouraging local businesses to donate items that will help the families' new houses feel like homes (Refugee Council, 2017). Such efforts not only begin the process of facilitating social interaction between refugee children and their new peers, but can also reach beyond the children to include refugee parents in the wider school community. For example, refugee parents can help with making bilingual signs or come in to give talks about their culture and language.

The added benefit of this is that it gives refugee children and parents alike the sense of being able to contribute and share something with their new neighbours – a key step in the process of integration so that they feel more like part of the community. This would also help to dispel misunderstandings in the surrounding community about the refugees' cultures and the reasons for their relocation to the UK. For refugees, most of whom will have experienced unimaginable violence and hardships, this would be an opportunity to reflect on their experience, their past life trajectory and maintain and cherish their home language and culture by sharing it with others.

What this essentially comes down to is the difference between cultural assimilation and cultural integration. By continuing to prioritise learning English while overlooking children's home cultures and languages, we thereby put pressure on refugee children to assimilate into British culture and abandon other sources of culture and language in order to do so. However, if we place the focus on cultural integration, this would not only provide a learning opportunity for monolingual British students but would simultaneously help refugee children to create social connections through sharing their culture, and therefore adapt faster to life in the UK while maintaining and nurturing their cultural heritage and home language. The sooner this process starts, the fewer social and cultural obstacles students – both mono- and multilingual – will need to overcome, and the smoother the process will be.

What is being suggested here is a process of mutual acculturation, whereby refugee children are encouraged to maintain and share their cultural heritage and home language for the benefit of both themselves and their peers. However, this is a two-way street that requires the participation and cooperation of monolingual British students and parents, the training of teachers, and the encouragement of the education system at large.

Four Keywords: Diverse, Inclusive, Innovative, Collaborative

In the context of the UK's multilingual classrooms, four pivotal keywords emerge: diverse, inclusive, innovative and collaborative. Firstly, our classrooms should encompass more than just celebrated Western European languages. We need to include the rich tapestry of languages spoken by the diverse peoples of the UK, including languages from Eastern Europe and Asia, for instance. This approach opens up language learning opportunities not only for the socially privileged but also for a wider spectrum of students, particularly those hailing from socially deprived areas.

Inclusivity goes beyond simply accommodating individuals born into heritage language backgrounds. It also extends its arms to English monolinguals from monocultural backgrounds, affording them an equal opportunity to immerse themselves in, learn from and celebrate the wealth of diverse languages and cultures. Furthermore, inclusivity extends its reach to those born elsewhere who have recently arrived in the UK, including, for instance, refugee children.

Within the pages of this book, I present arguments and strategies on how best to facilitate the integration of these individuals into UK society. It is not just about encouraging them to become English-only speakers but also about supporting them in maintaining and flourishing in their own languages. By adopting an inclusive strategy, we contribute to strengthening the UK's national assets of multilingualism and multiculturalism.

Multilingual Babies in the UK: Are We Ready to Raise Them as Multilinguals?

In 2022, there was a noticeable increase in the number of multilingual babies in the UK. Specifically, in England and Wales, 30.3% of all live births were to mothers who were born outside the UK, showing a rise from 28.8% in 2021 (Bradford & Stevens, 2023). This increase continues the ongoing trend of a growing percentage of live births to non-UK-born mothers. Moreover, in 2022, India emerged as the most common country of birth for non-UK-born mothers, surpassing Romania, and Pakistan replaced Romania as the most common country of birth for non-UK-born fathers (Bradford & Stevens, 2023). The multicultural landscape is particularly prominent in London, where two-thirds of live births occurred to parents where either one or both parents were born outside the UK. While parents generally aspire to raise their children as multilinguals, they often lack awareness of the benefits associated with multilingualism and may feel uncertain about how to proceed. Questions may arise regarding the feasibility of this endeavour and whether it might hinder their child's language development. Yet learning new languages, including heritage languages, does not interfere with their living languages. For example, in the UK, many parents give up teaching their heritage language because they are concerned that it might hinder their children's English proficiency (Karatsareas, 2018; McCabe, 2014; Weekly, 2020). However, studies have shown that this is not the case (De Houwer, 2005; Evans *et al.*, 2016; Field, 2011; Giguere & Hoff, 2020; Hoff, 2013; Hoff *et al.*, 2018; Mieszkowska *et al.*, 2017; Rodina *et al.*, 2023).

UK Language Learning Trends

The British Academy and University Council of Modern Languages (2022) published a report in November 2022 detailing their Universities and Colleges Admissions Service's (UCAS) analysis of admissions data from 2012 to 2021 concerning undergraduate modern languages courses in the UK. Their research focused on degree programmes, but they also note the existence of non-credit-bearing language learning, which is beyond the scope of their report. Their report aimed to examine the data on a granular level to provide a nuanced picture that goes more in-depth than simply stating the general decline of modern languages at university, as is often the case in media portrayals.

Their findings showed that single-subject degree courses have declined in numbers, while combined and joint degrees have remained fairly stable, albeit also showing a general downward trend. Those studying single-language degrees or combinations of languages exhibited the highest reduction. There is a less significant decline in the uptake of degree combinations with a language. In particular, the number of students studying languages with a social science has decreased over the last 10 years, but not to the same extent as single-subject courses, and the study of a language with an arts or humanities subject had remained relatively stable until the year prior to publication, when it saw a sharp drop. The three most commonly taught European languages – French, German and Spanish – have also experienced significant decreases in acceptance, where a language is named in the title of the degree.

The Joint Academic Coding System (JACS) subject group R, 'European languages, literature and related', witnessed a total of 34,005 acceptances in the 10-year period from 2012 to 2021; this corresponds to an overall decrease of 61%. French studies, German studies and Spanish studies remain the most popular European languages but have been in steady decline since 2012. Meanwhile, other languages in group R by and large have lower numbers and show greater fluctuations in acceptances.

JACS subject group T, 'non-European languages, literature and related', had a total of 10,880 acceptances in the previous decade. While the numbers are smaller than the R group, they are spread more widely across courses. Between 2012 and 2021, there was a 14% increase in the number of acceptances to group T degree courses. The two largest courses were Chinese studies (showing a 41% decrease in the period) and Japanese studies (showing a 79% increase in the period).

Delving into individual languages, in the 2021 UCAS admission cycle, 1685 students were accepted into a course with French in the title. This number has halved over the past decade, and fewer people are applying to such courses at university. With the exception of the 2020 cycle, the acceptance rate has remained between 0.15 and 0.17 during the 10-year period.

As for Spanish, in the 2021 UCAS cycle, 1670 students were accepted into courses with Spanish in the title. This indicates a clear shift in the distribution of students across language degrees in the UK. In 2012, there were 58% more students taking French courses than Spanish courses – now the two are almost equal. The overall decrease in the acceptance of students into courses with Spanish in the title was 23% in the last decade. This is in tandem with a 25% reduction in applications to Spanish undergraduate courses. What is particularly interesting about Spanish is the fact that there has been an increase in pupils taking GCSE and A-Level Spanish within the same period. While a slight lag is expected, the general trends show that pre-university formal study of Spanish is not translated into higher education statistics, with the acceptance rate of Spanish courses also remaining fairly stable. However, the increase in acceptances from 2012 to 2015, followed by a steady decrease, reveals a pattern that broadly fits with the trends in the 18-year-old population: mild increases between 2013 and 2015, then a dip in the numbers of the demographic ending in 2020.

Acceptances into courses with German in the title has reduced by 52% since 2021, mirrored by the decrease in applications to such courses. German GCSE and A-level entries have also dropped, but not to the same extent.

Turning to Portuguese, the number of acceptances into courses with Portuguese named in the title has reduced by 52% since 2012. Portuguese peaked in popularity in 2015, but since 2015, acceptances have followed a downward trend, again reflecting the changes in the 18-year-old population. It is important to note that the overall total acceptances for Portuguese-related courses in this period is 1660. Such a notably smaller cohort size would be susceptible to bigger percentage changes per year, with the closure of one department potentially having a significant effect on the numbers.

The last European language discussed in the report is Italian, in which the number of acceptances into courses with Italian named in the title has reduced by 58% since 2012. The trend in acceptances has varied over the past 10 years, showing steady decreases from 2017 to 2021. The total number of acceptances for Italian-associated courses over this period is 3610, indicating another small cohort that would likely face the same difficulties as Portuguese.

The number of acceptances into courses with Chinese and/or Mandarin in the title has decreased by 21%. Compared to other languages discussed, the overall number of applications has remained fairly stable, although the yearly percentage changes are notably varied. It should be kept in mind that Chinese and/or Mandarin courses showed smaller aggregate numbers; in 2021, there were only 320 acceptances. These trends differ from pre-university levels of study. For instance, in Scotland, there has been a great increase in entries for Chinese languages at Highers and Advanced Highers since 2016, but for the rest of the UK, entries dropped following 2019. The statistics for Chinese/Mandarin were particularly interesting because there was an overall decline, despite the increased emphasis placed on the language in recent years, such as through the MEP and the strategic importance of this language for the UK government.

The report also briefly discussed a 'with other' category, encompassing combinations of languages not with a social science, humanities, or arts subject (such as French and maths). For this category, acceptances have increased by 99%, but this only represents an absolute increase of 130 acceptances in the 10-year period.

There is also considerable variation in language learning across different regions in the UK. The three regions showing the largest declines in acceptances into language courses over the past 10 years are the East Midlands, East of England and the West Midlands, with the bulk of these decreases taking place at pre-1992 universities. The London region displayed the greatest reduction in acceptances in absolute terms, with 310 fewer students studying language courses. While the report claims that this is not surprising, as London has more institutions and students than any other UK region, scale is crucial here; no other region had over 300 language students accepted at post-92 institutions in 2021. Meanwhile, the northwest region is an outlier as it is the only region that seems to have experienced an increase in the number of acceptances from 2012 to 2021, largely driven by an increase in students studying languages with a social science. Part of the reason for the variation in language learning may be the disappearance of language learning at post-92 institutions in some regions, in turn affecting access to language studies.

Overall, we find that the demand for single-language or combined-language courses is in decline. However, for courses in which a language is taught in combination with other disciplinary fields, the trends are more ambiguous. The broad shift may indicate the changing attitudes and motivations of students, while also being influenced by external factors. For instance, the net decline of approximately 76,000 persons in the 18-year-old population from 2012 to 2021 may also play a role in the decreasing number of students taking up a language-related degree course, although the disproportion between the two remains an area to be explored.

Factors influencing student demand from 2012 to 2021 include Brexit, COVID-19, the introduction of alternative education routes, and a changing economy. Yet, the emerging demographic increase in this population (projected to last until 2030) has the potential to mitigate some of the negative trends found in the report. Further research is required to understand the factors influencing the trends and numbers stated in the report. As a result, there is a need for policymakers and universities to be receptive to these trends; it may very well be that non-European languages should become the focus, and steps must be taken in pre-university education in order to create such a change.

Why Does the UK Fail to Teach its People's Languages?

The UK fails to teach its people's languages. The 2021 language census shows that other than English (English or Welsh in Wales), the most common languages were Polish, Romanian, Punjabi and Urdu (Waddington, 2022). In 2011, only one of the top seven main languages spoken in England and Wales (excluding English and/or Welsh) was Western European: French. The remainder were Eastern European (Polish), South Asian (Punjabi, Urdu, Bengali, Gujarati) and West Asian (Arabic) (Potter-Collins, 2013). In 2021, French dropped from seventh to 12th place. However, Portuguese and Spanish climbed to fifth and sixth place, resulting in two of the top seven languages being Western European. The top seven languages spoken in England and Wales (excluding English and/or Welsh) as of 2021 in descending order were: Polish, Romanian, Punjabi, Urdu, Portuguese, Spanish and Arabic. Romanian as a main language displayed the biggest growth, rising from 0.1% in 2011 to 0.8% of usual residents in 2021. How then are these languages and their speakers cared for and accommodated in the broader UK society? It is surely fair to call these languages the UK people's languages.

These languages are largely ignored in foreign language education. If inclusion in the GCSEs or English Baccalaureate (hereafter, EBacc) is a sign of acknowledgement as part of the UK's languages, then Urdu, Punjabi and Polish are there. But what about Romanian? Since Brexit, we have had to work beyond Europe. Yet, this is not reflected in our language attitudes. Language matters, yet the languages that are offered are mostly Western European. The world is moving forward, but our thoughts are still Eurocentric. Asian languages are offered in some UK schools, but still in a very limited way. According to a recent British Council report, pupils from socially deprived areas have fewer opportunities to learn a language (Tinsley & Doležal, 2018) – a result that is not surprising. A taxi driver told me how frustrated he is in not being able to teach his daughter Urdu. Urdu is offered at the GCSEs, but not every school can offer it. In the recent House of Commons report on language teaching in England's schools, the languages mentioned above, the UK people's languages, are labelled as 'less widely spoken' languages (Long & Danechi, 2022: 23). My question here is, on what basis are these considered less widely spoken? These are the UK people's languages. But, of course, there is a resource problem: we cannot find the teachers. However, we may be able to find a solution to this problem through AI in the near future. The real problem is not about teachers or resources but our deep-rooted, Eurocentric attitudes. We need to diversify our language repertoires and innovate teaching methods to change our language attitudes to become more inclusive.

Policy and Curriculum

The holistic and multidimensional approach matters, particularly in studying young Asian multilingual children who grow up in the English-speaking world, as the languages and cultures they engage in are very different from each other. Although the young Asian population and Asian-English families are growing in the English-speaking world, to this day, research on multilingual children and their family languages remains predominantly Eurocentric. According to a report published by the UK's Department for Education, more than one in five children now have a mother tongue other than English, and this figure has risen steadily over the past few years (Gov.uk, 2023a). Some of the most commonly spoken languages in the UK other than English include Polish, Romanian, Punjabi, Urdu, Portuguese, Spanish, Bengali, Gujarati, French and Italian (Waddington, 2022). Notably, out of the top 10 most spoken languages in the UK, half are Asian languages, and yet there has been very little linguistic study of non-European and non-American multilingual households. In the UK, as is the case for many Anglophone countries, why is a 'modern language' taken to mean a 'European language' – a problematic assumption I have explored in an article written after I attended a Westminster Education Forum in 2017 (Kiaer, 2017). While the forum was dedicated to 'The Future of Modern Foreign Languages in Higher Education', the focus was staunchly on French, Italian and Spanish despite the diverse multilingual reality of the UK spanning more than just European languages.

The situation is similar in other English-speaking countries. According to Canada's 2021 census results published by Statistics Canada (2022), there has been an increase from 9.7% in 2000 to 12.7% in 2021 in the number of people who primarily speak another language at home other than English and French, in particular, languages from South Asia, East Asia, Southeast Asia and Central Asia. Among the top 12 languages spoken at home, the majority (nine) are Asian languages: Mandarin, Punjabi, Cantonese, Arabic, Tagalog, Urdu, Korean, Iranian Persian and Vietnamese. In the case of Australia, in the latest 2021 census, it was reported that the top five languages spoken at home in Australia, other than English, are Mandarin, Arabic, Vietnamese, Cantonese and Punjabi, all of which are Asian languages (Australian Bureau of Statistics, 2022). As for the United States, survey data on home language was collected by the American Community Survey (a subsidiary of the US Census Bureau) from 2009 to 2013, and out of the top 20 home languages (excluding English and Spanish due to the relatively large number of speakers), 12 are Asian, namely Chinese, Tagalog, Vietnamese, Korean, Arabic, Hindi, Cantonese, Japanese, Urdu, Persian, Gujarati and Bengali (United States Census Bureau, 2015).

On paper, the British government holds language learning in high esteem. The Ofsted (2021) website asserts, 'Languages are an integral part of the curriculum. Learning a language is "a liberation from insularity and provides an opening to other cultures". It helps to equip pupils with the knowledge and cultural capital they need to succeed in life. It encourages pupils to appreciate and celebrate difference'. The previous Conservative government set a goal of getting 75% of students to take a language GCSE by 2022 and 90% by 2025 (Department for Education, 2019). Thus, on paper, it seems that languages should be thriving. Yet, reality shows that this is far from the case. In 2004, taking a language at the GCSEs was no longer mandatory, and this has led to a rapid decline in the uptake of languages. Uptake at all levels almost halved within a decade, with GCSE entries falling from 76% in 2002 to 40% in 2011 (Tinsley & Doležal, 2018). In 1996, 40,000 students took a language at the A-levels, while only 27,000 did so in 2005 (Collen, 2020). The number of undergraduates studying a language fell from 160,000 in 2003 to 75,145 in 2019 (Muradás-Taylor, 2023). Therefore, the government's supposed support for languages has far from materialised in reality.

The current national curriculum is structured so that there is no mandatory language learning during Years 1 and 2 (ages 5–7). Years 3–6 must include the study of an ancient or modern language Years 7–9 make the study of a modern language compulsory, and Years 10–11 have no language requirement. The most troubling part of this structure is that there is no compulsory language learning between ages 5 and 7. All linguists, whether in the theoretical or applied fields, would heartily agree that the earlier a child is exposed to a language, the better. I am not suggesting that five-year-olds be taught other writing systems and grammars rigidly at such a young age, but rather, I am highlighting the importance of early exposure to and learning of a range of cultures and languages.

Furthermore, in theory, pupils aged 14 have the option to select a GCSE in the following languages: Ancient Greek, Arabic, Bengali, Biblical Hebrew, Chinese, French, German, Greek, Gujarati, Italian, Japanese, Latin, Modern Hebrew, Punjabi, Persian, Polish, Portuguese, Russian, Spanish, Turkish and Urdu. However, very few schools offer more than French, German and Spanish as regular classes. This is due to several reasons, such as lack of teachers, funding and uptake. Notably, such deficiencies do not affect all schools equally. In fact, over a third of state schools in England do not teach languages after Year 8, as they reduce Key Stage 3 to two years and spend three years on the GCSEs in a bid to rank well in national league tables. Notably, these schools tend to be located in the North of England and have a higher proportion of students who are eligible for free school meals, suggesting that this affects students from comparatively underprivileged backgrounds (Tinsley & Doležal, 2018). State schools receive far less funding, and therefore they require a certain number of students to take each class for them to run at the GCSEs and A-levels. Such quotas often mean that the few pupils who do want to study languages are unable to do so. In private schools, however, the story is different. Private schools can afford to fund classes for just a few students. Consequently, private school students make up a disproportionately high number of applicants to undergraduate language courses (Lanvers et al., 2018).

The EBacc was introduced in 2011 by the coalition government. To 'achieve' the EBacc, a student must achieve A* to C grades in English, mathematics, two sciences, a language, and history or geography. Rather than an award that a student can receive, the EBacc is a measure by which Ofsted assesses the academic attainment of secondary schools. The Department for Education (2019) describes the purpose of the EBacc as 'keep[ing] young people's options open for further study and future careers'. The EBacc is therefore a performance measure intended to promote the study of certain subjects at the GCSEs, including languages, with the goal of 90% of pupils studying the EBacc combination of subjects by 2025. However, languages are the only subject area preventing this goal from being met. Currently, there are only 21 languages in which there is a GCSE, including Ancient Greek, Arabic, Chinese, French, German and Spanish. The government's self-proclaimed aim is that 75% of pupils would study the EBacc at the GCSE level by 2022, and 90% by 2025. This target was staggeringly missed in 2022, with only 38.7% of pupils taking the required EBacc subjects (Gov.uk, 2023b).

The low EBacc figures are, in part, due to a lower interest in languages. To combat this, the government has tried to put measures in place. The MFL Hub programme began in 2018, managed by the National Centre for Excellence for Language Pedagogy (hereafter, NCELP) based at the University of York. During the first three years of delivery, the NCELP provided support to 36 partner schools via 9 lead schools with the aim of increasing the number of pupils opting to take a language GCSE by improving language teaching at Key Stages 3 and 4 in these schools (Marsden et al., 2023). In the fourth year of the contract, the NCELP delivered free continuous professional development (CPD) courses to language teachers nationally, prioritising curriculum design and pedagogy as well as support in implementing the revised French, German and Spanish GCSEs. The Department for Education agreed to a £0.3 million extension to the NCELP's contract, extending it from 2 December 2022 to 2 March 2023. The department recently announced a new contract for a national network of language hubs to be delivered by the University College London Institute of Education (hereafter, UCL IOE) (University College London, 2023). The contract commenced in March 2023 for initial implementation in schools from September 2023. Whether this will be effective remains to be seen.

Indeed, there are various programmes led by the department to improve the language learning landscape in England, such as the MEP and the Latin Excellence Programme (LEP). The £16.4 million MEP, delivered by the UCL IOE in partnership with the British Council, is the department's flagship Mandarin learning programme for pupils in state schools in England, with the aim of training fluent Mandarin speakers to meet the future economic and business needs of the country. Almost 10,000 pupils from 79 schools have benefited from this programme since it started in 2016 (British Council, n.d.). The programme is set to expand to 100 schools by September 2024 (British Council, n.d.). The LEP, delivered by Future Academics, is based on the successful MEP model and aims to increase uptake and attainment in GCSE Latin at state schools in England. This programme is one step closer towards reducing inequality in the provision of Latin between independent and/or selective schools based in the southeast and schools elsewhere in the country. Currently, over 2000 pupils from 18 schools are participating in this programme, and this is expected to increase to 40 schools by September 2023 (Bryant, 2021). In future years, pupils will also have the opportunity to take part in study trips to UK sites, such as Hadrian's Wall, and international locations including Rome.

No Fun, Feeling Disconnected

According to the 2015 Living Languages Report, one of the main reasons that puts learners off language learning is that language learning is perceived to be difficult and disconnected from 'real life' (The Guardian, 2015). Many feel that they are rehearsing the language rather than actually using it to carry out authentic real-world actions with a tangible end product. One solution to this problem is task-based language learning (hereafter, TBLL), a well-established approach that prompts students to achieve a goal or complete a task (Skehan, 1998, 2003). There is a clear psycholinguistic basis for adopting this approach in language teaching and extensive empirical support for its success (Ellis, 2003; González-Lloret, 2003; Smith, 2009). Meanwhile, content and language integrated learning (hereafter, CLIL) has become the umbrella term describing both learning another (content) subject such as physics or geography through the medium of a foreign language and learning a foreign language by studying a content-based subject. Language learning among the youth is still a problem – one that goes beyond the borders of Britain and affects young people worldwide. This is because AI natives have arrived, and old pedagogies are no longer applicable to them. CLIL and TBLL should be better incorporated into language education as part of innovating the system, such as through gamification, as they can help make the learning experience both fun and relevant.

What is more, the traditional image of students hunched over exam papers, scribbling away, may soon become a thing of the past. England's largest exam board, AQA, has announced plans to introduce digital testing for some GCSE subjects starting in 2026, with the possibility of expanding to other subjects, including English, by 2030 (Addley, 2023). This shift towards digital exams reflects the evolving role of technology in education and underscores the need for a re-evaluation of our educational methods. Writing and typing are undergoing significant changes, prompting us to rethink how we approach education in the digital age. Academics have argued that modern language teaching is 'under threat from tough exams' not only on the level of practical implementation, but also on the level of content (Bawden, 2019). How we formally assess languages also needs innovation to avoid putting off students from picking a language that could benefit them and society at large in the long term. It is not that desire has decreased; it is a matter of addressing and solving the problems in our methods of teaching and assessing languages.

The Continuity Problem

Often, UK school children are taught a second language but feel that they will never be able to speak the language at a useful level. The MEP is unique in that it has a clear commitment and goal, but other types of formalised language learning have problems in delivery. I once interviewed a girl called Rose in Year 7 who studied French at the French club once a week during her primary school years. However, when she went to secondary school, she started learning from scratch, as if she had no background in French at all. Rose's story is not uncommon among young people in the UK. Transitioning from one key stage to another often means that language learning constantly restarts from level zero. The National Curriculum for Languages, spanning Key Stages 1–3, provides a well-structured approach to language education, with specific objectives tailored to each age group, from ages 5 to 14. Theoretically, this curriculum was designed to foster curiosity, deepen students' understanding of the world, and promote the learning of foreign languages as a means of embracing different cultures. It outlines a progressive development of language skills, from understanding and responding to spoken and written language to confident speaking, fluent writing and an appreciation of literature in the studied language.

Key Stage 1 (ages 5–7):

At Key Stage 1, the curriculum aimed to introduce young students, typically aged 5–7, to language learning. The objectives included enabling students to understand and respond to spoken and written language, speak with confidence, write for different purposes and appreciate a range of writing in the studied language. While the plan was well set, the transition to Key Stage 2 often lacked continuity, leaving students ill-prepared for the challenges ahead.

Key Stage 2 (ages 7–11):

Moving on to Key Stage 2, which covers ages 7–11, the curriculum was intended to build upon the foundation laid down in Key Stage 1. However, Ofsted's (2021) report has raised concerns about the effectiveness of this transition. Language teaching encompassed both modern and ancient foreign languages, with an emphasis on practical communication for modern languages. Despite the well-intentioned plan, many students felt a lack of continuity between Key Stages 1 and 2, which made language learning less effective.

Key Stage 3 (ages 11–14):

In Key Stage 3, typically covering ages 11–14, the curriculum aims to further deepen students' language learning experiences. However, Ofsted's report indicated that students often perceived a disconnect between Key Stages 2 and 3. The objectives included ensuring that students understood and responded to spoken and written language, spoke confidently, wrote effectively, and appreciated literature in the studied language. Yet, the issues with continuity and delivery raised by Ofsted have made it challenging for students to transition smoothly into Key Stage 3 language learning.

While the National Curriculum for Languages outlined a well-designed plan, the effectiveness of this curriculum has been called into question, as indicated by Ofsted's (2021) recent report, which highlights a decline in language learning and critical continuity issues between Key Stages 2 and 3. Despite the well-intentioned plan set out for Key Stages 1–3, it appears that the actual delivery of language education may not have achieved its intended goals. In addition, according to a 2023 British Council report on the language trends of England, primary teachers stated that the constraints of time and lesson length inhibit pupil progress in language learning (Collen, 2023). The report also highlights that, as was the case in 2022, communication, collaboration and continuity remain issues that require attention in the transition from Key Stage 2 to Key Stage 3. It is clear then that continuity challenges have made it difficult for students to fully benefit from the curriculum's intentions, highlighting the need for a closer examination of language learning approaches within the education system.

2021 Language Landscape More Diverse than Ever

The UK 2021 Census was published on 29 November 2022 by the Office for National Statistics. Every 10 years, a census is carried out to provide estimates of the characteristics of all households and people in England and Wales. The most recent census data from England and Wales in 2021 showed a response rate of 97% of the usual resident population.

The data revealed that 91.1% of usual residents (52.6 million), aged three years and over, had English (English or Welsh in Wales) as their main language (Waddington, 2022). This was a decrease of 1.2% from 2011 (Potter-Collins, 2013). However, the results are limited in how accurate a picture they provide of the English-speaking population in Wales, as residents in Wales were asked if their main language was one other than English or Welsh. This means that we cannot determine how many residents in Wales consider Welsh as their main language. London was the region with the lowest percentage of people (78.4%, or 6.7 million) who claimed English to be their main language.

Of the 5.1 million people who did not report English (English or Welsh in Wales) as their main language, 17.1% said they could not speak English well, and 3.1% said they could not speak English at all. This data was gathered with the help of interpretation services and translation leaflets for households that did not have English as a main language.

In addition, for the first time, information was also collected on whether household members have the same or different main languages. Out of 24.8 million households across England and Wales in 2021, 69.8% were households of more than one person and, of these households, 6% had any combination of multiple main languages within the household.

The census data shows that, while English (English or Welsh in Wales) remains the dominant language in England and Wales as of 2021, the population is highly multicultural and multilingual. The capital and cosmopolitan hub of England, London, is a prime example of such linguistic diversity, with 21.6% of its residents not claiming English as their main language. According to the Office for National Statistics (n.d.), in places like Newham, a borough of London, over 34% of individuals and 44% of households do not have English as their main language. Indeed, non-Western European languages are spoken in households more so than Western European languages, continuing the general trend from 2011 to 2021. In fact, the problem still persists even after 20 years, as we examine Baker and Eversley's (2000) book titled *Multilingual Capital: The Languages of London's School Children and their Relevance to Economic, Social and Educational Policies*. Such statistics highlight a problematic disparity between how we perceive and treat non-Western European languages despite their clear prevalence. Not encouraging these people to speak their languages could create significant social problems.

Diversification is the Key

Compared to Western European languages, such as French, German and Spanish, non-Western European languages like Polish, Punjabi and Arabic are far less celebrated, particularly in formal public education contexts. Even though census data clearly reveals a greater population of residents in England and Wales who do not use Western European languages, their linguistic needs are not adequately met at a governmental or institutional level; many of these languages do not have a GCSE available and many are not even taught in schools. Rather, preference is still given to languages like French, German and Spanish. Indeed, such failure to meet the needs of those who do not speak a Western European language may be due to insufficient funding and poor policies. Students have commented on their disinterest in languages other than English, noting reasons such as how studying another language has little connection to real life and difficulties in finding and maintaining motivation to learn a new language (The Guardian, 2015).

Moving forward, researchers and policymakers should re-evaluate the ways in which non-European languages are viewed and treated at a societal level. English is the current lingua franca and, as such, it is undeniably useful for individuals to be proficient in English. We must work towards striking a proper balance between learning and maintaining English while continuing to celebrate our diverse population's home languages – many of which are not Western European. It is also worth considering the impacts of Brexit, which took place shortly before the 2021 census. Given that the UK is no longer in the EU, perhaps we need to seriously reconsider if, and in what ways, this will impact our language learning situations, particularly in formal contexts.

In the UK, there is a significant increase in diversity, with various cultures and languages enriching the nation's social fabric. However, despite this growing diversity, a concerning issue remains. The languages spoken by a majority of people in the UK continue to face marginalisation and are often overshadowed by dominant languages. One way in which this clearly manifests is in how the people's languages are not or are hardly taught. This marginalisation can lead to linguistic and cultural inequalities, where some languages and communities do not receive the recognition and support that they deserve, hindering their ability to thrive and contribute to the rich tapestry of the country. Diversifying is therefore the key because the languages of relevance and interest to a nation will always change. As more and more hybrid or unfamiliar language varieties arrive, we will be driven to embrace them and their speakers in order to create a welcoming environment that allows their speakers to thrive.

Stigma

At the school gate, one can see groups of parents and guardians huddled together in their own circles. For example, you are likely to find British parents talking among themselves, while South Asian mothers are together on the side. It is usually the case that British society considers English as an additional language (hereafter, EAL) children to be 'problem cases' that need to be 'solved'. However, a lack of fluency in English is not the source of the problem; English will be picked up through daily life. The real issue lies in a lack of proper appreciation for the linguistic and cultural roots of these children. In fact, English monolingual children can also be considered a problem in some regards. English monolingualism creates a language deficit problem. There are many reasons why English monolingual children should learn another language: for example, by remaining monolingual, they may lose out on opportunities to flourish on the global stage due to both linguistic and cultural communication barriers. In addition, English monolingualism may make children somewhat narrow-minded, as knowledge of other languages often goes hand in hand with knowledge of other cultures. This may mean that they are less likely to understand and connect with people from different backgrounds. Just as EAL children require support to adapt to English-dominant societies, English monolingual children also need help to understand our increasingly diverse, multicultural society.

There are numerous ways in which acquiring another language can be beneficial for English-only (EO) children. Whether students wish to stay in the UK or travel and work abroad, they will certainly come into contact with people of different cultural and linguistic heritages in the future. Therefore, even if monolingual students do not learn other languages to any significant degree of fluency, it is important that they learn the skill of cross-cultural communication and acquire an openness towards and acceptance of peers with different linguistic and cultural backgrounds for future studies, job prospects and to connect with the increasingly multicultural British society.

It is clear, therefore, that knowledge of other languages and cultures and related skills can only be beneficial, not only in creating greater social cohesion in the classroom and broader British society, but also in maximising one's future opportunities in a workforce that increasingly requires a globalised mindset. While London mayor Sadiq Khan made a valiant statement claiming that 'London is open to all people and all communities—we do not just tolerate each other's differences, we respect and embrace them' (Greater London Authority, 2016), this attitude of inclusivity, integration and celebration of diversity, while admirable, is still missing from the primary educational aim of rapid assimilation amid a widely held misconception of a bilingual 'deficit'.

'English-is-Enough' can Cause Deprivation

Quietly endorsing the 'English-is-enough' approach by not fostering children's growth in other languages during early childhood can inadvertently deprive young children of opportunities to flourish in languages other than English. This linguistic exclusivity may result in unintended consequences, such as fostering a sense of pride and limiting their understanding of the broader world. The 'English-is-enough' mentality was echoed in David Cameron's 2016 controversial policy on English language skills. Cameron suggested that a lack of English proficiency can potentially lead to extremism (Mason & Sherwood, 2016). Of course, English is important, but his words prioritised English and reinforced stigmatised perceptions of the languages spoken in Muslim communities. While young children may grow up and live primarily in an English-speaking environment, during the initial stages of their multilingual journey, their languages other than English also require nurturing. They should feel pride in these languages because, in doing so, they, their peers and their community can collectively build a more inclusive and diverse future. When children are confined to using only English and are not encouraged to develop proficiency in other languages, it can impede their ability to thrive in a diverse and interconnected global community. This exclusivity can foster a sense of pride, where children might believe that English alone is sufficient and that there is no need to learn or appreciate other languages. Additionally, this linguistic isolation can contribute to a lack of understanding and empathy towards individuals from different linguistic and cultural backgrounds, hindering effective cross-cultural communication and exchange.

Across the UK, we face a constant challenge to promote language learning. This is the case not only for second language learners but also for heritage language learners who are raised in a home where a language other than English is used and have some degree of bilingualism in the heritage language and English (Valdés, 2000). The sociolinguistic context of heritage languages means that they often have a low status in the community compared with the dominant language (which in the UK is English). They can even be perceived as a problem rather than a shared resource to be valued and utilised, resulting in language loss among younger generations.

Multilingual Injustice?

The British Council's 2021 report on language learning-related motivation and influences at Year 9 reveals important insights for future research (British Council, 2021b). It indicates that students across various socioeconomic backgrounds generally hold positive attitudes towards language learning. However, the report highlights a noteworthy trend: parents in higher socioeconomic groups (ABC1) are more inclined to encourage their children to learn a modern foreign language, suggesting a potential link between SES and language learning motivation. Furthermore, the United Nations' Declaration on the Rights of Persons Belonging to National or Ethnic, Religious, and Linguistic Minorities, Article 2, states that individuals who are part of national or ethnic, religious and linguistic minorities – referred to as persons belonging to minorities – have the fundamental right to embrace and express their own culture, practice their chosen religion, and communicate in their native language, both privately and publicly, without any hindrance or discrimination (Bielefeldt & Wiener, 2023). This underscores the importance of upholding language as a human right and emphasises the significant reasons for establishing and maintaining multilingual classrooms.

Gen Z and Alpha's Language Learning Journey: Learning Alone with AI

The often-mentioned challenge of the lack of language teachers remains significant; it is a recurring issue when we discuss the problems plaguing language education. This challenge is multifaceted, with two primary components that continually hamper the educational landscape: the scarcity of teachers and insufficient funding to support them. These issues are intertwined in a complex and sometimes vicious cycle that poses a substantial hurdle, and finding easy solutions proves to be a formidable task. The shortage of qualified language teachers results in understaffed classrooms and increased student-to-teacher ratios. This not only affects the quality of education but also places a heavier burden on existing educators, making it challenging for them to provide individualised attention and support to each student. Moreover, the lack of teachers can lead to the discontinuation of language programmes or the elimination of certain languages from the curriculum, further limiting students' options and access to language education.

However, it is important to recognise that Generation Z and Alpha – the primary demographic discussed in this book who are born as AI natives – are now taking charge of their language learning independently online. More is discussed in Chapter 6, specifically regarding innovation matters. When we delve into the topic of language teaching, it is worth noting that the landscape of language learning methods has undergone substantial changes. Generation Z and Alpha learners primarily engage in independent language study using internet resources and digital tools. AI in this context is a double-edged sword, presenting high risks and having the potential to serve as valuable educational tools when utilised effectively. While human teachers remain essential, AI-driven teaching can facilitate more diversified and individualised language learning experiences. Psychologically, traditional human teachers sometimes contribute to language anxiety in the classroom. In contrast, interaction with AI, especially among Generation Z and Alpha learners, tends to promote emotional stability, reduce anxiety and enhance overall enjoyment in the language learning process.

AI Natives and Their Literacy

'AI natives' are individuals who are born into a world where AI technologies are seamlessly integrated into everyday life, a term I introduced in *Conversing in the Metaverse* (Kiaer, 2024). They grow up with AI, becoming comfortable and adept at working with AI systems. AI natives heavily rely on AI as their primary source for seeking and accessing information, finding convenience in its quick and easy retrieval. Furthermore, they thrive on instant gratification and rewards facilitated by AI technologies. When AI natives learn English and other languages using the less interactive traditional method alone, they suffer from foreign language learning boredom. While AI natives may have an innate familiarity with AI, AI literacy education further enhances their understanding of AI concepts, ethics, and critical thinking skills specific to AI applications. These AI natives engage with AI technologies thoughtfully and analytically, actively considering and addressing the ethical implications associated with their use.

Methodological Innovation is Necessary

A significant contemporary obstacle arises with the advent of AI-native approaches, as it becomes increasingly challenging to apply and repurpose conventional methodological insights. The methods we previously employed, designed for a different technological era before the AI boom, may not seamlessly translate into the realm of 'digital' learning. Educational effectiveness can vary significantly from one platform to another, and even within the same platform, the specific product version and features can have a substantial impact. This complexity stands out as one of the major hurdles in effectively integrating research findings into classroom practices.

A Two-Track System

A two-track system, in particular, would help heritage learners and new arrivals maintain their languages, both old and new, while affirming their sense of identity. To achieve this, we must diversify the curriculum to include a wider range of languages. By gamifying language learning, we can also make it more fun – an aspect that is all the more important given that approximately one-third of the world's population identifies as gamers. By incorporating AI into language education, we would also be able to cater to AI natives. Adequate communication and collaboration between students, teachers, parents and those involved in developing language pedagogies would further reinforce the positives of language learning, making information readily accessible. Finally, such a system could help reduce inequality by offering more opportunities to learn new languages. There is a growing divide between the rich and poor in school language learning (British Council, 2018), but through a two-track system incorporating more gamified digital resources and AI-integrated resources, we can help tackle the imbalance in access to language education (see Chapter 6 for more). According to the Pew Research Centre (2015), the term 'generation' is used to classify people into age cohorts according to the specified 15- to 20-year period during which they were born. Of the recent generations, Baby Boomers are the most senior, having been born between 1946 and 1964, followed by Generation X, born between 1965 and 1980 and, subsequently, Generation Z, born between 1997 and 2012, is the most contemporary group after the Millennials who were born between 1981 and 1996 (Hecht, 2023). Just as each generation's demographics change, so should our approach to language teaching and learning. As AI natives make up the younger populations, we should incorporate AI into our language education in more innovative ways. From my own experience learning languages, I recall using cassette tapes, phrase books and dictionaries before moving on to MP3 players, but now all we need is a smartphone to download an app and dictionary, and we are ready to go.

3 Why Language Matters

Practical tips:
- **Keep an eye out for anxiety:** Train teachers to identify signs of anxiety during language learning. Offer calming strategies like deep breathing or journaling.
- **Increase foreign language enjoyment** (FLE): Frame language tasks as challenges or problem-solving exercises to make them more engaging and reduce anxiety.
- **Refrain from tying self-esteem to success:** Avoid making students think that learning a new language is the only way to have a successful career or life in the future. Instead, emphasise the value of language learning as a tool for personal growth and cultural understanding.

Language that Goes to Your Heart

Nelson Mandela (1995: 630), a native Xhosa speaker and the iconic anti-apartheid leader who later became South Africa's first black president, once famously said, 'If you talk to a man in a language he understands, that goes to his head. If you talk to him in his own language, that goes to his heart'. This powerful statement underscored the profound importance of language during his presidency. South Africa is home to a multitude of languages – there are 11 official languages in total – rendering its people inherently multilingual. However, this linguistic richness can come with challenges if not properly acknowledged and celebrated, potentially causing serious division. These challenges include communication barriers, social divisions, inequalities, cultural erosion and a lack of inclusivity among various language-speaking communities. Recognising and celebrating linguistic diversity is essential in South Africa to promote inclusivity, bridge cultural gaps, and ensure that all language communities are respected and represented. It is also crucial for building a more equitable and harmonious society. Language, as Mandela recognised, is not just a tool for communication; it also acts as a bridge that transcends boundaries, enabling South Africans to unite, comprehend each other's viewpoints, and forge bonds that have played a pivotal role in the nation's pursuit of unity and reconciliation.

Language as a bridge for uniting people is not limited to South Africa. In the UK, for instance, there is a considerable multilingual population representing a vast range of languages that would benefit from increased recognition and appreciation of their non-English linguistic inventory. Yet, for those who have only one language, namely English, in their inventory, learning another language would also be beneficial to them. In fact, there are many more reasons to explain why learning more languages matters – particularly from a young age. The early years of life are often considered the best time for language learning. During this period, typically referred to as the 'critical period' for language acquisition, children are highly receptive to learning languages. As outlined in the following section, there are several reasons why early childhood is an optimal time for language learning.

Why Should Young Children Learn Languages?

Eric Lenneberg (1967), a linguist and neurologist from the 1960s, popularised the concept of a 'critical period' for language learning. According to Lenneberg, there exists a biologically predetermined time frame, typically ending around puberty, during which language acquisition unfolds most naturally and effectively. This theory is rooted in the notion that the brain undergoes specific changes as a child matures, exhibiting high plasticity during early childhood, enabling it to adapt and reorganise neural networks to facilitate language learning. Support for this critical period theory is found in the observation that individuals who learn a second language (L2) early in life tend to attain near-native pronunciation and fluency (Hartshorne et al., 2018).

Young children's brains exhibit a remarkable quality known as neuroplasticity, which means that they can readily adapt and reorganise in response to new information and experiences. This inherent flexibility makes it significantly easier for them to acquire intricate aspects of language, including sounds, grammar and vocabulary in multiple languages. What further enhances their language learning journey is the natural immersion environment in which they often find themselves, where they are regularly exposed to and interact with languages, allowing them to effortlessly develop their language skills. Another notable advantage is their capacity to acquire native-like pronunciation and accents when they commence language learning at an early age. During this period, young children's vocal apparatus is exceptionally flexible, contributing to their ability to master nuances in linguistic sounds. The benefits extend beyond language proficiency. Early language learning is closely associated with cognitive advantages, such as improved problem-solving skills, heightened creativity and a more profound grasp of language structures.

Beyond cognitive benefits, early language learning can foster valuable social and cultural connections, as explained in more detail later in this chapter. Children who embark on language learning journeys at a young age tend to develop a deeper appreciation for different cultures and a broader worldview. Moreover, learning multiple languages at a young age can play a significant role in nurturing social and emotional development. It empowers children to communicate with a wider range of people and fosters a deep understanding of diverse cultural perspectives. In essence, young children's language learning journey is not only advantageous but also enriching on various levels.

Nevertheless, it is important to note that language learning can occur at any age, and individuals can become proficient in new languages throughout their lives. While the early years provide certain advantages, language learning remains possible and beneficial at later stages as well. The key is motivation, consistent practice, and effective learning strategies. As this chapter shows, there are numerous language learning benefits as evidenced by various studies, some of which will be explored in more detail shortly. However, it is also crucial to realise that what 'language learning' itself entails must be carefully re-examined in each situation. Language learning experiences need to embrace inclusive, innovative, and diversified approaches.

Early Second Language Learning: Psychological and Cognitive Benefits

Early language learning offers several advantages for cognitive development. Research has shown that it can lead to enhanced cognitive abilities, including improved problem-solving skills, language processing and creativity (Bialystok, 2011, 2018; Fox *et al.*, 2019). Moreover, learning a new language can enhance cognitive flexibility, enabling children to switch between different tasks or problem-solving strategies more effectively (Fox *et al.*, 2019; Nicolay & Poncelet, 2013; Sun, 2022). Additionally, some studies have suggested that early language learners may develop stronger memory skills, further contributing to their cognitive development (Brito & Barr, 2012; Fox *et al.*, 2019; Spence, 2022). Indeed, being bilingual can bring about huge benefits for the brain, including better concentration, problem solving, memory and creativity (Spence, 2022). According to Professor Li Wei, dean of IOE, UCL's Faculty of Education and Society, and Dr Frédérique Liégeois of the UCL Great Ormond Street Institute of Child Health, the bilingual brain boosts brain development, delaying dementia by 4.5 years and increasing neuroconnectivity (Black Lab Films, 2023). Studies from Canada and India also suggest that speaking two or more languages may delay the onset of dementia symptoms by up to five years, which underscores the potential benefits of language learning for dementia prevention (Alladi et al., 2013; Bialystok et al., 2007; Craik et al., 2010). However, the protective effect may be more significant when individuals are proficient in at least three to four languages. Interestingly, speaking two languages seems to specifically delay dementia onset in immigrants. While these findings are promising, further research is needed to fully understand how the number of languages spoken impacts dementia prevention.

Early Second Language Learning: Linguistic Advantages

Early language learning offers numerous linguistic advantages to children, as supported by research. One significant benefit is the development of enhanced phonetic skills, enabling children to discern and produce sounds that may not exist in their native language (Conboy & Kuhl, 2011; Goriot et al., 2020; Sundara et al., 2020). Additionally, while bilingual or multilingual children might have smaller vocabulary sizes for each language compared to their monolingual peers, some studies suggest that, collectively, they have a larger or comparable vocabulary size across their linguistic repertoire (De Houwer et al., 2014; Hoff et al., 2012; Siow et al., 2023). Exposure to multiple languages from an early age also nurtures a heightened sensitivity to languages, enabling children to grasp subtle nuances in both sound and meaning (Amelia, 2016; Byers-Heinlein & Lew-Williams, 2013; Oxford CLIL, 2018). Furthermore, early exposure to an L2 can facilitate continued language acquisition later in life, fostering a more robust linguistic skill set (Kuhl, 2011; Singh, 2018; Swanson et al., 2019). Another advantage is the development of pragmatic competence, which entails the ability to understand and interpret the communicative intentions of others. This skill tends to be particularly pronounced in bilinguals and multilinguals, as they must navigate various languages when conversing with different individuals (Fan et al., 2015; Groba et al., 2018; Siegal et al., 2010). Overall, these linguistic benefits highlight the importance of introducing language learning in the early years, as it significantly contributes to children's linguistic development and overall language proficiency.

Early Second Language Learning: Academic and Emotional Development

Bilingualism or multilingualism is correlated with improved academic achievement in various subjects, not just in language-related areas (Amelia, 2016; Fox et al., 2019; Sayer & Ban, 2013). Learning more than one language can enhance metalinguistic awareness, which is the understanding of language structure and use, positively impacting literacy development (Bialystok, 2007; Kieseier et al., 2022; Thomas,

1992). Additionally, knowing more than one language allows children to develop bi- or multiliteracy – a valuable skill in the 21st century that extends to various areas of development, including emotions and social skills (Dressler, 2014; Han, 2021; Ibrahim, 2017). Alongside academic attainment, achieving milestones in a new language, such as mastering new words or grammar rules, can boost confidence and self-esteem in children (Berlitz Singapore, 2023; Edge Early Learning, 2023; Tunçel, 2015). Furthermore, learning about another language and culture can increase empathy and understanding towards speakers of that language (Chen & Fang, 2022; Kamenetz, 2016; Spence, 2022).

Language Learning Pleasure

A study reveals that the process of learning a new language is remarkably pleasurable for humans. Researchers found that when adults successfully learned the meanings of new words, a part of their brain called the ventral striatum, known for its role in reward processing, lit up with activity (Ripollés *et al.*, 2014). This brain activation was similar to the response seen during unrelated reward tasks. Notably, the study also uncovered that the ventral striatum displayed increased functional and structural connections with language areas in the brain during successful word learning. This suggests a strong link between the brain's language regions and its reward system. These findings provide compelling evidence for the neural basis of reward and motivation during language learning. The close connection between language areas and the brain's reward system likely played a crucial role in our evolutionary advantage as humans, enabling us to acquire language skills successfully. However, it is important to acknowledge that language learning experiences can vary greatly from person to person. Individual situations and learning styles matter significantly in language learning, as will be discussed further in this chapter.

Well-being

Language learning has become an increasingly important aspect of modern society, with many individuals seeking to improve their communication skills and enhance their cultural understanding. However, beyond its practical benefits, language learning has also been found to have a positive impact on language learners' well-being. Research has been conducted to explore the impact of language learning on the psychological, social, and emotional well-being of language learners. From the positive psychology perspective, researchers stress the positive aspects of improved well-being in learners who engage in various activities. For example, Pikhart and Klimova (2020) explored how learning an L2 affects the quality of life for older individuals by investigating their subjective feelings and satisfaction levels. The study involved 105

Czech citizens who were aged 55 or older and enrolled in an L2 learning course. Two control groups were also used: one consisted of young adults aged 19–23, and the other comprised older individuals aged over 55. All participants were asked to complete an online questionnaire that was the same for each group. The results showed that learning an L2 had a positive impact on the overall well-being of older individuals, increasing their happiness, satisfaction and motivation to learn, and improving their mental health and social networks. For example, around 90% of the respondents were positive, showing that learning an L2 can reflect their desire to travel and discover new cultures. Although some respondents reported that learning a foreign language required a lot of time or that objective learning outcomes were weak due to cognitive decline, learning an L2 was still a meaningful activity for older individuals. Interestingly, when compared to young individuals, the older individuals showed overwhelmingly positive results in terms of subjective feelings of well-being and happiness. Overall, the study highlights the many benefits of learning a foreign language, both for personal growth and for improving one's quality of life. These findings are important because they show that good health and longevity are directly linked to well-being.

In relation to employment, S.H.O. Kim *et al.* (2012) explore the level of English proficiency, employment and overall sense of well-being among adult immigrants in Australia, which are closely interconnected. It has been noted that immigrants must satisfy their lower-level needs of attaining a job by speaking the target language for economic and social success (Smolicz & Secombe, 2003). The authors argue that possessing a strong command of the English language is arguably the primary means for immigrants to achieve happiness in Australia. Their findings suggest that immigrants who make more progress in improving their English skills are more likely to experience greater improvement in their happiness levels compared to those who do not make as much progress. Upon arriving in Australia, immigrants must have or work towards achieving a high level of English proficiency in order to secure a job or gain admission to further education programmes that can improve their job prospects. Once they have a job and a steady income, immigrants are better able to meet their higher-level needs, participate in Australian society, and experience a sense of well-being and happiness.

Against Marginalisation

Learning and embracing new languages offer significant benefits to individuals and societies. Moreover, they serve as a powerful preventive measure against marginalisation, particularly for marginalised children in our society. One of the primary advantages of language learning is the enhancement of intercultural competence. This increased competence leads to richer interactions among people from diverse backgrounds, ultimately reducing the potential for conflicts within families and divisions in societies. For instance, children growing up in a translingual couple's household, where multiple languages and cultures are celebrated, can develop a strong sense of cultural awareness, adaptability and empathy, thereby nurturing an openness to embracing diversity in their own lives and interactions and reducing tensions and misunderstandings stemming from unresolved language and cultural differences (Kiaer & Ahn, 2023b). Furthermore, language acquisition fosters emotional and cultural adaptability, significantly improving an individual's ability to navigate diverse environments. This adaptability positively impacts various aspects of life and prepares individuals for a better future. A society that values and promotes multilingualism becomes more enriched, inclusive and diverse. It fosters stronger intergenerational connections and emotional enrichment, contributing to the overall well-being and intercultural competence of its members. By recognising and embracing the languages of marginalised children, refugees and asylum seekers, we not only provide them with a sense of belonging but also proactively prevent marginalisation. This approach enhances their well-being and facilitates their integration into society.

From a broader perspective, language and intercultural skills play a pivotal role in our economy and society. We utilise this knowledge to positively shape our future. An exclusive focus on speaking English can lead to increased social problems and misunderstandings, potentially resulting in identity crises among our youth. Therefore, learning and embracing multiple languages serve as a powerful tool for personal growth and the promotion of societal harmony.

Job Market Competitiveness

When learners are at a crossroads of deciding what foreign language to learn, foreign language competency is often viewed as an advantage in job applications, with English language proficiency arguably being the key to success. Job candidates with high proficiency in EFL are often seen as well-rounded and competitive in the global job market, as English provides greater access to information from around the world and can enhance one's sense of personal value. The belief that English proficiency is essential for success in education and the workforce can motivate people to invest time and effort into improving their English skills. The acquisition of English language skills is prioritised by individuals seeking to increase their chances of success in these areas.

Park (2011) explores the significant role of English language proficiency as a crucial criterion for the employment of 'white-collar' workers in South Korea. English has become a symbol of success and upward mobility in South Korea and is viewed as a necessary skill for individuals seeking to advance their careers. English proficiency has become a form of 'linguistic capital' highly valued by employers, reflecting broader social and economic trends such as the shift towards a knowledge-based economy and global markets. However, English proficiency also acts as a marker of social class and privilege, creating a stratified job market. Despite the fact that English proficiency is seen as a necessary skill for career advancement, the emphasis on English proficiency has negative consequences. For instance, it reinforces existing inequalities in South Korean society. Private English education with 'native English speaker' teachers and study abroad programmes can be expensive and out of reach for many individuals. Those who have access to these resources are more likely to have better English proficiency and are thus better positioned to compete in the job market, while those who lack English proficiency are often marginalised and unable to access certain types of employment. Additionally, the focus on English has created unrealistic expectations for language learning, leading to feelings of frustration and anxiety among many individuals. While English proficiency is seen as a crucial criterion for success in the job market and education, the author also notes that the emphasis on English proficiency has the potential to create social and economic inequalities. Employers and policymakers must be aware of these issues and work to promote equitable access to English language education and employment opportunities.

Another interesting stand on foreign language learning in the area of job applications can be found in the Chinese context, particularly from the perspective of language learning materials for learners. Xiong and Yuan (2018) examined a series of English language textbooks used in Chinese schools through critical discourse analysis. They found that these English learning materials in China promote society as a collection of individual entrepreneurs, emphasising that competency in the English language can help individuals yield a 'good price' in the job market. Additionally, the textbooks suggest that every individual can achieve English competence to the same level, with little mention of a socially orientated approach to learning English due to the glorification of personal effort over group effort. Lastly, learners are encouraged to build a monolingual and monocultural virtual community while learning English, which may inevitably weaken their individual sense of belonging to the English language. They also highlight the influence of textbooks on shaping English language education in China, emphasising the importance of individual achievement in the job market over social and cultural aspects of language learning.

In the European job market, foreign language skills beyond English are highly valued among job seekers. While multilingualism is promoted on a supranational level, official EU documents are typically published in dominant European languages, such as English, German and French, indicating a lack of commitment to linguistic diversity. Although the

European Commission acknowledges the importance of teaching and learning additional languages, societal attitudes often restrict language learning to only English, as noted by Spolsky (2009). Kantaridou *et al.* (2018) found that although job advertisements in Greece did not explicitly require language skills, senior or high-skilled positions in specific industries such as law, shipping and engineering often demanded foreign language proficiency. Many employers may assume that applicants possess fundamental literacy skills, including language proficiency and computer knowledge. The authors suggest that the educational system offers more language choices, including economically and geographically significant languages such as Chinese. Additionally, the language policy should reflect the diverse interests and points of reference of students who are exposed to a multilingual environment from a young age. Hence, it can be concluded that language skills play a crucial role in determining an individual's competitiveness in job markets in a multilingual and multicultural environment. Employers consider language skills as a strong indicator of interpersonal and intercultural competence, and these skills have been shown to enhance communication, build relationships and promote diversity in the workplace. The reviewed studies also suggest that individuals with strong language skills are better equipped to adapt to new situations and are more likely to succeed in multicultural workplaces. The importance of language skills and the need for individuals to develop and maintain foreign language competence to thrive in today's globalised world is highlighted in the modern workplace.

Career Mobility

With the world becoming more interconnected, the ability to communicate effectively in multiple languages has become a highly desirable skill for professionals. Multinational corporations (MNCs) may expand their operations internationally, and thus the ability to work with colleagues and clients using foreign languages, English as a lingua franca (ELF) in particular, is becoming a critical competency for career success. It is not difficult to imagine that the existence of different languages in MNCs could be viewed as a communication problem, or as a 'language barrier' (Feely & Harzing, 2003: 38). Karhunen *et al.* (2018) also reviewed articles on the need for employees who are expected to be working globally with the requisite proficiency in foreign language(s).

Research has also shown that foreign language learning could benefit language learners in terms of career prospects. For example, Grosse (2004) investigated whether a competitive advantage could be derived in individuals' careers from their foreign language skills and cultural knowledge. They presented the results of an electronic survey of 581 randomly selected alumni of an American graduate school from the graduating classes of 1970–2002. The school required a minimum of four semesters of a foreign language for graduation. The respondents worked in firms of all sizes and in different positions. The results revealed that the more proficient in foreign languages the respondent was, the more likely they were to have received a competitive advantage. From the perspective of companies, the same trend applies: the better the employee knows the language and culture, the more likely the company is to recognise and reward those skills. The vast majority of respondents acknowledged that both foreign language skills and cultural knowledge had benefited them in their professional lives. The value of foreign language could even enhance one's credibility when working at an international business level, in the context of America.

Itani *et al.* (2015) also examined the significance of language skills in career development in today's job market. Based on survey data and open-ended responses from 96 employees who worked at different organisational levels in Finland's private and public sectors, the results revealed that employees with higher English and other foreign language competencies were perceived to be more endowed with three career competencies: 'knowing how' (i.e. work-related knowledge and skills), 'knowing why' (i.e. career identity and motivation), and 'knowing whom' (i.e. career-related social networks and contacts). Individuals would learn foreign languages as a strategic decision to invest in their career competences, and bilingual respondents who were fluent in both Finnish and Swedish demonstrated higher levels of physical career mobility (i.e. career moves that are performed between employers) and psychological career mobility (i.e. the mental preparedness and readiness to make a career move if a good opportunity arises). The authors also suggested that the possibility to use foreign languages at work is in itself an effective 'language teacher', which also increases job motivation (Itani *et al.*, 2015: 375). Latukha *et al.* (2016) further suggested that managers in Russia with high foreign language competencies had more horizontal, vertical, external and internal career mobility in comparison to their counterparts with low foreign language competencies.

Despite earlier research underscoring the importance of prominent language competencies, do these necessarily translate to job promotions and wage increases? Recently, Peltokorpi (2023) went beyond previous studies looking at the direct effects of foreign language competencies on subjective career-related benefits by exploring the relationship between the competencies of EFL and job promotions, wage increases and career satisfaction through career encouragement and internal social capital development in two independent studies conducted in foreign subsidiaries in Japan. By examining 499 participants who responded to surveys over a 12-month period in one of the studies, it was found that local employees' English language competencies are positively related to job promotions, wage increases and career satisfaction. In a multilingual workplace, local employees who demonstrate English proficiency are more likely to receive promotions and salary raises. This is because senior members tend to support those employees who possess the necessary skills and competencies, which could in turn enhance their 'visibility' in the workplace and their career success, differentiating them from local employees without such foreign language competencies.

To sum up, this section highlights how learning a foreign language can improve career mobility. The ability to communicate effectively in a foreign language allows individuals to access new job opportunities in MNCs, global non-governmental organisations and international branches of local companies. Learning a foreign language thus provides important career-related benefits to employees in the workplace.

Fluency is Not the Only Goal

A British Council (2023b) survey highlights that 26% of UK adults express regret for not achieving fluency in another language. Additionally, a quarter of respondents are inclined to make learning Spanish their New Year's resolution. The same survey indicates that London has the highest number of individuals proficient in foreign languages, with French and Italian being popular choices. A significant 24% of respondents believe that it is crucial for UK residents to learn a language other than English. Among the preferred languages, Spanish (25%), French (21%) and Italian (14%) top the list. French, Spanish and German are considered the most important languages for UK residents to learn. In the educational sphere, the popularity of Spanish is on the rise, as it has become the top A-level language in England and is expected to surpass French at the GCSEs by 2026. Interestingly, Chinese is seen as important by 25% of 18- to 24-year-olds, compared to 13% of those aged 35–44. Most people prefer learning through mobile apps (39%) or evening classes (35%).

Based on a comprehensive study involving over 669,000 individuals, it has been found that language learning ability remains robust until around 17.4 years of age, after which it gradually declines (Hartshorne *et al.*, 2018). This applies to both complex and simpler aspects of grammar, challenging previous assumptions about the timing of this decline. However, it is important to note that fluency, which is hard to measure and achieve, cannot be the sole goal of language learning. The study underscores the existence of a prolonged critical period for language acquisition that extends well into adulthood, impacting fluency and language learning capabilities.

Indeed, one assumption that people tend to make is that fluency is always necessary. However, this is not true; fluency is *not* always necessary. For many who learn an L2, there are other motivating factors such as developing intercultural competence, empathy and solidarity. In the case of the UK particularly, it would be unrealistic to expect pupils to suddenly speak foreign languages to the same level that others – such as students in Singapore – speak English. One explanation for this is that, while many of us would generally agree that learning another language is beneficial, the reasons *why* it is beneficial have not been adequately conveyed to the public. In addition, the current educational framework for language teaching and learning in the UK has significant room for reform, given that learning of foreign languages has taken a backseat to other subjects as English is the current lingua franca.

Post-Brexit Language Education Needs Diversification

As the UK charts its economic destiny, it becomes increasingly evident that investing in a comprehensive and inclusive global language education initiative is paramount. While English retains its status as a global lingua franca and a valuable asset, the aspiration for fluency in the languages of diverse nations may not be a practical goal for the entire UK workforce. Nevertheless, cultivating a more receptive attitude and fostering intercultural competence is both feasible and essential. This approach gains particular relevance in the context of negotiations within the Comprehensive and Progressive Agreement for Trans-Pacific Partnership (CPTPP) and similar international agreements (Webb, 2023b). While not every member of the UK workforce may attain fluency in the languages of all member countries of these international agreements, possessing a nuanced understanding of their languages and cultures can significantly enhance the depth and effectiveness of negotiations on a global scale. It enables more meaningful communication, serves as a demonstration of respect for international partners, and contributes to the construction of robust relationships grounded in trust and mutual comprehension.

By placing a strong emphasis on the development of comprehensive and inclusive global language education and intercultural competence, especially in this post-Brexit era, the UK can position itself to thrive in a global marketplace that extends well beyond the confines of Europe. This strategic approach aligns seamlessly with the UK government's vision of an 'Indo-Pacific tilt', as outlined in the Integrated Review, reaffirming the nation's commitment to nurturing enduring and prosperous partnerships with countries worldwide (Cabinet Office, 2023). Moreover, by focusing not just on written languages but also on immersing the population in other languages and cultures, celebrating diversity and passing on the rich cultural heritage, the UK can transform its multilingualism into a valuable asset. This goal can perhaps be achieved not by training new linguists but by revitalising our heritage languages. In doing so, we would help heritage language speakers and new arrivals to maintain their home languages and affirm their sense of identity (see Chapter 4 for more). Imagine former Prime Minister Rishi Sunak being able to communicate fluently in Punjabi. It may be more efficient to train someone without prior knowledge of Punjabi to learn it rather than relying solely on English for communication.

Nick Gibb, minister for school standards, said: 'Our economy needs people who can communicate across the globe and trade with overseas businesses. This programme is about ensuring we have the next generation of young people with the languages needed to compete on the world stage' (University College London, 2023). The programme that Gibb refers to is a new nationwide language hubs programme, which intends to provide thousands of students across England with quality language teaching through a centre of excellence. Such incentives seem to be a response to the ever-decreasing interest in formal state language education. For example, the uptake of modern foreign languages (MFLs) at GCSEs and A-levels has declined significantly since 2004. According to the British Council's 2022 survey, across all school types, increasing numbers of schools are reporting no school exchanges abroad (Collen, 2022). The government is currently on track to meet its EBacc target, whereby 90% of pupils take five EBacc subjects by 2025 in all subjects except languages, which is currently at less than 50%. The uptake of languages is lowest in areas of socioeconomic deprivation. Korean as a foreign language (KFL) learners represent a striking counterpoint. Its popularity and profile are increasing with the spread of South Korean popular culture in the UK (Frenchin-Pollard & Bartlett-Imadegawa, 2023). KFL is taught in extracurricular contexts emphasising task-based learning and cultural creative approaches to foreign language study.

Consequently, it is important to promote not just L2 learning but also heritage language learning in order to ensure that our younger generations do not miss out on the various advantages associated with multilingualism. These include intellectual growth, increased understanding of other cultures and customs, a broadened view of the world, and economic benefits, as Foreman-Peck and Wang (2014) estimate that a shortage of language skills among young British people costs the UK economy around £48 billion a year, or 3.5% of the UK's gross domestic product (GDP). There has been a growing interest in heritage language learning (see Trifonas & Aravossitas, 2018) and the unique challenges faced in teaching these languages. However, resources and funding remain limited, particularly in community centres where heritage languages are typically taught. Additional practical steps to aid in the diversification of post-Brexit language education at a governmental level include the creation of a bank of knowledge on language research, which could inform future language policies, such as the role of home, heritage and community languages within the language hubs programme. Following this, policy partners could share this knowledge more widely within the languages team, for example, with the curriculum strategy team, and the international strategy and partnerships team. The tools shared with the Department for Education analysts and social researchers can also be used in future research and evaluation work. In turn, this has the potential to better inform future business cases and submissions to ministers on language pedagogy in the UK.

Post-Brexit UK Trade Diversified

In the wake of Brexit, the UK has taken significant steps to broaden its economic horizons by forging new trade alliances beyond Europe. This strategic decision aligns with the UK's overarching goal of expanding its global trade presence. To this end, the UK has successfully inked several noteworthy trade agreements. In 2021, the UK–Australia trade agreement was signed, followed by the UK–New Zealand trade agreement in 2022 (Webb, 2023a). These agreements officially came into effect at the end of May 2023, representing significant milestones in the UK's evolving global trade strategy. Furthermore, the UK has ventured into the realm of digital trade, signing two important digital trade agreements. In February 2022, a digital trade agreement with Singapore was formalised, entering into force on 14 June 2022 (Department for Business and Trade & Department for International Trade, 2022). Subsequently, on 20 March 2023, a digital trade agreement with Ukraine was signed, further expanding the UK's presence in digital trade (Department for Business and Trade & Department for International Trade, 2023). As of July 2023, the total UK trade in goods with non-EU countries stands at £19.4 billion in terms of exports, while that with EU countries stands at £14.9 billion (HM Revenue & Customs, 2023).

Amid the rapidly evolving global landscape of the post-Brexit era, the UK made a pivotal strategic move by joining the Asia-Pacific trade bloc known as CPTPP in July 2023 (Webb, 2023b). This trade bloc comprises 11 other nations, including Australia, Brunei, Canada, Chile, Japan, Malaysia, Mexico, New Zealand, Peru, Singapore and Vietnam. The UK's inclusion in this diverse and influential global coalition underscores its recognition of the importance of diversifying trade partnerships beyond the confines of the European sphere. In summary, the UK's post-Brexit trade strategy is marked by diversification, with a focus on expanding its trade relationships and forging new economic alliances well beyond the borders of Europe.

'The Economic Value to the UK of Speaking Other Languages'

The chapter now delves into one study that highlights the economic value of speaking other languages in a UK context. Ayres-Bennett *et al.*'s (2022) study aims to evaluate the economic value of foreign languages to the UK and the potential economic benefits of improving language education in schools. The skill to communicate in different languages is a highly valuable asset amid our increasingly globally integrated market. Indeed, the UK is at an advantage compared to many other countries since English is the current lingua franca. Yet, this does not mean we should rely on English too heavily because of the influence of other economic superpowers such as China, where English is not the official or main first language. Since 2004, the UK has shown a notable decline in the overall uptake of languages, as evidenced by the decrease in entries for the GCSE and A-level examinations. This may very well be a problem for the UK's ability to compete in the global business community. While there has been increased funding in schools for language education, we find a lack of evidence conveying the potential economic benefits of enhanced foreign language skills. Ayres-Bennett *et al.*'s (2022) study aims to fill this gap by showing the economic importance of investing in other foreign languages in the UK. It is useful to the area of international economics and language policy and particularly relevant to those working in language policy and language education.

Currently, we already have evidence suggesting that languages play an influential role in international trade. This is because having a common language can reduce trade barriers and promote preferential trade cooperation agreements. Furthermore, empirical studies show that learning additional languages enhances human capital, as multilinguals potentially earn higher wages and have better labour market outcomes than their monolingual peers (Laitin & Ramachandran, 2022; Schroedler, 2018). In the UK specifically, there is mixed evidence on wage returns for speaking an additional language apart from English. This may be because of an undervaluation of language skills by employers, an unwillingness of businesses to invest in these skills, and a mismatch between the actual L2 proficiency level and the proficiency level necessary in professional settings among the UK population. The UK has also focused on hiring people from abroad with the needed language skills, rather than recruiting existing UK residents.

Ayres-Bennett *et al.*'s (2022) study applies the 'gravity model of trade' to analyse the association between the ability to communicate in a spoken language and bilateral trade flows. There were three key findings. Firstly, sharing a spoken language can reduce trade barriers; the study observed an increase in bilateral trade in mining and energy as well as services, when a proportion of the population of two countries can communicate with each other through a common spoken language, all other variables being equal. Secondly, through their sensitivity analysis comparing the relative importance of English versus other languages regarding bilateral trade flows, they found that while English plays an important role in business relations worldwide, it is not the sole driver of trade flows in sectors like mining and energy and services; other languages matter equally – if not more – in reducing trade barriers. Finally, they found that UK exports are predicted to increase if there are more languages spoken that are shared with trading partners. The study estimates that the complete removal of language barriers with other Arabic-, Chinese-, French-

and Spanish-speaking countries could increase UK exports annually by approximately £19 billion.

To quantify the economic benefits of language education for the UK economy, Ayres-Bennett *et al.* (2022) assess how UK economic activity would change between now and 2050 if more UK pupils at Key Stages 3 and 4 could speak an additional modern language to a level suitable in a business setting. As a baseline, they used the projection of the UK economy under current levels of language education provision in schools. In their hypothetical scenarios, there was an emphasis on improving language skills in four modern languages (Arabic, Mandarin, French and Spanish) for UK pupils aged between 11 and 16 at Key Stages 3 and 4. While there are various ways in which this can be practically achieved, their scenario attempted to broadly mirror that of the MEP, which aims to enable pupils in Key Stages 3 and 4 to achieve at least a B1 level in Mandarin according to the CEFR.

They found that a 10-percentage point increase in UK pupils in Key Stages 3 and 4 learning any one of the four languages translates to a cumulative GDP increase over 30 years ranging between £623 million (the lowest conservative estimate for Spanish) and £944 million (the highest conservative estimate for Arabic) through a reduction in non-tariff trade barriers related to languages alone. They also found a positive impact on consumer welfare effects, witnessing a cumulative increase in UK welfare by 2050. As an example, for Mandarin, the estimated cumulative welfare gain is between £1817 million and £1886 million. Assessing the potential human capital effects associated with learning languages, they further found an estimated cumulative increase in the UK's GDP by 2050. Using Mandarin as an example, this increase was estimated to be between £11,518 million and £12,354 million, with the estimates for Arabic being between £11,769 million and £12,613 million.

To understand the magnitude of the quantified economic benefits, they must be set against the cost of achieving them. The estimated costs were based on publicly available information about the MEP and discussions with MEP stakeholders; a central cost estimate per student per year for Mandarin of at least £480 was therefore applied. However, Spanish and French would likely cost less to run because they are already established in many UK schools, whereas Arabic will cost more than the MEP because it would involve starting with an even smaller base in UK schools.

The primary takeaway from the cost–benefit analysis is that investing in language education is most likely to return more than the investment cost. Promoting Mandarin, Arabic, French, or Spanish would result in benefit-to-cost ratios of at least 2:1, meaning that spending £1 could return about £2. This study aimed to highlight the value of improving the quantity and quality of language provision in the UK. Their findings suggest that there are identifiable returns for investing in language education that are not just economic, as it would also produce a labour force with the language skills necessary for the UK to compete in an increasingly globalised world.

Ways to Build an Inclusive, Diverse Language Learning Classroom

Language or language learning encompasses more than just vocabulary and grammar; it should also include non-verbal and cultural aspects of communication as a whole. In this broader context, cultural activities can also be regarded as integral parts of the language learning process. This perspective highlights that language acquisition goes beyond words and verbal language, incorporating the cultural context and non-verbal elements that enrich one's ability to communicate effectively in a given language. While the general public's knowledge of language learning may be limited due to personal experiences that were far from ideal, this can change. Nurturing an inclusive and diverse language pedagogy can serve as a powerful tool in diminishing radicalism, racism and social divides within society. Here, we elaborate on various approaches to achieve this goal.

Promoting cultural understanding

Inclusive language pedagogy extends beyond teaching the language itself; it encompasses the culture and values tied to it. When individuals delve into different cultures through language, they cultivate a profound understanding that diminishes stereotypes and prejudices. This newfound comprehension fosters empathy and contributes to the dismantling of barriers that fuel racism and social divisions.

Fostering communication

Language is the gateway to communication, and effective communication among people from diverse backgrounds promotes social cohesion. Inclusive language pedagogy actively encourages students to engage with peers who hail from various cultural and linguistic backgrounds, fostering a sense of community and reducing divisive lines.

Empowering marginalised groups

Inclusive language pedagogy places a strong emphasis on languages and dialects spoken by marginalised communities, validating their languages and identities. This validation empowers these groups, reducing feelings of marginalisation and mitigating the risk of radicalisation.

Challenging stereotypes

Language pedagogy serves as a powerful tool to challenge and debunk stereotypes and biases prevalent in society. By employing inclusive teaching materials and methods, educators can guide students to critically analyse and question existing stereotypes. This cultivates more informed and empathetic individuals.

Enhancing critical thinking

Inclusive language pedagogy fosters critical thinking and open-mindedness. Exposure to diverse perspectives and instruction in analysing language and discourse critically equips students to identify and confront discriminatory rhetoric and ideologies effectively.

Creating inclusive learning environments

Inclusivity in language education extends beyond the classroom to encompass the creation of safe and welcoming learning spaces. Educational institutions that prioritise inclusivity send a resounding message that discrimination and intolerance have no place, thereby discouraging radicalism and extremism.

Global citizenship

Learning multiple languages and delving into various cultures through inclusive language pedagogy nurture a sense of global citizenship. When individuals consider themselves part of a global community, they are less likely to harbour extremist or divisive ideologies.

Promoting tolerance

Inclusive language pedagogy underscores the values of tolerance and respect for diversity. These values, when integrated into education, wield a lasting influence over students' attitudes and behaviours, fostering social harmony and minimising radicalism.

Building inclusive societies

Ultimately, inclusive language pedagogy contributes to the creation of more inclusive societies. By nurturing inclusivity and diversity in education, we move closer to a future where individuals from all backgrounds are esteemed and honoured. This, in turn, leads to a reduction in radicalism, racism and social divisions.

Language Matters

In summary, inclusive and diverse language pedagogy transcends the mere teaching of language skills; it actively promotes cultural understanding, effective communication, critical thinking and tolerance. These qualities serve as potent instruments in reducing radicalism, racism, and social divides by encouraging empathy, respect and unity within society. The benefits of language learning, particularly from a young age, are manifold, spanning cognitive, emotional, social and other domains. With regard to the economic advantages of a bilingual and multilingual UK population, we must, however, keep in mind that the UK cannot simply model what non-Anglophone countries have done to achieve fluency in English as an L2. The UK requires different methods – ones that should make the most of a diverse, multilingual population. Rather than placing the emphasis on training monolingual English speakers to achieve fluency in a language like Mandarin Chinese for the economic growth of the country, it would be far more feasible and achievable for heritage language speakers of Mandarin Chinese instead to maintain and develop their linguistic repertoire. Heritage speakers would likely be better negotiators in foreign languages compared to Anglophone speakers who have had to learn a foreign language from scratch. Of course, this does not diminish the previously discussed advantages of learning an L2 at whatever age and with whatever background one may have. Yet, we must remain acutely aware of the need to develop context-sensitive language learning packages, so to speak, in order to yield optimal results. This involves carefully innovating current language policies and education, ensuring that language education is not discontinuous or unstructured as has often been the case in the UK; one hour a week of French vocabulary games and miscellaneous grammar activities will not give the results we seek. Returning to the words of Nelson Mandela, 'If you talk to a man in a language he understands, that goes to his head. If you talk to him in his own language, that goes to his heart'. Maintaining, promoting and valuing bilingualism and multilingualism on both individual and social levels is key to developing a more interconnected, equitable and harmonious society.

4 Why Home and Community Language Matters

Practical tips:
- **Bridge the gap:** Encourage students to share aspects of their home and community languages in the classroom. This can involve short presentations, cultural objects, songs in their native tongues, and creating a language map with pupils showcasing the languages represented in the classroom.
- **Provide family language policy (FLP) support:** Offer resources or workshops for parents on strategies to maintain their heritage language at home. This could include bilingual storytime or encouraging grandparents to speak their native language with younger generations.
- **Celebrate multilingualism:** Organise events that celebrate the diverse languages spoken in your classroom community. These can include a language fair, poetry readings, or presentations on different cultures.
- **Embrace technology:** Utilise online resources, apps and language learning platforms dedicated to heritage languages.
- **Collaborate with the local community:** Partner with local cultural organisations or community centres that offer programmes or events in students' home languages.
- **Normalise code-switching:** Create a classroom environment where students feel comfortable using both their home language and the target language, acknowledging the benefits of translanguaging.
- **Challenge stereotypes:** Discuss the importance of valuing all languages, regardless of their perceived prestige or dominance.

'The Limits of My Language'

As Ludwig Wittgenstein (1922: 115) writes in his *Tractatus Logico-Philosophicus*, 'The limits of my language mean the limits of my world'.

This quote serves as a reminder that the language of emotion is often deeply tied to one's native tongue, rendering it inherently untranslatable. This awareness holds significant importance for intercultural couples (IC), as it highlights that their emotionally rich communication may not be fully expressed through words. Yet, Wittgenstein's words apply to us all; the more languages we have in our repertoire, the richer and more diverse our understanding of the world. This is why it is crucial to invest in language education and appreciation to expand our linguistic knowledge and skills.

Who is a Multilingual?

According to the Oxford Companion to the English Language, 'multilingualism' is defined as follows:

> The ability to use three or more languages, either separately or in various degrees of code-mixing. There is no general agreement as to the degree of competence in each language necessary before someone can be considered multilingual; according to some, a native-like fluency is necessary in at least three languages; according to others, different languages are used for different purposes, competence in each varying according to such factors. (McArthur *et al.*, 2018)

In line with this definition, we see that multilingualism is not necessarily about fluency, specifically traditional notions of native-like fluency. In this book, we consider a multilingual as someone who has linguistic competence in two or more languages, thus also encompassing bilinguals, applicable to specific situations or all situations. We will not adopt the view that a multilingual must be fluent in two or more languages. Following this understanding of what makes a multilingual, I further suggest that in the UK, almost everyone – if not everyone – is multilingual to an extent; in our increasingly interconnected and globalised nation, even a British child born and raised in an English-speaking environment would inevitably be exposed to and pick up other languages from their surroundings, whether or not intentionally.

Foreign, Home, Heritage or Community Language?

The value that we place on our languages can be seen specifically in the terminology that we use to describe them. MFL is often used as a department name in schools and universities, but this term is not without issues. Firstly, many MFL departments in universities exclude Asian languages. For example, the University of Oxford and the University of Cambridge both have a modern languages faculty and an

Asian and Middle Eastern studies faculty, which separates Asian languages from European languages in a problematic manner. The term 'foreign', which admittedly is used less commonly these days, has an othering effect, separating UK students from languages in a manner that does not reflect their multicultural reality. 'Home language' (HL) and 'heritage language' are also commonly used terms. These terms imply a hierarchical order of languages. Home and heritage languages are implied to be secondary to the main language, English. Such terminology does not encourage the study of language nor emphasise its importance. 'Community language' is another common term. For language learning, it is a better term in the sense that community plays an important role in facilitating language acquisition through social interaction, and mutual understanding within the community is important for fostering cohesiveness and preventing prejudice from developing. For older students who are considering which subjects to take for the GCSEs and A-levels, 'community language' may not be such a great term. It once again fails to emphasise the necessity of language and how it can help students in their adult lives. In Australia, language subjects are simply referred to as 'languages' with no additional description. Perhaps the UK should adopt this neutral stance to avoid influencing our perception of language study with loaded terminology.

Language, with its inherent ability to forge connections, can also, unfortunately, be a tool for division and discrimination. This dynamic is not isolated to English-speaking countries like the United States, the UK and Australia, but is a global occurrence. Overemphasis on national languages sometimes encourages an exclusionary form of nationalism. In various contexts, such as those found in English-speaking countries, there are nuances in the definitions and valuations of foreign, home, heritage and community languages. The act of categorising and labelling languages, although designed to protect them, can inadvertently serve as a mechanism for 'othering'.

Firstly, the Collins Dictionary (n.d.) defines a 'community language' as 'a language spoken by members of a minority group or community within a majority language context'. This term is widely used in the UK, referring to the languages of various immigrant communities which account for more than 5.5% of the population (BBC, 2014). Such a term creates the impression of inclusivity and being welcomed, as 'community' fosters a sense of belonging. However, Li (2021) argues that the choice of label is not motivated by reason but reflects the UK's Eurocentric bias towards languages that are not indigenous to Europe. He warns against such arbitrary classification, especially if it accords prestige to certain languages over others, as it will lead to an imbalance in support across languages. He encourages a wider, international outlook regarding languages, which embraces multilingualism and languages in minority groups.

The term 'community language' originated in Australia to denote the non-English or Aboriginal languages used by the people (Clyne, 1991: 3), preferred over other terms such as 'minority' or 'immigrant' languages. These terms can result in their invisible stigmatisation by implying that they are spoken only by a small number of people and are not worthy of mainstream attention. According to NALDIC (2011), the term 'community language' 'avoids many of the negative connotations which these other terms have attracted and draws attention to the fact that languages are used in a range of shared social and cultural contexts'. However, as Li (2021) noted, the term is not unproblematic – such marginalisation still prevails through the use of unnecessary classifications. There is a close link between community languages and one's ethnic background, as Community Languages Australia (n.d.) states that community language schools were formerly referred to as Australia's ethnic schools, in which emphasis was placed on a student's linguistic and cultural heritage in such an educational setting, intending to reflect Australia's multiculturalism. Interestingly, Lo Bianco (1987: 8) describes community languages as having been 'modified to express the new experiences of their speakers and, as such, have evolved features such as pronunciations, new words, metaphors, and intonations which mark them as truly Australian'.

Compared to the UK, the United States makes less use of the term 'community languages'. According to the National Foreign Language Resource Centre, the description of these languages seems to highlight the places in which these languages are spoken, such as radio stations, local newspapers and 'only in groups of speakers who may be clustered in particular areas or come together for activities such as religious worship or cultural festivals' (Menacker, 2001: 2). They further state that some community languages like Japanese and Hawaiian are taught more than others, with some not being taught at all. In Canada, this term is used even more rarely (Cummins, 1992).

New Zealand has also adopted this term, as community languages are distinct from English and indigenous varieties, evidenced through the website of the Ministry of Business, Innovation and Employment. They provide a list of more than 200 languages and mention that community languages are from several regions and differentiated from indigenous varieties such as Te Reo Māori and New Zealand Sign Language (Ministry of Business, Innovation and Employment, n.d.a, n.d.b, n.d.c). The term is also used in a range of other countries like Ireland and Nigeria (Brann, 1994; Department of the Environment, Climate and Communications, 2021).

The term 'home language' is also used across the globe, such as in Australia, Singapore, South Africa and Ireland. For example, St Joseph's Institution International (n.d.), an international school in Singapore, prefers to use 'home language' rather than 'mother tongue' or any other term to denote the language learned first, the language known best and/or the language used the most. This was to distinguish it from the Singapore Ministry of Education's term 'mother tongue language', used to refer exclusively to the government-approved additional language that Singaporean citizens and permanent residents learn alongside their HL. In South Africa, Australia and Ireland, the term is broadly understood as the dominant language spoken in a household (Aistear Siolta, n.d.; Australian Bureau of Statistics, 2021; Staff Writer, 2019). In the UK specifically, 'home language' is often used synonymously with 'community language' (Ward, 2014), while stressing the home environment in which these languages are learned and mostly used. The HHCL (Home, Heritage and Community Languages) Advisory Group (n.d.: 4) cites the UNESCO definition of a HL and notes how it can also be referred to as 'mother tongue', 'first language', or 'native language'. The classification of HLs is perhaps less problematic than community languages, but it is not without its pitfalls; again, it hints at an underlying prejudice towards non-Anglophone speakers, in which their language may be limited to the home and other particular contexts.

In addition to the above, another commonly seen term is 'heritage language'. The Cambridge Dictionary (n.d.) defines this as 'a language that someone learns in the home as a child, but that may not fully develop because the person uses a different language in other situations in their life'. This classification overlaps greatly with community language and HL, and is also used internationally, including in Australia, New Zealand, the United States, Canada, Singapore and India (Alliance for the Advancement of Heritage Languages, n.d.; Borneman, 2018; Centre for Development of Advanced Computing, n.d.; Cummins, 1992; Our SG Fund, n.d.; The Office of Ethnic Affairs, n.d.). In the UK, heritage languages include Polish, Urdu, Turkish and Arabic, which are widely spoken in home settings but differ from the majority language dominant in larger society. GCSE and A-level qualifications are available for a small selection of heritage languages spoken in the UK; organisations such as Hampshire Services and the British Council encourage children to complete these qualifications where possible. Yet, while they acknowledge the value of these heritage languages, their provision in public spaces and awareness about them are lacking.

It is noteworthy that in numerous English-speaking regions, European languages often do not dominate discussions about home, heritage and community languages, despite their substantial presence. There is a certain irony in the observation that in some areas where Asian populations may surpass Western European ones, more educational attention and investment are often directed towards Western European languages. Languages related to home, community and heritage, on occasion, tend to be marginalised and go uncelebrated, especially in areas where discrimination towards certain language groups persists. Therefore, challenging and dismantling the stigma attached to them is crucial to paving the way towards inclusivity. In so doing, we enable languages to be channels of unity and connectivity, rather than to be used as vectors of division and exclusion.

This issue is not restricted to North America, the UK, or Australia; language discrimination is indeed a worldwide phenomenon. Across the globe, in varied sociocultural contexts, languages can be both a marker of identity and, paradoxically, a basis for exclusion. Addressing these disparities and biases at a global level necessitates a comprehensive understanding of how languages can be preserved, celebrated and made inclusive, ensuring that they unite rather than divide. Languages have been stigmatised and marginalised (as discussed in more detail in Chapter 3), echoing post-colonial discourses. However, times are changing – and indeed have changed – and we need to adapt accordingly. The UK population today is highly multilingual; even those who might claim to be monolingual English speakers cannot deny that they are surrounded by multilingual environments, whether through school, work, the internet, or more.

Myth: Learning Heritage Languages Harms English Learning

Contrary to the widespread myth, learning new languages, including heritage languages, does not interfere with the learning of wider or dominant languages. For example, in the UK, many parents give up teaching their heritage language because they are concerned that it might hinder their children's English proficiency. However, studies have shown that this is not the case, as will be explored in more detail below.

Challenging marginalised multilingualism: A perspective on anglo-eurocentric ideology

Mills (2001: 387), among others, points out that the majority of studies on childhood bilingualism are dominated by accounts from middle-class, professional, and academic parents from Europe and North America. Two decades have passed since Mills' study and the situation has not changed much. Several other scholars have also echoed Mills' views. Montanari and Quay (2019: 399) advocate for a shift away from a 'Eurocentric ideology', which they argue has been the backbone of research on multilingualism to date. Lanza and Gomes (2020: 167) note that scholarly debates on FLP still largely adopt a Eurocentric approach and argue that documenting the 'social reality' of multilingualism and family multilingualism requires looking not only at northern (Eurocentric) perspectives, but also at views from the Global South. They also claim that, at least for the 20th century, discourses of multilingualism from non-Eurocentric regions, such as Asia, Africa 2 and Latin America, have been 'appropriated' in Europe and North America before being recirculated back to those aforementioned regions (Lanza & Gomes, 2020: 166). An understanding of Asian–English multilingualism is not easily translatable to Eurocentric approaches due to complex, pragmatic aspects that are rich in Asian languages unlike in English and other European languages. In Korean, for example, you cannot produce a grammatical sentence without knowing whom you are speaking to and where you are speaking. For every utterance, one needs to know the relationship between themselves and the hearer, otherwise, one cannot be sure of how to even start talking. In this book, I hope to contribute to the diversity of this field by tackling pragmatic issues that are mostly relevant in Korean and further Asian–English multilingualism. This includes pragmatic adjustment and translanguaging to express emotions, attitudes and social interactions observed in Korean-English children and their families. In doing so, this book aims to raise awareness of the necessity of researching Asian–English multilingualism.

In today's world, being multilingual does not necessarily require full fluency in multiple languages. It encompasses a broader perspective. Individuals can be considered multilingual if they have exposure to languages beyond their native tongue. This exposure can take various forms. For some, it begins from birth, growing up in households with parents and caregivers who speak languages other than English. Others may find themselves in multilingual communities where various languages coexist. Yet, even beyond these family and community connections, the desire to voluntarily learn and immerse oneself in different languages signifies a mindset of multilingualism. It is about embracing the idea of navigating and appreciating the richness of linguistic diversity. For many children in the UK, their lives are intricately interwoven with languages and cultures from around the world. Whether it is a connection to their heritage, engagement with a diverse local community, or simply a personal preference to explore and learn, the ability to pick up languages is essential. It empowers them to fully realise their potential in a super-diverse and super-digital world.

In essence, being multilingual is not solely about fluency but is also about the openness and willingness to engage with different languages and cultures. It is a valuable skill that enhances our understanding of the world and fosters meaningful connections with others in an increasingly interconnected global society.

A Taxi Driver's Frustration

I was in a taxi, and the driver expressed deep frustration; he lamented that his daughters could not speak Urdu, and he saw no way for them to learn their heritage language at school. He explained that they could not afford to visit his home country, Pakistan, where they could naturally pick up the language. This frustration was palpable, and it highlights a larger issue in the UK. Some ethnic groups, like the Chinese, Japanese, and Korean communities, are quite proactive in teaching their heritage languages to their children. In East Asian communities, for example, there is often structured support for language education. However, for many other communities, the provision of heritage language learning operates primarily on a community basis rather than through governmental support. This means that not all communities have the same opportunities, and as a result, some individuals can become very discouraged. It is crucial for parents, children, and the community to understand the importance of their children learning these languages. It is not just about language; it is also about staying connected, building solidarity and ensuring that children have a strong and clear sense of identity. They also need to recognise that if English is the only language their children have access to, it can lead to isolation, conflicts and various challenges in their relationships and in the broader society, as this book explores in detail.

Home, Heritage and Community Language Matters

Promoting home or heritage languages can be a rich and valuable investment in children's holistic development, offering them a wealth of experiences, connections, and skills that span across various facets of their lives. Some of the key benefits of learning these languages are outlined next.

Cognitive development

Being bilingual in both the heritage and majority language can promote cognitive flexibility, enabling children to adapt to varied tasks and think from multiple perspectives (IRIS Center, n.d.; Leonard *et al.*, 2020; Sutton, 2021). In addition, a strong foundation in a heritage language can enrich memory, as children might associate words or phrases with personal experiences, stories, or cultural rituals (Huang *et al.*, 2022; Mårtensson *et al.*, 2012; Morales *et al.*, 2013).

Linguistic development

Engaging actively in two languages often leads to the acquisition of more diverse vocabulary, as children can draw from both linguistic pools (De Houwer *et al.*, 2014; Hoff *et al.*, 2012; Siow *et al.*, 2023). Being bilingual from an early age, especially in a heritage language and the dominant community language, can also foster heightened metalinguistic awareness, giving children insights into the structure and nuances of both languages (Leonard *et al.*, 2020; Song, 2016; Sutton, 2021). Furthermore, early heritage language learning can enhance phonetic skills, enabling children to perceive sounds at a level that is better than or as good as native speakers in both their heritage language and dominant language (Chang, 2016; Chang & Weiss-Cowie, 2021).

Societal and social development

Heritage languages play a pivotal role in connecting children with their grandparents or older family members who might not be proficient in the community or dominant language, fostering deeper family bonds (Huang & Liao, 2024; Kwon, 2017; Leonard *et al.*, 2020). Alongside strengthening familial relations, a strong grasp of the heritage language can bolster cultural identity, enabling children to engage more deeply with their cultural roots and traditions (Cho, 2000; Huang & Liao, 2024; Leonard *et al.*, 2020). Children who speak their heritage language can also gain opportunities to engage with a broader spectrum of the community, bridging both the heritage language speakers and the majority language group (Lee & Suarez, 2009; Triebold, 2020; Wong, 2021). Moreover, developing proficiency in their heritage language allows children to become more desirable in the job market through their ability to access speakers from their heritage language community in future professional contexts (Cho, 2000; Huang & Liao, 2024; Kwon, 2017).

Academic development

Proficiency in a heritage language, in addition to the community language, can facilitate bilingual academic skills, enabling children to excel in diverse educational settings (Kwon, 2017; Lee & Suarez, 2009; Prevoo *et al.*, 2016). Furthermore, knowledge of the heritage language can lead to the development of literacy skills in multiple languages, which can be academically and professionally advantageous in the long run (Papadopoulou *et al.*, 2022; Raising Children Network, 2023; WIDA, 2014).

Emotional development

Recognising and valuing their unique linguistic abilities can boost children's self-esteem and emotional resilience, particularly in diverse settings (Little, 2023; Wang *et al.*, 2022; Yu, 2015). Engaging with stories, experiences and histories through their heritage language can also cultivate empathy and solidarity, not just within their community but also towards other communities with similar experiences (Fan *et al.*, 2015; Huang & Fang, 2024).

Intercultural development

Children proficient in their heritage language often display a nuanced understanding of multiple cultures, fostering intercultural sensitivity (Patel, 2023; Raising Children Network, 2023; Sutton, 2021). With the world becoming more interconnected, having proficiency in a heritage language further provides children with a global perspective, enabling them to understand and navigate cross-cultural scenarios effectively (Patel, 2023; Sutton, 2021).

UK Language Learning Trends

In 2023, a report on language trends in primary and secondary schools reveals some noteworthy patterns. Nearly 9 out of 10 primary schools have students for whom English is an additional language (EAL), reflecting the rich linguistic diversity within these educational settings (Collen, 2023). Importantly, this diversity is viewed as a valuable opportunity rather than a challenge. Another positive trend is the increased collaboration between primary and secondary schools regarding language education, ensuring a smoother transition for students as they progress through their education. French continues to hold its position as the most popular language at Key Stage 3, closely followed by Spanish, with German also making a strong showing, particularly in independent schools. Remarkably, Spanish maintains its dominance at A-levels, indicating a sustained interest in advanced Spanish language education. Despite the challenges posed by the COVID-19 pandemic, schools' international engagement is on the rise, highlighting their resilience in maintaining global connections and cultural exchanges. Additionally, the report underscores the potential influence of parents' attitudes on language learning, particularly during a child's formative years, emphasising the role that parents can play in shaping their children's interest in language studies. Overall, these trends shed light on the diverse linguistic landscape of 2023 and the evolving dynamics of language education in schools.

Home: A Space beyond Family

The concept of 'home' goes beyond just one's blood relatives and physical residence; it can encompass a sense of belonging within a community. This broader notion of home suggests that a community, such as a Chinese community centre, can become a home for individuals from various backgrounds. HLs do not necessarily have to be intricately tied to one's heritage; they can be diverse and multifaceted. An experience that exemplifies this occurred during my fieldwork at a Chinese community centre in Camden. Surprisingly, the tai chi teacher was English, and within the same community centre, there was a mix of individuals, including third-generation Chinese individuals and Malaysian women who all engaged in learning Chinese. It was a remarkably inclusive and harmonious setting, where solidarity transcended ethnicities and languages. 'It's like a family, it's like a home' – this is how one individual I interviewed described the centre. They continued by saying: 'I think it's a part of their home life or daily life, especially for those who live on their own'. The centre itself felt like a welcoming home for everyone involved, and the languages spoken within its walls were not limited to just one; they encompassed a multitude of languages, including English, Mandarin Chinese and Malay, reflecting the rich tapestry of diversity and interconnectedness within the community.

In essence, home and community can extend beyond the confines of blood ties and physical dwellings. They represent places where individuals can find comfort, a sense of belonging, and a safe space to connect with others who share common interests or backgrounds. This inclusiveness and diversity within a community can foster a deep sense of home, where individuals come together to support and nurture one another, creating a strong and welcoming sense of belonging that transcends traditional notions of family and residence.

'Pride, Prejudice and Pragmatism: Family Language Policies in the UK' (Curdt-Christiansen *et al.*, 2023)

In the UK however, stigma persists towards heritage, home and community languages – specifically for non-Western European languages – as discussed in more detail in Chapter 2. This acutely affects heritage language speakers, particularly parents deciding on the language(s) spoken in the home. Curdt-Christiansen *et al.* (2023) investigate how mobility and changes in sociocultural contexts impact FLP in the UK. They aim to understand the reasons behind the different types of language practices and language management activities, exploring how the ideological constructs of *pride* (why parents want their children to learn their HL, usually tied to cultural connections and pride), *prejudice* (when differences are shown through language, race, culture, and values) and *pragmatism* (how families deal with their HL) are directly related to attitudes towards the development of children's HL. In doing so, they examine how transnational families in the UK find pride in their children's multilingualism, and how their experiences of raising multilingual children come into conflict with institutional policies and societal discourses that marginalise minority languages, leading to hierarchies of languages and resulting in the loss of HL development in the home. They show that the interplay of these three constructs creates FLPs – mirroring the ways in which social inequalities are reproduced. Their study falls within the area of FLP and the increased interest it has received in recent years, drawing on Spolsky's (2009) triadic model of language policy: language ideology, language practice and language management. They show that raising multilingual children and HLs have effects far beyond the family domain and are closely intertwined with sociopolitical factors. The study found that migration, social values, raciolinguistic policing in public education, and linguistic loyalty all affect FLP regarding language choice and maintenance. Their results indicated that different beliefs about language prestige and language privilege have implicit effects as evidenced by survey and interview data. Most families reported a strong pro-multilingual ideology, affirming that speaking more than one language had a positive impact on their children, and displayed a strong belief against prejudice statements. The findings showed that migrant families are aware of the advantages of bi/multilingualism but note discrepancies in how society views HLs; they disagree that HL learning is a private matter and that speaking other languages is unacceptable in the UK. There were positive pride responses concerning the relationship between HL maintenance and identity. However, pragmatism overtakes pride in the maintenance of HLs when comparing two prejudice statements and two pride statements on the benefits of bilingualism, which show a lower percentage of positive responses.

The results displayed an inconsistency in the distribution patterns of responses on whether prejudice is implicitly reflected in responses to pride (i.e. participants generally do not believe in the prejudice that using the HL can be disadvantageous for their children, but a minority strongly agree that they feel comfortable using the HL in public). This finding is explored more in interviews, which highlighted a 'fear' of being 'othered', revealing a deep-rooted prejudice from UK society concerning an implicit hierarchy of languages with English at the top. For instance, one interviewee showed covert pride in speaking Polish, but this pride is challenged in the public space to avoid overt prejudice. The use of the HL in public was found to be influenced by such fear of othering, as well as personal experiences (such as working as a migrant person). There was further inconsistency between the prejudice statement 'Learning non-English home language(s) is a private matter that should be done only at home' and the pride statement 'More governmental support is needed for maintaining home languages for minority groups in Britain'. This may indicate pragmatic concerns as public funds are needed for different minority language programmes, along with prejudice suggested through an implicit hierarchy of languages where certain languages are deserving of more public funds than others.

The findings also showed patterns of language change from the parent's generation to that of the children. For instance, depending on the type of activity (such as helping with their child's school homework and speaking to their child), the percentage of mixed English used by the parents varies. This may suggest a pragmatic act to unconsciously align their language practices with those of the school. Parents' self-reported that language practices after the birth of their first child also changed to accommodate societal language practices, influenced by invisible prejudice, as approximately 50% of parents changed practices, with more starting to use English more than the non-English HL. This may indicate invisible prejudice and seeking of a pragmatic solution. These findings are supported by the interview data, with parents feeling worried about their child's English language development and the pressure from a mainly monolingual public education, revealing competition between minority and dominant languages, which lead many parents to make the pragmatic decision to stop HL learning.

The results also showed that parents are aware of the importance of giving children exposure to the HL. However, the top choices (including frequent visits to their home country) were all temporary, periodic activities that can be affected by other factors like travel bans and finances, leading to inconsistent language experiences. This was further supported by the interview data in which the researchers could see the emotional reactions from some parents towards the pragmatic decision to lose their children's HL.

The findings indicated internalised prejudice against minority languages, promoted by public education, which links the loss of the HL to pragmatism and attempts to maintain pride in speaking the language(s) that is/are lost. The study shows how policies and structures normalise linguistic prejudice in families in the UK, as reflected in language ideologies, practices and management. Experiences of 'othering' and pride contradict each other, thereby forcing FLP to give in to pragmatic measures. While most families did not overtly subscribe to a prejudice ideology, instead showing pride, they viewed such pride as non-essential and challenged in the public space. The study highlighted the tensions existing between pride, prejudice, pragmatism and language practices; language practices change according to covert and overt prejudices, and there is conflict between what they view as pride and actual practice. Although parents believed that learning the HL is beneficial and a matter of pride, they also noted little time and few resources for their children to engage in HL learning as a result of HLs remaining marginalised in the UK public education system, leading parents to concede to pragmatism and give up the HL.

This study contributes to research on the multilingual development of children in transnational families. Importantly, Curdt-Christiansen *et al.* (2023) show that FLP alone cannot save minority languages; institutions and ideologies need to legitimise these languages as linguistic resources and languages of pride. They call for more research exploring how institutionally sanctioned language practices and raciolinguistic ideologies interact with FLP in highly diverse societies like the UK and advocate for more studies on home–school collaboration to understand how the positives of legitimising HLs in school contexts can generate increased opportunities to develop multilingualism and pride as a multilingual.

The Language of Culture

Culture and language are inextricably linked. Culture is co-constructed through language and other symbolic systems, such as images, videos and even social media. According to Kramsch (1998: 10), culture can be defined as 'membership in a discourse community that shares a common social space and history, and common imagining. Even when they have left that community, its members may retain, wherever they are, a common system of standards for perceiving, believing, evaluating, and acting. These standards are what is generally called their *culture*'. Culture provides you with a way of thinking, behaving and apprehending the world around you. We are both the actors and creators of culture. With every act of language, we both consolidate and develop what it means to belong to our respective cultures. Culture is now seen as a heterogeneous entity. We rarely belong to just one culture: we all have a unique combination of national, regional, ethnic, occupational, professional, gendered and generational belonging. Our culture is linked to our sense of self-identity and often provides us with legitimacy.

In intercultural couples (IC), co-constructed culture is highly significant. Both partners in an IC contribute their own culture to the relationship, and the couple must work out how the two cultures can co-exist and eventually even combine them to live harmoniously. The shared culture in an IC must be worked out via a process of negotiation rather than domination. In this way, the challenges that ICs face are related not just to the linguistics of their communication, but also the cultural context of their communication. Culture is expressed in all aspects of life. In this chapter, we see culture as expressed in cooking and cultural activities. In negotiating these everyday occurrences, couples embark on a journey of co-constructing their culture together. In this pursuit, no one culture should take centre stage. Instead, both cultures should be incorporated to some extent, so that the couple constructs a shared culture between them in an egalitarian manner. Coming from two different cultures can be difficult, but it can also make a couple's lives richer and more diverse. For ICs, transculturation, that is to say, 'cultural transformation marked by the influx of new culture elements and the loss or alteration of existing ones' (Merriam-Webster, n.d.), is inevitable. Transculturation is even further enabled due to easy access to social media and the online world. Learning about another culture and accessing its cultural content has never been so easy.

Conflicts in Intercultural Families: Avoiding Intergenerational Breakdown

Effective parent–children communication is of paramount importance, and this extends to grandparent–children and wider family communication as well. Language plays a crucial role in these interactions as it serves as the foundation for understanding, connecting and harmonising within the family unit. Without effective language communication, there is a risk of experiencing conflicts, divisions and social discord among family members. The consequences of inadequate communication can be particularly challenging for parents, as they bear the burden of navigating these complexities and ensuring the well-being of their family.

In his 2017 work, Baldwin explores the intricate relationship between culture, communication, and family dynamics, highlighting the critical role that families play in reflecting and transmitting cultural idiosyncrasies. These processes yield noticeable differences among families grounded in diverse cultures. Baldwin (2017) further elucidates the pervasiveness of intercultural communication within families, especially in instances where parents hail from distinct cultures and children are subject to various cultural influences due to immigration or globalisation, or within colonised or diasporic contexts.

Through its profound influence, language serves as both the cornerstone of culture and a mirror of societal dynamics. During their formative years, children are predominantly shaped by their parents' and caregivers' language. However, these dynamics often undergo significant changes as children grow, especially within migrant families. They frequently transform into cultural mediators, acting as bridges between their family culture and the broader multicultural society in which they live. Hua (2008) delves into this complex negotiation of multiple languages within families. Hua investigated the intricate relationship between social interaction and sociocultural values by analysing conflict talk samples between parents and children in Chinese diasporic families in the UK. Hua's study reveals how conflicts are managed using codeswitching, how personal values and identities are negotiated in bilingual interactions, and how bilingualism itself gives rise to new family dynamics and values. Similar to Hua (2008), Rubino (2015) scrutinises how code-switching between three languages – Sicilian, Italian and English – is used to negotiate intergenerational conflict in a Sicilian-Australian family with historical ties to Sicily in Italy. She found that the trilingual alternation functioned to construct and negotiate parent and child identities during interaction, where instances of conflict become emblematic of tensions surrounding the intergenerational process of enculturation and acculturation in the family.

Hua (2010) has also investigated interculturality and seeks to contribute to this field by looking at how different generations of diasporic families negotiate their sociocultural values in interaction. Hua focuses on the use of address terms by Chinese diasporic families living in the UK, viewing language as more than a reflection of sociocultural ideas, but as something that informs them. Hua examines the use of Chinese and English by the older and younger generations of families, discussing the older generations' use of English pronouns and terms of address as a 'they'-language, with younger generations viewing English as a 'we'-language. Both generations employ address terms in either English or Chinese selectively to portray their feelings regarding family values (based on either their Chinese or British cultural heritage). Intergenerational conflicts are commonplace and can permeate all aspects of daily life, from holiday traditions to meal choices. Li and Hua (2013) examine an instance where a Chinese mother and her British-born Chinese son have a disagreement over the appropriate dish for Christmas dinner, showcasing the complexity of navigating multicultural and bilingual family dynamics.

Understanding the inherent connection between discourse and culture is crucial in comprehending the role that language plays within a culture.

As children mature and gain more influence within their families, these dynamics continue to evolve. Thus, it becomes essential for families to cultivate a culture of active listening, negotiation and mutual respect. Intergenerational conflicts often surface in intercultural families, particularly in in-law relationships. An Asian-Western couple living in Singapore who were part of Kiaer and Ahn's (2023b) case study perfectly illustrate this complexity. After deciding to live with the wife's parents to economise, the couple found themselves confronting different cultural views on personal boundaries. The wife's Asian culture lacks strict physical boundaries, contrasting sharply with the husband's Western culture, which emphasised personal space. The husband's discomfort became apparent when his private workroom was entered without permission, underscoring the potential complexities and tensions within intercultural families. To mitigate these tensions, the couple opted to spend some time in Sri Lanka.

Translanguaging emerges as a potential catalyst for conflict resolution in these situations. It can help relax the rigidity of family relationships, fostering an interactive learning environment where no party wields dominant authority. This co-learning process is perceived not as a rigid teaching model but as a journey of mutual exploration and understanding. By engaging in this collaborative process, parents, children and other family members co-create and co-shape their languages and cultures, forging unique familial identities. Shared cultural activities, like cooking together or learning martial arts, serve as powerful tools in this journey, reinforcing solidarity and reducing conflicts. Although the power of language is dynamic and evolving, the importance of understanding, acceptance and mutual respect remains constant and critical for successful intercultural family relationships.

Making Language Learning Relevant for Multilinguals: The Australian Model

On a societal level, to practically achieve better recognition of and to nurture home, heritage and community languages, we can turn to Australia as an example (as will be discussed in more detail in Chapter 7). Australia's language policy, known for its multicultural and multilingual approach with English as the *de facto* national language, provides valuable lessons for the UK, given their shared English background. Australia's language policy development, spanning assimilation, multiculturalism and a focus on foreign language education, offers a framework for the UK to consider (Wang, 2010). Notably, Australia's emphasis on Asian languages like Chinese and Japanese for tapping into economic opportunities in the region, and their flexible foreign language curriculum, diverse content, and investment in education, are aspects that the UK can learn from to enhance its own language education system. By improving home, heritage and community language education and appreciation, we will be able to make language learning relevant to our children's lives.

5 Psychology of Language Learning

Practical tips:
- **Go beyond words:** Integrate non-verbal cues like gestures and facial expressions into language instruction for a more holistic learning experience.
- **Emphasise the importance of original thinking:** Encourage quality thinking rather than rote manipulation of formulas. This can be achieved by incorporating communicative teaching methods and reducing the use of rote learning techniques in language classrooms.
- **Make it relevant:** Utilise TBLL and CLIL to enable students to learn and use the target language to complete actual activities or tasks. Additionally, interactions with materials and speakers of the target language can aid in showing the relevance of learning the language. This will help connect language learning to real-life scenarios and other subjects.

Why Learn Languages?

In this chapter, we delve into the psychology of language learning, exploring the intricate factors that drive individuals to study languages. We examine the roles of individual differences in shaping the language learning process, delving into the following topics: motivation, fandom learners, solidarity learners, individual differences, foreign language anxiety (FLA) and enjoyment (FLE), among others. Each of these aspects plays a crucial role in understanding the psychology behind language learning and the diverse motivations that propel individuals on their linguistic journeys.

The Foundation: Motivation Theory

Gardner's motivation theory, developed in 1972 by Robert Gardner and Wallace Lambert, is a cornerstone in the field of language motivation research. According to their perspective, motivation plays a pivotal role in the success of language learning, transcending natural abilities. Their theory highlights the notion that learning a new language is not solely about mastering the language itself; it also involves forming a connection with a different culture.

Within Gardner's framework, two distinct types of motivation come to the forefront, each with its own unique examples:

Integrative motive

This aspect centres on the desire to belong to a specific community or culture. For example, imagine a person who decides to learn Spanish because they have always been fascinated by the rich cultural traditions of Spanish-speaking countries and want to immerse themselves in these cultures by understanding the language. In this case, the integrative motive is the driving force behind their language learning journey.

Instrumental motive

Instrumental motivation, on the other hand, is driven by practical goals. For instance, consider someone who learns Mandarin Chinese because they anticipate better job opportunities in an increasingly globalised job market by being bilingual. Here, the instrumental motive is clear: it is about advancing one's career prospects through language proficiency.

Gardner's theory comprises four key components:

(1) Integrative motive: This aspect centres on the desire to belong to a specific community or culture, emphasising the importance of cultural integration in language learning.
(2) Socioeducational model: Gardner and Lambert introduced this model to underscore the societal and educational factors that influence language motivation. For example, if a society values bilingualism and offers educational programmes that encourage language learning, individuals may be more motivated to acquire a new language.
(3) Attitude/motivation test battery: A tool designed to measure the levels of motivation, this battery aids in assessing and understanding the motivational aspects of language learning. It might include questions like, 'How strongly do you feel about becoming part of a particular culture through language learning?'.
(4) Extended second language (L2) motivation construct: This component expands upon the fundamental concepts of Gardner's theory, providing a comprehensive perspective on language motivation.

For example, it may consider how motivation evolves over time as an individual becomes more deeply engaged with the language and culture.

The Process-Orientated Model

The process-orientated model, developed by Dörnyei and Ottó in 1998, views motivation as a dynamic and evolving process. This model outlines motivation as a series of steps, which can be illustrated with examples:

(1) Goal setting: The first step in the process is setting clear and achievable goals. For example, a student who sets a goal of achieving a certain proficiency level in French within six months has established a specific language learning objective.
(2) Taking action: After setting goals, learners take action by engaging in language learning activities. This could involve attending classes, practicing conversation with native speakers, or using language learning apps and resources.
(3) Evaluating progress: As learners progress, they continuously evaluate their advancement towards their goals. For instance, if a student aiming for French proficiency notices improvement in their conversational skills and vocabulary, it serves as positive feedback that they are moving in the right direction.

Dörnyei and Ottó emphasise that motivation changes as learners move through these stages and can be influenced by various factors, such as the learning environment and emotional factors. However, it is essential to acknowledge that this model has its limitations, as it does not consider hidden or irrational motivations and tends to isolate motivational actions from other ongoing activities. Gardner's theory emphasises the significance of culture and identity in language motivation, while Dörnyei and Ottó's process-orientated model focuses on how motivation evolves as learners progress through clear steps, illustrated with examples, and how motivation is influenced by various external factors. These two perspectives provide valuable foundations for understanding the intricate nature of motivation in language learning.

Your Future Self

Dörnyei's L2 motivational self system (L2MSS) is outlined in his 2009 work. At the core of this theory lies the concept of the 'future self'. It is the gap between someone's present self (their actual self) and the person they aspire to become in the future (their ideal or 'ought-to' self) that serves as the driving force for motivation among learners. Here is a breakdown:

Ideal self

This is a learner's personal vision of who they want to become. It is like a mental image of their desired language proficiency and abilities. For instance, someone learning French might envision themselves as a fluent speaker, comfortably navigating conversations with native speakers.

'Ought-to' self

In contrast, the 'ought-to' self is influenced by external factors, primarily the social environment. It is what learners believe they need to be based on societal or cultural expectations. Using the same example, if society places a high value on bilingualism, a learner may feel they 'ought to' achieve a certain level of proficiency to meet these expectations.

In simpler terms, according to Dörnyei (2009), learners are motivated by a desire to become the person they want to be (ideal self) or the person they believe they should be based on external influences (ought-to self). This perspective highlights the power of personal aspirations and societal pressures in driving motivation in language learning.

Motivation: Belonging to a Community

In a study by MacIntyre *et al.* (2017), a different facet of L2 motivation, termed 'community-level motivation', is explored. This motivation is distinct from the ideal L2 self and integrativeness, as it represents a collective mindset deeply rooted in the shared geography, history and cultural practices of a heritage community, specifically focusing on the Gaelic community in their research.

This concept aligns with Ushioda's (2009) person-in-context relational model, which perceives motivation as organically evolving from the close interaction between individuals and their cultural and historical contexts. In simpler terms, learners who are influenced by community-level motivation envision themselves as integrated members of the community in the long run. The power of surrounding sociocultural traditions, such as music and dance, can explain that the ought-to self is not necessarily seen as an unwanted obligation to integrate, but rather a welcome, albeit challenging, obligation for learners to learn the language to carry forward the traditions of their specific community – in this case, the Gaelic community.

The study suggests that current assumptions about L2 motivation are often based on the premise that English is a static source of motivation. However, this might not hold true for languages other than English (LOTE), where motivation can have fragmented sources. For instance, in the case of community-level motivation, social circles (fandom) and a sense of uniqueness from others (feeling cool when learning a foreign language (FL)) can be significant motivators. Learners in a fandom context possess a shared understanding of the target language's history, norms and culture, which further strengthens their motivation to be a part of this community.

Dörnyei and Ushioda (2011) also emphasise that perceived social norms that do not align with one's self-image can be counterproductive in terms of motivation. This highlights the importance of considering the intricate interplay between an individual's motivation and their cultural and community contexts when studying L2 motivation.

Digital Motivation

Adolphs *et al.* (2018) report on the visual representation of language learners' ideal L2 selves digitally, arguing for the use of technology-based approaches as a potential means to create effective visualisations of their ideal selves and to serve as a powerful motivator. Previous studies like C. Kim *et al.* (2012) have also demonstrated that virtual characters or avatars can represent ideal selves. Dörnyei and Kubanyiova (2014) also assert that digital technology can have a considerable motivational impact on learning.

Motivation Research: Imbalance between English and Languages Other than English

In their 2017 paper titled *The Motivational Foundation of Learning Languages Other than Global English: Theoretical Issues and Research Directions*, Dörnyei and Al-Hoorie (2017) address a critical issue in the field of L2 motivation research. The authors argue that the long-standing and unquestioned dominance of English has created an imbalance in L2 motivation research. This dominance has led to a disproportionate focus on the motivation to learn English, while other languages, referred to as 'languages other than English', have been overshadowed in research. This oversight is despite the awareness of global geopolitical factors, such as the influence of globalisation, and sociopolitical factors, including the promotion of multilingualism. Dörnyei and Al-Hoorie advocate for full linguistic justice in the realm of L2 motivation research. They emphasise that English should not and cannot be the sole conceptual anchor in the theoretical foundations of L2 research. In essence, their argument underscores the importance of recognising and researching motivation in the context of learning LOTE, ensuring a more balanced and comprehensive understanding of language learning motivation across diverse linguistic backgrounds.

Motivation: A Complex Story

In a study by Thompson and Vásquez (2015), the concept of an 'anti-ought-to self' is explored, shedding light on the intricate nature of language learning motivation. One illustrative case involved an American learner of Chinese who was initially discouraged and advised to choose a different language due to perceived difficulties. However, this learner persisted and used the doubts and challenges as motivation to prove himself. The doubts, rather than hindering his progress, actually served as a driving force. Similarly, in a UK context, Oakes (2013) reported that learners of LOTE reject the notion of a monoglot culture in England. This rejection highlights the awareness of inadequate FL skills in the UK and a desire to challenge the status quo. Nevertheless, it is important to note that these findings are drawn from case studies and may not be universally applicable.

The study prompts the exploration of whether participants, especially those born and raised in the UK, exhibit similar rebellious behaviour that unintentionally leads to language learning motivation. This suggests that motivation in language learning is a multifaceted and complex phenomenon influenced by various factors, including societal expectations, challenges and personal determination. In essence, this research emphasises that motivation in language learning cannot be simply categorised; it is a complex and dynamic interplay of factors, where even doubts and resistance can fuel learners' determination and drive to succeed.

Additionally, Ushioda's (2012) work delves into the fascinating realm of religion and faith-based motivation in language learning. Ushioda notes that when language learning motivation is intimately bound up with one's Christian faith or sense of Christian vocation, this motivation becomes exceptionally powerful and sustaining. The L2MSS is framed in terms of an individual's self-related beliefs, visions and aspirations, making room for personal beliefs in divine sources of motivation and religious ideals. In religious contexts, language learning often plays a crucial role in nurturing faith and spirituality. For instance, there is a certain amount of linguistic ritual involved in religious practices for followers to acquire, further emphasising the interconnectedness of faith and language learning.

Motivation in language learning is therefore a multifaceted and dynamic phenomenon, encompassing various sources of inspiration, including personal beliefs, challenges and faith-based motivations. These diverse facets contribute to the complex tapestry of language learning motivation, which continues to diversify at a rapid pace.

Language Learning: Beyond Pragmatic, Instrumentalist Needs

In Lo Bianco's (2014) work, the concept of 'super-diversity', as introduced by Vertovec (2006), takes centre stage. This concept highlights a shifting landscape where traditional boundaries of nations, languages, and cultures are becoming increasingly fluid and evolving. This transformation is driven, in part, by the expansion and blending of digital technologies, underscoring the growing complexity of societal structures and interactions in today's globally interconnected world. Lo Bianco argues that if researchers approach language learning motivation solely from an instrumentalist perspective, viewing language learning as having purely pragmatic value, they may limit their investigations to theoretical accounts related to self-states or future goals. This narrow focus could lead to a restricted understanding of how individuals and societies engage with language diversity.

Furthermore, Lo Bianco suggests that an overly instrumental approach, as seen in communicative language learning, may contribute to the challenges faced by modern language education in Anglophone contexts. This is evident in the demotivation among young learners to study languages other than English, resulting in low levels of FL competency and enrolment rates. In contrast, non-Anglophone countries tend to prioritise FL learning due to institutional curriculum priorities, particularly English, and individual motivational priorities. Furthermore, Lo Bianco points out that language education is often perceived as a tool driven by narrowly defined economic interests, sometimes in contrast to a more humanistic, cultural and intellectual approach. This tension highlights the ongoing debate about the purpose and value of language learning in an evolving global context. To address these complexities, Cook (2016) proposes a 'linguistic multi-competence' framework as an alternative way to theorise motivation. This framework considers the intricate realities of communication in today's globalised yet increasingly pluralistic and diverse societies. Rather than focusing on individual language systems in isolation, it encompasses 'the total system for all languages (L1, L2, Ln)' within a single mind or community and their interconnectedness (Cook, 2016: 7).

Why Invest in Language Learning?

In Norton's (2013) exploration of language learning, the concept of 'investment' takes centre stage. This term is defined as 'the commitment to the goals, practices and identities that constitute the learning process and that are continually negotiated in different relations of power' (Darvin, 2019: 245). It challenges traditional theories of motivation by highlighting the complex identities of language learners and the nuances they encounter in their learning journey. For example, it may explain why highly motivated learners sometimes resist opportunities to speak when they feel marginalised, a phenomenon particularly relevant in the context of LOTE.

Learners invest in language learning because it offers them access to a broader spectrum of symbolic and material resources. This, in turn, enhances their cultural capital and social power. Norton (2013) emphasises that this investment is closely intertwined with learners' identities and their position in the social world. It determines their access to communities, social networks and their interactions with speakers of the target language. To establish a powerful identity in these contexts, learners must secure more influential positions that enable them to engage in speaking, reading and writing in the target language.

Building on this idea, the concept of 'imagined communities' comes into play. Norton argues that language learning investment goes beyond affirming existing identities and empowering learners to assert their right to communicate. It also involves enabling learners to imagine new identities and affiliations. This concept draws inspiration from Wenger (1998), who stressed the importance of gaining membership in a community of speakers through engagement and imagination, as well as Anderson (1991), who conceptualised nations as imagined communities united by a shared sense of belonging. In the realm of L2 investment, 'imagined communities' refers to groups and networks that learners aspire to join, extending beyond local relationships. By aspiring to be part of these communities, learners invest in an L2 to gain entry and actively participate with others.

Social Media and Language Learning

As social media is becoming increasingly intertwined with our modern life, engaging billions of users worldwide, it could be an engaging and effective platform to integrate into language pedagogies. Lambton-Howard *et al.* (2021) examine the role of social media features in language education through the perspectives of students and teachers by carrying out two workshops at a UK university in 2019. One notable finding from their research emphasised the sense of ownership these young people felt towards social media: 'social media is their space'. With this, there came the corresponding need to navigate the appropriateness of social media communication between learners and teachers, which currently stands as a grey area without clear agreed-upon boundaries. The study also found that social media allowed for the prioritisation of authentic communication through a more immersive learning experience. Lambton-Howard *et al.* recommend better integration of social media features, such as group text, images and video, to make language education more comfortable and accessible to learners. They also propose creating learner-led and learner-owned social media spaces, designing structured pathways that enable authentic social media use through group structures and sizes, and incorporating social media in traditional and new methods of assessment. Evidently, social media seems to be a tool with significant positive potential that has not yet been fully unlocked in the realm of language learning. In this globalised, super-digital age, we must creatively innovate how we teach languages to digital natives, as former methods may no longer be the most effective for younger generations.

Fandom Learners: The Case of K-Pop

Fandom learners are characterised by their high level of enthusiasm and proactivity in their language learning journey. They are often at the forefront of language learning trends, utilising a combination of social media and AI-assisted learning methods to enhance their language skills. This involves learning languages through means that reduce anxiety while maximising enjoyment in an environment that is as free from judgement as possible. Fandom learners are not passive language enthusiasts; they actively engage with the language they are learning. In the case of fandom learners of Korean, they immerse themselves in the culture, media, and content associated with their favourite K-pop groups or interests. This active engagement includes watching K-dramas, listening to K-pop music and participating in online fan communities. Social media platforms, particularly Twitter (now known as X), play a central role in the language learning process of fandom learners. They use these platforms to connect with fellow fans, share their language learning progress, and engage in discussions related to their interests. Twitter's immediacy and global reach make it an ideal platform for connecting with other fans and accessing authentic language content. What is more, fandom learners often leverage AI-assisted learning tools and language learning apps to enhance their language skills. These tools offer personalised learning experiences, adaptive content and gamification elements that align with the preferences of tech-savvy learners. AI-powered chatbots and language learning apps provide instant feedback and practice opportunities, making the learning process more interactive and enjoyable. Consuming a wide range of content in the target language is also integral to a fandom learner's immersion in the FL. They watch subtitled videos, read lyrics and engage with fan-translated materials to gain exposure to the language. This diverse content consumption allows them to learn in context, reinforcing their language skills through real-world applications. Indeed, fandom learners are highly motivated to excel in their language learning journey. They set clear goals for themselves, driven by their desire to better understand their favourite content and connect with their idols. This intrinsic motivation fuels their dedication and persistence in language learning.

In summary, fandom learners are characterised by their active, goal-orientated and tech-savvy approach to language learning. They harness the power of social media, AI-assisted tools, and authentic content consumption to immerse themselves in the language and culture of their chosen fandom, making language learning an integral part of their fan experience. In light of these concepts, learners who identify as fans may negotiate their position of power within communities and social networks, particularly within their fandom interest group. Being part of a fandom group can significantly influence how language learners interact with speakers of the target language. Drawing from investment theory, fandom language learners strive to claim empowered identities as 'fans', which enhances their ability to communicate in the target language. Consequently, they consistently invest time and effort in language learning to strengthen their position in the social world.

K-wave fandom's language

For many youths worldwide, including Millennials and Generation Z, the K-wave fandom's language is their language – although not exclusively so, as the fandom encompasses a wide range of age groups. What is particularly interesting is that for such people, Korean is not their heritage language; they are breaking the boundaries of more traditional concepts of language learning and motivation. Through translingual, transcultural media, they learn the language to sing with their idols, watch exclusive fan content, and even buy merchandise from official websites in Korean – all of which may act as a gateway to immersing themselves, often as part of a wider community, deeper in the language even outside the realm of K-pop.

Online communication is an important aspect of intercultural communication. The internet has made it possible for people to connect with others from all over the world, whether it be family, friends, or colleagues. As Kiaer and Ahn (2023a) discuss, one area where this is particularly evident is in K-content fandoms, where fans of K-pop idols, K-actors, K-dramas and K-films come together online. Being part of a K-fandom often involves engaging with internet culture, such as uploading pictures of K-idols on social media or discussing the latest happenings. To highlight just how global K-fandoms are, the top 10 markets tweeting about K-pop in 2020 were (1) Indonesia, (2) Thailand, (3) South Korea, (4) the Philippines, (5) the United States, (6) Brazil, (7) Malaysia, (8) Japan, (9) Mexico and (10) India (Kim, 2021). From a small subculture previously popular only in Asia, K-content has exploded in popularity all over the globe.

As mentioned, Twitter serves as a vital platform for K-fandom discussions, allowing fans to connect and communicate easily with each other. K-fandoms hold significant value on Twitter, with #KpopTwitter generating over 7.8 billion tweets in 2021 alone (Kim, 2022). The majority of the top 20 most retweeted tweets of all time belong to the popular K-pop boy group, BTS (Boyd, 2023). Twitter has even established a dedicated K-pop team, led by Yeonjeong Kim, who heads Global K-pop Partnerships. On Twitter, K-fans engage in discussions related to the K-wave, including Korean culture, using a unique online language that is specific to their shared culture. For instance, particular emojis hold significant meaning within the K-fandom. The blue heart emoji, for example, symbolises BTOB, while Cherry Bullet fans use a combination of cherry and pistol emojis to refer to their favourite K-pop girl group (Laure, 2023). Likewise, fans of Twice use a lollipop emoji to represent the group, and BTS is indicated by a purple heart (Laure, 2023).

Reddit is another platform that fandoms typically use to discuss and debate. It is a forum platform in which users can open a thread, often by asking a question, and respond to or discuss these threads. Reddit serves as an important platform for fans from all over the world to discuss their favourite K-pop groups, K-films, or K-dramas. Compared to Twitter, Reddit's forum-style layout means that fans use it for debate and negotiation. It is a site on which users explain things to each other, rather than simply sharing their love for their favourite K-content. Reddit is an important archival space where global fans exchange and negotiate both culture and language.

Being a fan of any form of K-content or K-celebrity typically involves some level of exposure to the Korean language. The more K-media grows, the more fans are exposed to K-culture and K-words. Notably, K-content does not necessarily expose fans to Korean high culture and history; rather, it exposes them to a new form of 'K-', which is commercially and globally informed. As a result of exposure to K-culture and K-words, K-fans often mix Korean words and non-verbal expressions into their online communication. This happens in one of two ways. Firstly, fans may mix their local language and Korean together. For example, it is particularly common to see a mix of Malay and Romanised Korean on Twitter. Secondly, global fans tend to communicate using English, as English is the lingua franca of the internet, so fans will often communicate in English and Korean, regardless of whether or not English is their first language.

K-wave fandom's language learning motivation

Following the discussion above, it is clear that Korean language learning has experienced significant growth and global popularity, with notable trends and factors contributing to its prominence in language education. The influence of K-pop and K-wave, driven by social media platforms like Twitter, has played a pivotal role in amplifying the appeal of the Korean language. Social media platforms, particularly Twitter, have been instrumental in expanding the reach and influence of K-pop and K-wave culture. They serve as hubs for fans to access information, news, and updates about their favourite artists and events, thus increasing the global visibility and popularity of Korean entertainment. This digital phenomenon has significantly shaped the K-pop and K-wave fandom and their global impact.

One can also observe Korea's growing importance in language education; the surge in Korean language learning reflects the language's remarkable growth and global appeal. In South and Southeast Asia,

Korean stands out as a preferred choice for FL learning, particularly in the Philippines, while also gaining traction in countries like Thailand, Indonesia and Pakistan (Ministry of Foreign Affairs and Korea Foundation, 2023). Duolingo's 2022 report ranks Korean as the seventh most-studied language on the platform, second only to Japanese among Asian languages (Blanco, 2022). This popularity solidifies Korean's position in contemporary language education.

Zooming out to consider the broader Korean wave – Hallyu – one striking example of Hallyu's impact on language learning is the surge in learners reported by Duolingo during the peak of *Squid Game*'s popularity in 2021 (Zabell, 2021). This Korean drama series achieved global recognition and sparked increased interest in learning the Korean language. Fans turned to language learning platforms like Duolingo to further explore the language and culture. K-pop fandom's influence, the global rise of Korean language learning, India's recognition of the Korean language (Sharma, 2021), and Hallyu's impact on language learning all contribute to the unique and dynamic landscape of Korean language education. The interplay of identity, power and community belonging within fandom language learning contexts adds depth to the motivation and enthusiasm of learners, a number of whom are not heritage speakers and might easily say, 'I want to learn Korean just so I can watch K-dramas without the subtitles!'

BTS effect

Within the domain of K-pop, one group in particular has led to an unprecedented rise in Korean language learners from overseas: BTS. The ARMY fandom, united through their interest and appreciation for the popular boy band BTS, has built an international community wherein individuals not only 'fanboy' and 'fangirl' over their favourite artists but also learn the native language of their idols together. On one occasion, ARMY popularised the phrase *soboksobok*, a lyric from one of BTS member Jimin's Christmas songs released on SoundCloud (Kiaer, n.d.). In a subsequent interview, Jimin explained that *soboksobok* is an onomatopoeic word meaning 'falling', but gently, as snow does. Both Korean and international fans have since regularly started using '#soboksobok' in their social media posts, demonstrating the global linguistic reach of BTS. On another occasion in 2018, overseas ARMY flocked to social media, posting their handwritten BTS lyrics in Korean with the tag '#방탄때문에_한글배웠다' (#I learned-Korean-because-of-BTS) (National Hangeul Museum, 2021). Noticing the trend of more Korean language learners being motivated by BTS, during COVID-19, Big Hit Entertainment, BTS's management company, launched a web series to help fans teach themselves Korean. Through 30 lessons hosted by BTS on the social media app Weverse, international fans keen on learning Korean could do so in a fun, content-based manner while belonging to a global community (Savage, 2020). On 9 October 2021, BTS also greeted their fans through a YouTube video on Hangeul Day, a day celebrating the creation of the Korean writing script called Hangeul, thereby supporting ARMY's study of Korean (KBS News, 2021). While official statistics are difficult to obtain, scrolling through ARMY's posts on social media shows an abundance of Korean language learners, driven at least initially, by their love for BTS. This is what I term the 'BTS effect'.

If You Like It and Love It, Then You'll Learn It

In Pavelescu and Petrić's (2018) study, the profound impact of 'love' on language learning emerges as a central theme. The findings reveal that 'love' serves as an enduring force that sustains learners in their journey of acquiring an L2 or FL, particularly English. This love is not necessarily an emotional attachment to the language itself but rather a deep affection for English that empowers learners to be proactive in motivating themselves. It drives them to engage with the language in enjoyable ways, such as through reading literature, and encourages their active involvement in FL learning. Importantly, this affection for English often stems from out-of-school experiences, such as online or internet-based communication with other users in English. The study highlights the crucial role of love in language learning, demonstrating that when learners genuinely appreciate and enjoy the language, their motivation becomes a driving force that helps them overcome challenges and remain engaged.

Additionally, the study underscores the significance of the learner–teacher relationship in fostering positive emotions in the learning of English as an FL. Numerous studies have corroborated this, emphasising that enjoyment in FL learning is strongly linked to teachers who are supportive and encouraging (Ahmadi-Azad et al., 2020; Jin & Zhang, 2021). This aspect of teacher–student interaction appears to be an irreplaceable component of language learning, potentially challenging the idea of AI teachers fully replicating these interpersonal dynamics.

Furthermore, Dewaele and Pavelescu's (2021) study sheds light on the impact of learners' interest in the topic(s) being taught on their FL learning experience. Lack of interest can lead to negative reactions, while computer-mediated communication with foreign friends appears to create less anxiety-provoking situations. This research, in conjunction with other studies, suggests that learners can adopt different roles, from being 'safe players' in the classroom to emerging as 'fighters' outside the classroom. These roles are shaped by various factors, including their level of interest and the context in which they use the language.

In essence, these studies collectively emphasise that love and enjoyment play pivotal roles in motivating language learners. When learners have a genuine affection for the language and enjoy their learning experiences, their motivation becomes a powerful driving force, encouraging active engagement and endurance in the language learning journey.

Solidarity Learners

The act of studying Ukrainian by over 1.3 million people worldwide following Russia's invasion of Ukraine in February 2022 serves as a powerful example of how language learning can be a means to build solidarity (Higgins, 2023). In times of crisis and conflict, people often turn to language as a way to show support and empathy towards affected communities (Briant, 2016). This surge in interest and active engagement in learning and using Ukrainian during the crisis period demonstrates how language can become a symbol of unity and solidarity, transcending geographical and cultural boundaries. It signifies the human capacity to express empathy and support through linguistic means, highlighting the role of language learning as a form of collective response to global events.

Indeed, the motivation for language learning is often closely tied to building human relationships; the more you share, the more you care. Children who speak their heritage language, for instance, seek to establish connections with their relatives back in their home country. Additionally, forming friendships with people who share similar interests or showing solidarity has become an increasingly important motivation for language learning. On the other hand, learning languages can also be driven by the desire to explore new cultures, discover new worlds or even transform oneself.

Individual Differences: Motivation

People often learn languages for various reasons. It could be a deep appreciation for the culture associated with a language, or it might stem from having friends who speak a particular language. Learning and sharing languages can be a profound way to express solidarity. However, it is essential to realise that the concept of solidarity goes beyond words. It encompasses non-verbal language and shared experiences, both of which play a significant role in building connections and fostering a sense of unity. Engaging in cultural activities, celebrating national festivals, and participating in customs and traditions together can be just as impactful in creating solidarity as linguistic communication (Kiaer, 2023a: 131–132). When individuals or groups make an effort to learn and speak each other's languages, it symbolises a commitment to understanding and respecting different cultures. However, solidarity does not stop there; it extends to actively participating in cultural events and traditions. These shared experiences deepen cultural understanding and showcase respect for the heritage and values of others. One way of achieving this is through more personalised language learning with the help of AI, as Chapter 6 discusses in more detail.

Individual Differences: Foreign Language Anxiety

Individual differences matter, perhaps most prominently in the realm of L2 learning. Every student brings a unique blend of personality traits, motivations, and aptitudes to the classroom. Zoltán Dörnyei's (2005) seminal work on the subject has been instrumental in highlighting the depth and significance of these differences in the language acquisition process. However, a pressing dilemma emerges: How can a teacher, already navigating the diverse demands of an entire classroom, be expected to tailor instruction to each individual's nuances?

The more we explore this topic, the clearer it becomes that we might inadvertently be placing added pressures on teachers and educational institutions, who are already grappling with heavy workloads and numerous responsibilities. While the importance of individualised instruction is undeniable, there is a crucial need to balance this understanding with the real-world constraints that educators face daily. This juxtaposition between idealised teaching approaches and the realities of classroom dynamics presents a pivotal challenge in the discourse on L2 education.

FLA refers to feelings of tension, apprehension and fear experienced by individuals when learning or using an FL. The severity and manifestation of this anxiety can vary based on several factors, including cultural, individual, pedagogical and environmental influences. Past studies, like those by Horwitz (2001) and Lu and Liu (2011), have shown that students who feel very anxious in FL classes often have a harder time learning. On the other hand, Ely (1995) suggested that if students are moderately comfortable with the uncertainties or ambiguities in the language they are learning, it can actually help their progress. This makes sense since learning a new language can present many unknowns, which could be stressful. So, while too much anxiety is detrimental, a moderate level of comfort with language uncertainty can be beneficial.

Language anxiety, often referred to as FLA, is shaped by a multitude of factors. While individual experiences play a significant role, broader cultural contexts, like those in Northern Europe and Asia, also have a notable influence (see Table 5.1).

However, it is important to remember that regardless of the regional context, individual differences such as personality, prior experiences and personal beliefs about language learning play significant roles in determining FLA. Some children might be more resilient or have higher self-efficacy, leading to lower anxiety levels. It is crucial to understand that these are general observations, and there will be individual and contextual exceptions. Not every child in East Asia will experience high levels of FLA, and not every Northern European child will be anxiety-free. The overall societal, educational and cultural context plays a role, but individual factors can mediate or amplify these effects.

Table 5.1 Cultural differences affecting FLA between East Asian and North European contexts

	East Asian context	Northern European context
Cultural expectations and pressure	Countries such as China, Japan and South Korea often have strong societal expectations regarding educational achievement. The competitive nature of the education systems and the importance of exams might increase anxiety levels among students, especially when they are expected to excel in FLs like English.	In countries like Sweden, Denmark and Norway, there is generally a more relaxed and student-centred educational approach. Moreover, the exposure to English (through media, for example) is high, leading to lower FLA when learning this language.
Pedagogical approaches	Traditional language teaching methods in some East Asian countries can be teacher centred and reliant on rote memorisation. This might not provide students with ample opportunities to practice speaking, potentially increasing their anxiety when they need to communicate in the FL.	The teaching approach is often more communicative, emphasising interaction and practical use. This might reduce anxiety as students are more accustomed to using the language in real-life contexts.
Prior exposure to the language	While there is increasing exposure to English through media and other outlets, it might still be limited compared to Northern Europe.	Many children grow up watching English TV shows, listening to English music and using English on the internet. This high level of exposure from an early age can make them more comfortable with the language.
Attitudes towards errors	In some cultures, making mistakes, especially in public, can be a source of shame or embarrassment. This fear of making errors can amplify FLA.	While no one likes making mistakes, there might be a more forgiving attitude towards errors, viewing them as part of the learning process.

Case study: FLA and learning English in Taiwan

In their 2004 study, Chan and Wu delved into the world of young students in Taiwan to understand how they felt about learning English. They focused on a group of fifth graders spread across 205 elementary schools in Taipei County. To ensure a comprehensive understanding, they meticulously selected 18 classes from 9 different educational districts, which encompassed 601 students. Alongside this broad student sample, they paid particular attention to 18 students who felt especially anxious about English, as indicated by their questionnaire scores. They also had conversations with all nine English teachers teaching these classes.

To gather a wide array of data, Chan and Wu (2004) used a combination of techniques: they distributed questionnaires, conducted interviews, observed real-time classroom interactions and collected relevant documents. Their findings painted a vivid picture. They found that a significant portion of these young learners exhibited clear anxiety when faced with English. Delving deeper, they identified six distinct factors rooted in the students' experiences with English that seemed to be at the heart of this anxiety. One standout discovery was that students who felt more anxious tended to perform worse in their English studies.

Diving into the specifics, several factors served as anxiety triggers: students felt inadequate due to their perceived low English skill levels; they were afraid of being judged for their mistakes; competitive class activities ratcheted up the tension; some students naturally had anxiety-prone personalities; and added pressure came from the students' own high expectations and from their parents. Certain classroom situations also heightened their nerves, especially tests, public speaking in English, spelling challenges, moments when English seemed too complex to understand and interactions with fluent English speakers.

However, amid these challenges, there was a glimmer of hope. Both the students and their teachers found that when classroom instruction balanced both English and their native language, it seemed to soothe some of the students' anxieties. Despite this, Chan and Wu (2004) observed a gap: many teachers seemed unaware of the depth of anxiety that their students experienced.

Given these findings, Chan and Wu (2004) proposed several actionable steps. They believed that if teachers became more attuned to recognising and addressing this anxiety and adopted clearer English teaching techniques, it could make a world of difference. They also advocated for more interactive English class activities and a deeper involvement of parents in their children's English learning journey. By sharing their feelings, students could also contribute to a more understanding environment. In essence, the study highlighted the need for a shift in the classroom atmosphere, aiming for a more relaxed and effective space for English learning.

Areas of Language Learning that Can Cause FLA

Language learners often experience various forms of FLA that can hinder their progress and confidence in language acquisition. These sources of anxiety can manifest in different aspects of language learning:

(1) Speaking and oral production: FLA can stem from the fear of negative evaluation, especially in group settings where learners worry about making mistakes. Pronunciation concerns, such as having an accent or mispronouncing words, can also contribute to anxiety.
(2) Listening comprehension: Difficulty in understanding spoken language, particularly when spoken quickly or with unfamiliar accents, can lead to anxiety. Learners may fear missing vital information or responding inadequately.
(3) Reading and writing: Some students may fear misunderstanding texts or struggling to express themselves clearly in writing. Concerns about grammar, vocabulary choices and writing conventions can heighten anxiety levels.

(4) Tests and examinations: Language tests can be anxiety inducing, especially if they involve oral examinations or timed written components.
(5) Cultural sensitivity: The fear of making cultural mistakes or misinterpreting cultural references can increase anxiety, particularly in real-world communication settings.
(6) Classroom dynamics: The teacher's approach, feedback style, or classroom management can influence FLA. Peer dynamics, such as competitive environments or unsupportive classmates, can also exacerbate anxiety.
(7) Personal perfectionism: Some learners strive for perfection in their language endeavours, which can increase anxiety especially when faced with challenges or mistakes.
(8) Prior negative experiences: Negative past experiences, like being ridiculed for language mistakes or struggling in previous courses, can carry anxiety forward into new learning contexts.

To address FLA effectively, educators should recognise these potential sources of anxiety and implement strategies to create a supportive, positive and encouraging learning environment. This approach can help reduce anxiety levels and promote a more conducive atmosphere for language acquisition.

The Dance between Anxiety and Motivation

In the intricate world of language learning, two prominent factors play pivotal roles: the palpable anxiety many students grapple with and the driving force of their motivation. Yet, while these forces often present themselves as if on opposite ends of a see-saw, the real story lies in the vast sea of individual differences. Imagine a classroom, bustling with students each carrying their own set of aspirations, fears and experiences. For one student, the thrill of mastering a new phrase might eclipse any fleeting anxiety. For another, the mere thought of a spoken exercise could evoke a paralysing fear. This individuality is what makes language learning both a deeply personal journey and a challenging group endeavour. However, in a typical classroom, striking the right balance becomes a Herculean task. With the often-skewed ratio of students to teachers, educators find themselves navigating a labyrinth of varied learning paces, distinct comfort zones and a spectrum of motivations. While some students might be buoyed by an intrinsic love for the language, undeterred by any anxiety, others could be operating under external pressures, making them more vulnerable to bouts of nervousness. The real challenge emerges when we consider how a singular teaching approach, no matter how well-intentioned, might resonate differently across this diverse group. A method that emboldens one learner might inadvertently intimidate another. What is more, in these bustling classrooms, teachers, despite their best efforts, might find it daunting to tailor their pedagogical approach to each unique learner.

In essence, the dance between anxiety and motivation in language learning is not just a two-step action; it is a complex choreography, influenced by individual rhythms and the broader dynamics of the classroom. Recognising and honouring these individual differences, while navigating the practical realities of group instruction, remain one of the most profound challenges – and opportunities – in the world of education.

Foreign Language Enjoyment

Alongside FLA, however, is FLE – an emerging construct in the realm of second language acquisition (SLA) which has been identified as an influential factor in language learning outcomes. The following factors show how FLE impacts language learning.

Cognitive and emotional engagement

Enjoyable experiences tend to be more memorable. When learners enjoy the process of language learning, they are more likely to remember linguistic elements, facilitating vocabulary acquisition and grammar retention. Enjoyment can also lead to a surge in positive emotions, which have been shown to improve cognitive processes integral to language learning, such as attention, memory and problem solving.

Motivation

Enjoyment can serve as a powerful intrinsic motivator. Learners who derive pleasure from language learning are more likely to stay motivated over the long term, even in the absence of external rewards. This increased motivation can lead to extended engagement, more frequent practice and persistence in the face of challenges, all of which enhance learning outcomes.

Reduced anxiety

Positive experiences in the language learning process can counterbalance and mitigate feelings of FLA. Reduced anxiety can free up cognitive resources, allowing the learner to process and produce the language more effectively.

Risk-taking and exploration

Learners who enjoy the language learning process are often more willing to take risks, such as attempting to use new vocabulary or structures. This risk-taking can accelerate language development as it often leads to meaningful feedback. Enjoyment can also inspire learners to explore the language outside of formal settings, like engaging in conversations with native speakers, consuming media in the target language, or participating in language exchange events.

Relationship with the teacher and peers

FLE can foster a more positive relationship between students and teachers, as well as among peers. Positive classroom dynamics and relationships can further enhance motivation, increase participation and provide a supportive environment for collaborative learning.

Resilience and persistence

The journey of language learning is filled with challenges. Learners who enjoy the process are more likely to display resilience, persisting even when faced with setbacks or plateaus in their progress.

Holistic development

Beyond linguistic competence, FLE can also contribute to the holistic development of the learner, fostering cultural appreciation, increasing intercultural competence and enhancing social skills.

The Value of Teaching and Learning Heritage Languages

Teaching heritage languages brings multifaceted benefits, not just to individual learners, but also to society as a whole. Foremost among the beneficiaries are the parents, who often cherish these languages as a vital link to their own history, culture and identity. Beyond the immediate family, the wider society, especially communities with a rich heritage, feels a profound sense of loss when younger generations are not acquainted with these languages. Heritage languages play a pivotal role in intergenerational communication, such as in parent–child communication through speaking shared LOTE. They bridge the gap between generations, fostering deeper connections and understanding. When these languages are not passed down, it can lead to a sense of disconnect, both within families and the broader heritage community.

Moreover, for societies at large, it is essential to recognise the implications of heritage language-speaking children communicating exclusively in English or any dominant language. When children are distanced from their heritage languages, it can lead to issues of identity and belonging. Over time, this disconnect can exacerbate societal conflicts as individuals grapple with their opposing dual identities. Thus, it is evident that the true beneficiaries of heritage language preservation and instruction extend beyond individual learners. The societies in which these individuals reside, with their richness of culture and history, stand to gain the most. By embracing heritage languages, societies can ensure a more cohesive, integrated and harmonious future. Yet, it is important to bear in mind that heritage language learners' motivation differs somewhat from general language learning motivation, and nurturing their language may require an alternative, tailored approach.

Addressing the Word Gap

Dr Dana Suskind, founder of the Thirty Million Words Initiative, emphasises the crucial role that parents play in their children's early language development. Inspired by the 1995 study conducted by researchers Betty Hart and Todd R. Risley which revealed a 30-million-word gap between children of different socioeconomic backgrounds, Dr Suskind highlights the significance of conversations, rich vocabulary and open-ended questions in shaping a child's future success (CI Guest, 2016). The term '30-million-word gap' (often shortened to just 'word gap') was originally coined by Betty Hart and Todd R. Risley (1995, 2003) in their book *Meaningful Differences in the Everyday Experience of Young American Children*, and subsequently reprinted in the article *The Early Catastrophe: The 30 Million Word Gap by Age 3*.

Healthy development and education are closely linked, with early language environments and parent–child relationships impacting long-term well-being. To support children's success, families can follow the 3Ts strategy: Tune In, Talk More, and Take Turns. In addition to parents, schools, teachers, healthcare providers, and childcare providers also play essential roles in fostering social interaction and communication for young children. Dr Suskind emphasises the importance of early intervention, spreading awareness about optimal brain development from birth, and government policies supporting initiatives like Thirty Million Words on a national scale (CI Guest, 2016).

Building Bridges with Translanguaging: Solidarity and Connection in Linguistic Diversity

In today's distinct linguistic era marked by exceptional complexity and diversity, it is necessary to explore new avenues for facilitating communication and preserving cultural traditions. This necessity is especially pronounced within intercultural families, where language variations often create an array of communication challenges. Amid these conditions, a more adaptable and flexible linguistic practice is needed, and this is where translanguaging can play a pivotal role. Translanguaging presents a framework that liberates individuals from rigid linguistic structures and conventions, catalysing freer dialogue and more dynamic interaction between languages (García & Li, 2014). Rather than necessitating a stringent switch from one language to another, translanguaging artfully integrates an individual's diverse linguistic resources into a single, comprehensive semiotic repertoire. This allows one to flexibly select, assemble and reassemble components from their linguistic reservoir, navigating social or political barriers with ease. By leveraging all available linguistic components, translanguaging promotes fluidity in communication, ensuring the interaction is both natural and seamless.

Translanguaging paves the way for a more accepting linguistic environment. It offers the older generations, such as parents and grandparents, an opportunity to let go of strict demands for perfect language practice and to instead cultivate a more open and inclusive linguistic atmosphere. It accommodates an environment where the authenticity of a language is no longer a prerequisite, and a greater emphasis is placed on the fluid exchange of ideas and thoughts.

Therefore, translanguaging provides the younger generation with a liberating space for linguistic expression. It ensures that they can communicate without the dread of being judged or chastised for using unconventional grammar or mixed vocabulary. This opens avenues for them to express themselves more freely, fostering an environment that appreciates and respects linguistic diversity. The shared understanding and mutual respect that translanguaging promotes can significantly alleviate communication-related stress. It paves the way for more effective, enriched dialogue by dismantling the barriers between what might be seen as right and wrong language practices, replacing them with a harmonious coexistence of varied linguistic resources.

The ethos of translanguaging promotes more open and welcoming intergenerational dialogues. The adoption of such a practice is vital not just within homes, but also in schools, communities and societies in general. This acceptance and normalisation of diverse language practices foster a sense of belonging among speakers of different generations and cultural backgrounds, promoting mutual respect and understanding (Jo et al., 2023).

FLA in UK Primary and Secondary Education

In the context of language anxiety within UK primary and secondary education, it is vital to acknowledge the profound impact that FLA has on students' language learning journeys. Translanguaging practices and the exploration of identity emerge as pivotal elements in alleviating this anxiety, thereby cultivating a more inclusive and nurturing educational atmosphere. By adopting a translanguaging pedagogy, educators are equipped to forge classrooms that encourage students to utilise their entire linguistic repertoire. This approach significantly diminishes the stress commonly associated with learning new languages by validating all forms of linguistic expression. Moreover, a deeper understanding of the interplay between identity and language in diverse educational settings enriches our approach to teaching languages. Recognising and addressing the complexities of maintaining multiple languages helps students foster a strong, positive language identity. This, in turn, enables them to better manage the pressures and anxieties of language learning. Such a nuanced and supportive approach not only enhances the language learning experience but also promotes a more inclusive and empathetic environment in UK schools, ultimately benefiting both students and educators alike. This alignment of translanguaging and identity exploration with educational strategies is essential for framing our discussion pertaining to providing a comprehensive perspective on how these practices can transform language education and alleviate anxiety among learners.

Safe Talk, Safe Space

Creating a safe space for conversation holds paramount importance in parent–child relationships, especially in intercultural families. Among the myriad of opportunities for such exchanges, mealtime talk is particularly enriching. This setting is what Li (2011) labels a 'translanguaging space', which Kiaer (2023a) further elaborates upon, terming it a 'translanguaging haven'. These are socially constructed environments in which individuals strategically utilise their diverse linguistic resources in a creative and critical manner. Unlike transient discussions, mealtime talks offer regularity, fostering an atmosphere of safety and familiarity. Amid the daily whirl of life, these shared meals present crucial opportunities for an engaging, reciprocal dialogue between parents and children, thus deepening familial bonds and nurturing mutual linguistic growth. Blum-Kulka (1997) underlines the significance of these mealtime interactions, illustrating their role as a nexus of socialisation. They cultivate crucial conversational competencies, such as storytelling, topic introduction and active participation. In addition to bolstering children's skills, these discourses enable parents to grasp their children's evolving worldviews. Within this shared mealtime space, a culture of learning and open debate thrives, benefiting both parents' and children's communication skills and sociocultural comprehension (Bova, 2021). Despite cultural differences in narrative styles and norms of politeness, mealtime talks can potentially foster bilingual dynamics in immigrant families and endorse adherence to wider social norms. Research suggests that these routine mealtime interactions significantly contribute to comprehensive linguistic and sociocultural development for not only children but also all participants, emphasising the reciprocal benefits of parent–child communication (Hu et al., 2021).

'Language of Solidarity'

The term 'language of solidarity', which I have coined, is often referred to as the mother tongue, but it does not necessarily indicate the very first language to which one is exposed. Rather, it is the language wherein children forge their relationships with their proximally closest individuals – parents, carers and family. The existence of this language, or these languages, is pivotal, serving to cultivate relationships between parents, children and the community. Shared languages can evolve into 'mentalese', a mental language where children develop their thoughts and expressions. Sharing languages is of substantial significance, impacting children's linguistic, cognitive and social development, as well as their identity formation. It is equally essential for parents to feel connected and supported by their children.

For many Korean children for instance, Korean acts as the language of solidarity. It is crucial that it be well preserved and nourished. English can be effectively built around this foundational language of solidarity. The boundaries between English and Korean will perpetually be tested in our multilingual, highly mobile society, which is encouraging news for English learners. Our children must understand that English is one of the languages they must live with, alongside Korean. They need to feel as at home with English as they do with Korean.

Language Maintenance: Identity and Solidarity

Language maintenance is a key factor in establishing connections between generations, fostering a sense of identity and promoting solidarity within intercultural families and the broader community. Rich and clear two-way communication is crucial between children and adults. Shared languages between parents and children act as threads of cultural continuity, reinforcing familial bonds. However, maintaining this continuity amid the current surge in multiculturalism and multilingualism, fuelled by the rapid pace of globalisation, is a challenging task. It necessitates significant dedication to preserving one's heritage language, a commitment which can occasionally ignite conflict within the family. Kiaer (2023a) discusses the lengths to which some families go to sustain this commitment to preserving heritage languages. She details the experience of a family that undertook a four-hour drive every Saturday morning so that their children could attend a Korean school in London. This example underscores the significant efforts that families make to uphold their linguistic and cultural ties. It is essential to recognise that not all families choose the same path. There are families that decide to forego language maintenance for various reasons. One instance from the same study highlights a family that chose not to speak Korean at home because the English-speaking father felt isolated. This decision brings to light the intricacies involved in balancing multiple languages and cultures within a family setting.

These instances demonstrate that there is no universally correct approach to language maintenance within intercultural families. Each family operates within its unique circumstances, shaping its language policies and decisions accordingly. Nevertheless, these examples collectively emphasise that heritage language maintenance is not a trivial task. It is a significant commitment that requires thoughtful decision-making and concerted effort. Despite the potential challenges, children from intercultural families often exhibit a strong desire to learn and maintain their heritage language. This drive is frequently fuelled by their aspiration to forge deeper connections with their extended family and the wider heritage community. For instance, Hua and Li's (2016) study on Chinese families in the UK identifies several key motivators, including the role of grandparents, a desire to reconnect with their place of origin, perceived future opportunities tied to bilingualism, and an underlying dissatisfaction with life in their host country. Huang and Liao (2024), on the other hand, found that while Chinese parents in Australia had a great influence on their children with regard to maintaining the heritage language, the children themselves had a more central and direct role in this, which is impacted by factors like the yearning to continue their parents' culture and affective elements related to learning and utilising Chinese, such as self-confidence derived from others' feedback about their language competency.

The complexities of identity and language maintenance are analysed by Hua (2010), who explores how terms of address and intergenerational discourse shape sociocultural identities within diasporic families. The study underscores the dynamic nature of the intercultural process, highlighting how younger generations actively adapt and redefine societal norms. Kiaer (2023a) reaffirms these findings, shedding light on the motivations of Korean–English bilingual children to improve their Korean language skills. The primary reasons include their ability to converse with relatives in Korea, recognition of their Korean heritage and nationality, and a general desire to interact more effectively with Koreans. This body of research collectively highlights the multifaceted nature of intercultural family communication and the pivotal role of language maintenance therein.

'Why are They so Passive, Shy, and Unengaging?'

'Why are they so passive, shy, and unengaging?' This is what I heard from my friend who was a primary teacher in South London, where most of her pupils were from the Urdu- and Bengali-speaking communities. She mentioned that although most of them were doing quite well academically, she felt that many were creating some distance from her. She mentioned that some were not even looking at her when she talked to them in person. This story reminded me of my own experience in the UK. Once I was invited to my husband's friends' home. I did not know them well, so I spent most of the time listening rather than talking, as I thought it would be good and respectful to do so. However, I later found out that they thought I was a bit angry because I was quiet. I was shocked because that was not what I had meant to convey – rather, I wanted to show them respect. The same may be the case for Urdu and Bengali children in South London. Nevertheless, I want to emphasise that I am not criticising individual schools or teachers; compared to politicians, for instance, I think they are making remarkable efforts to welcome children from diverse backgrounds. Indeed, interpretations can be very different depending on the situation and the person. Yet, this sort of misunderstanding is born out of ignorance. One way to mitigate this problem is by improving intercultural understanding through better appreciation and understanding of FLs in the UK, particularly heritage languages.

Understanding Differences in Educational Settings

It is important to recognise that cultural norms and expressions of respect can vary significantly across different regions and communities, especially in Asia. In some Asian cultures, pointing at people or objects with the index finger can be seen as impolite. Instead, it is customary to use the entire hand or gesture with the chin; this may be translated into the classroom. The significance of eye contact can also differ substantially between cultures. While Western cultures generally view sustained eye contact as a sign of confidence and attentiveness, some Asian cultures consider it impolite or confrontational. In addition, the manner of verbal communication can differ greatly. Western cultures often favour direct communication, while Asian cultures may employ indirect communication, especially in hierarchical situations. In the Middle East, elaborate metaphors or allegories may be used in expressions, which could be misunderstood if taken too literally. Furthermore, in South Asia, as well as in East Asia, there are cultural traits that might be misconstrued as passivity or shyness, but they are often rooted in a deep sense of respect. In South Asia, such as in India, Pakistan and Bangladesh, it is not uncommon for people to display deference and respect by being polite, reserved and not overly assertive in communication. This demeanour can sometimes be mistaken for passivity or shyness in the diaspora, especially in educational settings. For example, children may refrain from asking questions or appearing too forward in front of authoritative figures, like British teachers. However, this is usually a sign of respect for the teacher's knowledge and authority rather than a lack of engagement or interest. Similarly, in East Asia, particularly in countries like Japan, China and South Korea, children often show respect by listening attentively and not interrupting the teacher. Silence during classroom discussions is seen as a sign of attentiveness and respect for the teacher's words. British teachers, who may come from a different cultural background, might misinterpret this silence as disengagement or indifference.

Understanding and respecting these cultural differences is vital for effective cross-cultural communication. It helps to prevent misunderstandings and fosters cultural sensitivity and appreciation, promoting positive interactions between individuals from Western European cultures and those from Asian and Middle Eastern regions. It is crucial for educators like British teachers to be aware of these cultural differences and not mistake them for a lack of interest or engagement. Instead, recognising that this behaviour stems from a different cultural expression of respect can lead to more effective cross-cultural communication and a better understanding of students' intentions and attitudes. Improved awareness of individual differences stemming from one's cultural and linguistic background, alongside the psychology of language learning, is crucial in creating more welcoming and diverse language classrooms. Encouraging open dialogue and creating an inclusive classroom environment where students feel comfortable expressing themselves in their own way can help bridge these cultural gaps and foster a more productive learning experience.

6 Digital Innovation Matters

Practical tips:
- **Prepare for digital assessments:** Familiarise yourself with digital and online exam formats and incorporate technology into classroom practices.
- **Incorporate AI-assisted teaching and learning:** Integrate AI-powered language tutors and tools to personalise learning, enhance speech practice, provide immediate feedback and create a non-judgemental environment for language learning. AI can also assist in creating and grading rubrics, saving valuable time for teachers.

Background: Why AI?

Take a look at Figure 6.1, generated by the AI system DALL-E which makes use of deep learning methodologies to produce images from natural language descriptions.

Notice in particular the inclusion of paper and a brush in response to the prompt 'children's education'. Next, compare the image in Figure 6.1 to a photograph I took of my daughter completing her school homework.

In Figure 6.2, we can see the use of a stylus – not a brush, pencil, or pen. When I was learning English, my main tools were paper dictionaries and textbooks, then cassettes and DVDs as time passed. Yet today, such resources have become almost obsolete. The methods have clearly changed. Making language learning relevant and fun again is not an option but an obligation.

For the younger generations, apps like Quizlet, Memrise and Duolingo have become cornerstones in their language learning journey. Even in some classes, teachers encourage the use of these digital platforms to enhance the learning experience. Paper dictionaries, while they still have their place, are increasingly being replaced by online dictionaries. Indeed, most students nowadays learn languages using online resources. Self-study is both possible and sustainable because of the availability

Figure 6.1 Image generated by the AI system DALL-E using the prompt 'children's education'

and accessibility of such materials. In recent years, the way people learn languages has changed dramatically; it is almost impossible to imagine a world without the internet and apps. The key question now is as follows: How do we use AI effectively and constructively in a language classroom?

The integration of AI tools in educational settings is no longer an optional choice but a fundamental norm. The rise of Generation Alpha and their increasing comfort with AI-driven learning, particularly accelerated by virtual practices necessitated during the COVID-19 pandemic, has made them true AI natives. Within language classrooms, a significant portion of learning now unfolds through digital AI interfaces. While some teachers may initially hesitate to embrace this shift, adapting to it becomes essential when engaging with and effectively educating these AI-native learners. Indeed, ethical concerns and reservations persist, but the undeniable reality within language learning classrooms is the emergence of overwhelmingly positive aspects. For instance, individual differences are one of the biggest challenges in language learning, but they can be mitigated with the aid of AI. AI technologies help create a less anxiety-inducing environment for students while enabling personalised

Figure 6.2 My daughter doing her homework on a tablet

learning experiences. For educators, the benefits extend to time saved on tasks such as grading, marking and generating reports by utilising AI-powered rubrics designed for various facets of language learning. It is crucial to reframe the dialogue around AI, particularly generative AI like ChatGPT, in the classroom. Rather than focusing on concerns about plagiarism, educators should emphasise its role in enhancing the learning process. Notably, current AI plagiarism detection tools are still not considered entirely reliable, further underlining the necessity of shifting towards more formative assessment methods and the development of effective writing skills (Kiaer, 2023b).

The conversation surrounding the use of generative AI in educational settings needs a transformation, moving away from apprehension and blame, and instead shifting towards empowering our students to harness these tools effectively. Personalised teaching is the key to making language learning more engaging and effective, while also reducing the burden on human teachers through the potential of automating marking and assessment; this is all achievable with the help of AI. This chapter delves into the multifaceted landscape of incorporating ChatGPT-like generative AI in the modern classroom, exploring its potential, challenges and the imperative role it plays in shaping the future of education.

Generation Z and Generation Alpha as AI Natives

My daughter Jessie was born in 2012, and her schooling was interrupted by COVID-19. For almost two years, she took lessons virtually – that is to say, one-third of her primary school education was online. Even now, a lot of her schoolwork requires using the internet. For her, it is the norm. From an early age, she has been able to use a computer and iPad, getting by with emojis when she could not yet write. She and her friends play together on Roblox, a metaverse platform that most parents do not even know about. They were introduced to autocorrect mechanisms from a very young age. Jessie often asks me why she should learn spelling when Siri can always tell her the correct spelling and the autocorrect function is always available while typing. This is not an easy question for me. She, along with many of her friends, meets her overseas grandparents and relatives digitally more than physically. Jessie and her friends' lives are accompanied by some form of AI, whether or not consciously. It is the way their lives are formed.

The term 'digital native' was originally coined in 2001 by Marc Prensky (2001). In his article 'Digital Natives, Digital Immigrants', Prensky defined 'digital natives' as young people who grew up surrounded by and using computers, mobile phones, and other tools of the digital age. The devices and technologies that Prensky was referring to at that time are very different from the devices and technology now. After all, in 2001, we only had dial-up internet connections and primitive computers and mobile phones. Since then, the digital experience has undergone dramatic changes, leading me to coin the term 'AI native' to emphasise this shift. Generation Alpha (those born after 2010) and Generation Z (those who precede Generation Alpha) are all considered to be AI natives. For AI natives like Jessie, AI is their playmate and virtual reality is their playground; it is an integral part of their day-to-day experience, which, of course, involves learning. They are born into a world where interacting with AI is natural and commonplace. For them, simply banning AI or the usage of AI would seem largely unfair. It is like banning a dictionary for the pen-and-paper generation or banning the use of Google in doing homework. We need to teach these children how to use AI well. For instance, teachers can advise AI natives not to rely on AI entirely but to use it partially to maximise their performance. It is also the teacher's role to teach AI natives that AI – though it is named 'intelligent' – can lead them to the 'unintelligent' path if not used carefully. In principle, human teachers need to understand the digital bliss and digital trouble that AI can bring forth in their classrooms.

Although Generation Alpha and younger generations will live with AI daily, when we introduce them to super-smart and powerful AIs like ChatGPT, we need to do so gradually and in a very timely manner. To be honest, I think that ChatGPT-like AI should be introduced later, if possible, except in some unusual circumstances. This is because, in order for these younger generations to be truly AI competent, they need to be acquainted with basic learning practices, and their minds need to grow and mature so they can properly manage the data and protect themselves from dangers like deep fakes.

Of course, in teaching AI natives about AI, I often realise that I have nothing much to teach them when it comes to AI – they know AI better than me! In this chapter, I introduce some data I collected from a week-long intensive workshop in the Czech Republic. All the participants were in their early 20s. My plan was to teach them how to use different digital tools, but within the first hour, I realised that they did not need me; they were able to explore these digital spaces with ease and enthusiasm. Thus, I realised that my role was not to teach digital skills or tools, but rather to introduce them to these technologies. As Generation Z, they were born to explore digital spaces, and this is even more so the case for Generation Alpha. For them, AI competence is an essential ability in their lives. It is the ability to live life making productive use of AI tools at their disposal. AI competence is something that Generations Alpha and Z will naturally acquire, though it will be needed by the rest of the population too.

In educational spaces, we must ensure that teachers understand AI and have AI competence so that they can help their students to use it effectively for their educational benefit. This is an important part. Furthermore, when AI natives learn English and other languages using the less interactive traditional method alone, they may experience increased foreign language learning boredom. To motivate AI natives effectively, it is essential to find suitable ways for them to learn, which involves alleviating foreign language learning boredom. Human teachers who have the sole responsibility of directing, inspiring and motivating their students also need to help students use AI for their good, instead of misusing it. For instance, human teachers can assist learners in using ChatGPT-like AI as their unintimidating teaching assistant (TA) who is available 24/7.

Before and After ChatGPT: The 'Wow' Effect

Figure 6.3 was drawn by one of my students during a digital humanities class discussing different platforms; it captured their reaction

Figure 6.3 A drawing by a student in reaction to AI tools during one of my digital humanities classes

towards ChatGPT, which I would assume is very similar to many of our own. Sabzalieva and Valentini (2023: 5) describe ChatGPT as a 'language model that allows people to interact with a computer in a more natural and conversational way'. This image expresses the 'wow' effect, a sense of craziness and shock that is coupled with the advent of ChatGPT. Indeed, living in the post-ChatGPT era where LLMs are on the rise, the opportunities, both for good and bad, are vast – overwhelming, even. However, as a linguist and language educator, I want to emphasise the great potential of ChatGPT as a constructive language learning tool. I have witnessed first-hand its successful use across the world, particularly in countries belonging to the Global South. ChatGPT can be a tool to help equalise the language learning playing field when used properly. For instance, if developed correctly in the right direction, generative AI can play a transformative role in rubric-making and grading students' language skills. Once they are trained to use the software, teachers can learn how to design more personalised language learning curricula and make rubrics using AI tools.

Teachers' Perceptions of AI in Education

Educators are increasingly incorporating AI-powered tools into their teaching and administrative processes. The emergence of technologies like ChatGPT has ignited discussions about the role of AI in education. However, there are mixed opinions among educators regarding AI's impact. Some educators view AI as a positive force that will revolutionise education by tailoring it to individual students' needs. They believe that AI can make learning more relevant and adaptable. The effectiveness of AI, in their view, depends on how it is integrated into instructional methods, and they advocate for embracing and understanding AI as an integral part of modern education. They also suggest that assessment methods should evolve to accommodate AI's presence and that students should be taught how to use AI effectively. Furthermore, some educators see the potential benefits of AI when used correctly. They believe that AI can enhance the curriculum and are willing to embrace it for the betterment of students' education. At the same time, there is recognition that AI can have both positive and negative effects, such as aiding teachers while also enabling cheating. Some educators express concerns about AI in education. They worry that technology may hinder critical thinking and problem-solving skills among students. There are concerns that AI could exacerbate mental health issues and lead to students relying on AI for answers without truly understanding the underlying knowledge. Additionally, there is a fear that over-dependence on AI may result in a lack of decision-making skills. Overall, while AI is intriguing, there is a consensus among educators that it should complement traditional teaching methods rather than replace teachers entirely.

Broadly speaking, human teachers have been hesitant to embrace digital advancements. They are often afraid and reluctant to face the realities of AI in the classroom, especially when compared to the younger generations who are at home in the digital world. Teachers often feel uncomfortable and clumsy when using online platforms, while digital platforms are considered fun by Generations Z and Alpha. In language learning, gamification is a huge trend for this exact reason. Simply saying, 'AI is not my cup of tea' is not an option in this AI era. Teachers must be proactive and face AI, rather than ignoring it. In my recent survey and in-depth interviews, I discovered that it is the teachers themselves who find AI empowerment in the classroom unsuitable for students at all stages of education. There are, of course, other questions that bother human teachers. Would ChatGPT-like AI demotivate students and make them all lazy? What if they stop learning? Will AI teachers as smart as ChatGPT replace human teachers? There are no clear-cut answers to these questions. We need to critically engage with these questions and find the most suitable model that will make learning efficient, enjoyable and sustainable. According to feedback I received from the participants in my digital language learning programme, I can confidently state that using ChatGPT does not discourage language learning, especially for advanced beginners who are already motivated to learn. However, my sample size was quite small, and more studies are needed to confirm this. Nonetheless, contrary to popular belief, using ChatGPT does not cause everyone to stop learning or lose motivation to continue learning.

Limitations of Human Teachers

Teacher availability is often cited as one of the major problems that the UK education system faces. This problem is primarily due to difficulties in funding, making it hard to employ new teachers, a lack of specialised teachers for certain subjects, and the sheer diversity even within a single UK classroom. In 2018–2019, the pupil-to-teacher ratio in the UK was 16.4 students for every teacher (Clark, 2023). While some may argue that a shortage of teachers persists and this ratio requires improvement, one must keep in mind that there is no ideal ratio; even if teaching and learning took place one-to-one, the situation would still be far from perfect because of individual differences and factors like foreign language anxiety. While human teachers may be reluctant to embrace new technology in the classroom, developing a model with more personalised teaching tailored to the individual is the way forward. This can be achieved with the help of AI, as human teachers can be trained to make AI their constantly available and reliable TA, ready to give customised feedback to the pupil.

Using AI Tutor Bots in Speech Practice

Engaging in speech practice, especially when learning a new language, can be a challenging yet essential part of the learning process. As mentioned, one of the persistent challenges in language education is the teacher–student ratio, which often limits the amount of individualised speaking practice students can receive in a traditional classroom setting. Many language learners possess a strong willingness to communicate and express themselves verbally, and when they lack ample opportunities to do so, it can lead to frustration and hinder their progress.

AI tutor bots offer a valuable solution to the challenge of speech practice in language learning. They provide learners with a convenient, personalised and supportive environment to enhance their speaking skills. By adopting AI technology, students can gain the confidence and proficiency needed to communicate effectively in the target language. This is where AI tutor bots come into play and offer a significant advantage. AI-powered language tutors can provide an effective and efficient solution to enhance speech practice. From a practical perspective, AI tutor bots offer round-the-clock availability, allowing learners to practice speaking whenever it suits them, addressing the constraints of traditional classroom schedules. These bots adapt to each learner's individual needs, tailoring exercises to match their strengths and weaknesses, ensuring engaging and relevant speech practice. They provide immediate feedback on pronunciation, grammar and vocabulary, helping learners to correct mistakes in real time and enhance their learning effectiveness. Moreover, AI tutor bots create a non-judgemental environment, reducing anxiety for learners who might be self-conscious about speaking in front of others. They offer diverse conversational scenarios, preparing learners for various real-world interactions, and track progress over time, enabling goal setting and progress monitoring. Additionally, their consistent and standardised instruction ensures that all learners receive the same level of attention and guidance.

Human Teachers vs. AI Teachers: Division of Labour

AI-assisted learning through the advent of LLMs like ChatGPT is a game changer in our language learning landscape. In the past, those who held the power were the ones with access to specialist libraries and language resources, and this created a knowledge gap. However, with the advent of the internet, information has been democratised and is becoming more accessible to all. The challenge for ordinary people is figuring out how to use this information effectively. AI has the potential to not only bridge this gap but also provide advice for maximising the utilisation of this information. From now on, the question is not about what humans can do, but about how AI can be used to assist us. At the end of the day, the quality of the work may be the only thing that matters. The best outcomes will likely be human led and AI assisted. Instead of giving up on defining and developing 'human values' for AI, closing the door to the possibility of bringing AI into spaces like our classrooms, we should actively engage in this process while being assisted by AI. It is crucial that we actively work towards finding a division of labour between humans and AI-based digital humans, learning to coexist alongside AI in a productive and mutually beneficial way.

Banning ChatGPT cannot be the solution to a change in the balance between human workers and AI assistants. Rather, we must critically think of new and productive ways to engage with smart AI. We need to rethink education, not only in terms of exams and assessments but also in how we view traditional classrooms and educational institutions. All of us, without exception, must think about how we can live alongside smart AI and benefit from its potential while preventing possible harm and danger. We need to work together to build a healthy, sustainable AI culture that benefits all of humanity.

In the domain of language education, AI can be a valuable tool for teachers. Rubrics are a proven and effective way to assess and provide feedback on essays or written response questions. However, many teachers shy away from using them due to the time required to create and grade using rubrics. With AI-assisted rubrics, teachers can now generate standards- and grade-aligned rubrics with ease, saving valuable time. Additionally, assisted rubrics can also support the grading process, enabling teachers to generate AI-suggested scores and feedback for student essays based on the provided rubric. This not only expedites the grading process but also provides teachers with a valuable starting point for grades and responses. Teachers can personalise and adjust scores and feedback before returning them to students. The Languages Gateway (n.d.) is a right move towards positively changing the UK language education landscape to accommodate the digital age in which we now live in and will continue to live in. However, we should develop this even further to make it more accessible in content and format, ensuring continuity for learners. Given the rapid pace at which AI and other digital tools are evolving, we must keep pace – it is a matter of urgency.

AI Reform: Now is the Time

Teachers might wish to use AI detection tools like GPTZero to prevent the use of ChatGPT for academic purposes, but this is only a temporary fix. AI language capabilities are fast evolving, and soon GPTZero will become ineffective for detecting AI plagiarism. Instead, teachers must educate their students on why it matters that they do the work themselves. To facilitate this, teachers must rethink what authentic writing means and re-evaluate and address their own assumptions about AI, which may be hindering their decision to incorporate it into their classrooms.

No matter how many times we as teachers might email Google, OpenAI and companies of the like about our concerns relating to AI, I am certain that the big corporations will not respond. Although unfortunate, this is a fact that we need to accept. As such, teachers need to start formulating their own response to the developments in AI as individuals, as part of their department, and as part of their overall school. Nationwide and global change is progressing too slowly. Our students are now at risk of being deceived by deep fakes and influenced by false information. If big tech companies are not going to act, then teachers, educators and policymakers need to take action instead. We must teach our students about these platforms, highlighting when it is appropriate to use them and making students aware of the dangers. This requires teachers to first engage with and explore AI, and then design educational programmes for students. Teachers need to be at the forefront of this issue. They are the only ones who can tailor-make teaching methods that implement AI in a healthy and productive way.

Incorporating AI-Driven Learning: Embracing the Norm in the Modern Classroom

The Technology Acceptance Model (TAM) is a framework used to understand why people embrace new technology. It focuses on two main factors: perceived ease of use (how user-friendly a technology is) and perceived usefulness (how much a technology benefits users) (Davis, 1989). According to the TAM, if people find a technology easy to use and believe it is valuable, they are more likely to use it. This model was initially developed by Fred Davis, who is a key figure associated with the theory. His groundbreaking research in the late 1980s laid the foundation for TAM. Since then, various researchers have contributed to the development and refinement of the model, but Fred Davis' work remains central to its origins. TAM helps businesses and researchers predict and improve technology adoption, making it a valuable tool for ensuring that new technologies meet user needs and are successful in the market. This model is an important framework for those working at the interface between AI and education to develop technologies that cater to the UK's language teaching and learning needs.

I strongly believe that, although there is much to discuss, it is important to teach our young AI natives to use AI, and use it well, rather than shutting it out entirely. It is important for educators like us to convey to others that banning AI is not the answer. Instead, we should work together with AI to teach students how to use it properly. Teachers should not view ChatGPT as a competitor, but rather as their faithful TAs, whom they do not have to pay. While TAs cannot replace teachers, they can assist them in various ways.

ChatGPT emerges as a significant asset in foreign language education, offering a variety of services such as writing assistance, language translation, language discussion partnerships, digital tutoring, article summarisation, personalised learning and research assistance (Skrabut, 2023). In the context of writing, ChatGPT stands out as a valuable feedback tool, providing insights into grammar, vocabulary and sentence composition (Ferlazzo, 2023). Through AI like ChatGPT, teachers can tackle the issues of individual differences in the classroom to provide more individualised and effective language education. Both in terms of efficiency and performance, the combination of human and AI teachers is ideal. While there will inevitably be thoughtful trial and error in finding the right balance between the two, we cannot keep the door closed to AI much longer. We must face this era head-on, navigating the digital era with discernment, innovation and excitement, to create a better language learning environment for both teachers and students.

Language Assessment in an AI Age

The traditional image of students hunched over exam papers, scribbling away, may soon become a thing of the past. England's largest exam board, AQA, has announced plans to introduce digital testing for some GCSE subjects starting in 2026, with the possibility of expanding to other subjects, including English, by 2030 (Weale, 2023). This shift towards digital exams reflects the evolving role of technology in education and underscores the need for a re-evaluation of our educational methods. The act of writing and typing is undergoing significant changes, prompting us to rethink how we approach education in the digital age.

The question of how to approach education assessment in the age of advanced AI is one that we must address head-on. The transition away from pen-and-paper assessments in the wake of the COVID-19 pandemic has only accelerated the need for new and innovative solutions. It is clear that we cannot go back to the old ways of assessing student performance, nor can we simply hide from the implications of these technologies. Our students are more tech-savvy than ever before, and some may already be using these tools to their advantage. As educators, it is our responsibility to stay ahead of the curve and find new ways to assess student learning and performance that are fair, rigorous, and truly reflective of what our students know and can do. We must embrace the challenges presented by these technologies and find ways to harness their power for the betterment of our students and our educational system as a whole.

It is easy to blame technological advancements for the challenges facing our educational system. However, it is important to recognise that we cannot simply reject the use of generative AI in education. Instead, we must strive to create an ecology in which we can coexist with AI in a way that is beneficial for all. To achieve this, we must find the right division of labour between AI and ourselves. In the sphere of education, this means separating the roles of knowledge memorisation and knowledge application; the very parameters of education must be reset to reflect this. Instead of solely teaching students to memorise facts and acquire basic skills, we must focus on teaching them how to use knowledge and data to gain insights. The ability to use data is becoming increasingly important, as it is more valuable than simply memorising facts.

AI advancements mark the end of traditional teaching methods and call for a new approach to education. It will take time to fully understand and implement this new approach, but now is the time to begin the process. As a parent, I am worried about what will happen if my daughters become aware of these technologies and begin to use them for their homework. They are growing up in a digital world and, for them, the computer is an integral part of their daily lives. It is only a matter of time before they figure it out and start using these technologies to their advantage. Some schools have already made moves to ban ChatGPT on their school internet networks, but what good will this do? Children will still be able to access ChatGPT on their home networks. Generations Z and Alpha are digital natives. Policymakers rarely belong to the digital native generations, but they need to understand the perspective of Generations Z and Alpha to make productive decisions. Restriction is not the way forward. Rather than trying to seize control, policymakers must consider how we can best live together with AI.

The way we approach exams and homework is undergoing a radical change that is imminently approaching. From 2025, South Korea plans to adopt AI-powered textbooks, replacing traditional paper textbooks (Lee, 2023). The country's education ministry intends to provide students with digital tools customised to their individual learning levels to enhance their study of maths, English and information technology. Following a first phase of implementation, the authorities will determine whether to extend this programme to other subjects.

Generation Alpha, who care for their virtual pets and butterflies, are doing maths in the metaverse as if it were a game. Generation Alpha, who are AI natives, are learning in ways their parents could never have imagined. It is important that we adapt our exams and homework to this new paradigm as learning undergoes a radical transformation. The transformative nature of learning should drive the transformation of homework and exams.

Assessing language proficiency for languages other than English is a complex task. While there is a framework in place for European languages, such as the Common European Framework of Reference for Languages (CEFR), in my experience, this framework does not work well for many non-European languages. Even in English, many major exams, such as the Test of English as a Foreign Language (TOEFL), can feel limited in their ability to accurately determine a test taker's linguistic competence. The challenge of language assessment is particularly significant for non-European languages, where there is often greater variation in dialects, vocabulary and grammar (Kiaer, 2020: 3). It can be difficult to develop assessment tools that accurately capture the richness and complexity of these languages. The diversity of language backgrounds and learning contexts can further complicate the assessment process.

I believe that AI-powered tools, such as ChatGPT, can be incredibly helpful not only for language learning but also for providing detailed, individually tailored assessments. For instance, suppose you use ChatGPT to learn a new language for a year. It would be able to precisely assess your level of proficiency in a way that traditional tests are incapable of doing by analysing your history of studying the language on ChatGPT, likely derived from your previous prompts that have been stored on the platform. Currently, every conversation on ChatGPT is stored in a navigation bar on the left, so that users can revisit their past chats with ChatGPT. Personalised assessment would help you identify your strengths and weaknesses and tailor your learning strategy accordingly. In this way, we are not saying goodbye to assessment, but rather saying goodbye to old ways and welcoming a new and better way of assessing and improving language proficiency.

Teaching requires creativity, and every teacher must find ways to bring out their students' potential and assess them effectively. Homework and exams are essential tools for assessing students' understanding of a subject and providing them with feedback for improvement. However, traditional methods of homework and exams may not always be effective in capturing students' language proficiency, as they may not reflect real-life language use. I believe that it is crucial to design homework and exams that simulate real-life situations and allow students to apply their language skills in meaningful ways. This may involve the use of interactive, AI-powered tools like ChatGPT. By taking a creative and modern approach to homework and exams, we can better prepare our students for real-world language use and enable them to reach their full potential.

A Personalised Learning Pathway

Individual differences in language learning refer to the varying attributes, traits and cognitive processes that influence how individuals acquire and use a second language (Dörnyei, 2005; Skehan, 1991). These differences can encompass a wide range of factors, including but not limited to personality traits, motivation levels, cognitive aptitude for language learning, preferred learning styles, and even creativity. Individual differences have significant implications for language development and instruction (Bates et al., 1996; Dörnyei & Skehan, 2003). Researchers have explored various aspects of individual differences, such as learning styles, motivation, learning strategies and foreign language aptitude (Dörnyei & Skehan, 2003; Ehrman et al., 2003). While some areas have received more attention than others, such as affective factors, learning styles and learning strategies, they are interconnected and play a crucial role in shaping language acquisition (Ehrman et al., 2003). Understanding these individual differences is essential for educators and researchers as it guides the development of effective and tailored language learning experiences for diverse learners, including those from unconventional populations or individuals with language disorders (Bates et al., 1996). Indeed, researchers and educators alike recognise the importance of acknowledging and accommodating these differences to create tailored and effective language learning experiences for diverse learners, whether they are children, adults or individuals from different linguistic backgrounds or cultures.

This is why developing a model of language education that enables more personalised feedback is a crucial step forward. For our AI natives, whose lives are intrinsically interwoven with technology, we must innovate our pedagogies to create a language learning environment that is suited to their needs – not the needs of previous generations. This is possible through the thoughtful incorporation of AI into classrooms.

Concerning motivation in language learning, it has become even more diversified in the AI age. With the advent of technology and AI-assisted learning tools, learners now have access to a wide range of motivational factors and resources that contribute to this complexity. An overview of how the AI age has diversified language learning motivation follows.

Personalised learning

AI-powered language learning apps and platforms offer personalised learning experiences. Learners can tailor their language learning journey to their specific interests, goals and proficiency levels. This personalised approach increases motivation as learners engage with content that resonates with them.

Gamification and rewards

Many AI-assisted language learning platforms incorporate gamification elements, such as points, badges and leaderboards. Learners are motivated to complete lessons and achieve milestones to earn rewards and recognition, making the learning process more engaging and enjoyable.

Instant feedback

AI chatbots and language learning assistants provide instant feedback on pronunciation, grammar and vocabulary. This immediate feedback loop keeps learners motivated to improve and refine their language skills.

Access to authentic content

AI algorithms can curate authentic and up-to-date content in the target language. Learners can access news articles, social media posts, podcasts and videos, allowing them to engage with real-world language usage. Exposure to authentic content keeps motivation high as learners see the practical value of their language skills.

Language exchange and social learning

AI platforms facilitate language exchange and social learning. Learners can connect with native speakers or language partners through AI-driven language exchange apps. This social interaction fosters motivation by providing opportunities for meaningful conversations and cultural exchange.

Adaptive learning

AI systems adapt to learners' progress and preferences. They identify areas where learners may be struggling and provide targeted exercises and practice materials. This adaptive approach keeps learners challenged and motivated to overcome obstacles.

Cultural and contextual learning

AI can provide cultural insights and context-specific language learning. Learners can gain a deeper understanding of the cultural nuances associated with the language they are learning, enhancing their motivation to connect with different cultures.

Visual and interactive learning

AI enables the creation of visually engaging and interactive language learning content. Learners can engage with multimedia resources, interactive exercises, and immersive virtual environments, making the learning process more dynamic and motivating.

In the AI age, motivation in language learning is not limited to traditional factors but is enriched by technology-driven enhancements. Learners benefit from a diverse range of motivational sources, which contribute to a more dynamic and multifaceted approach to language learning. As a result, language learning has become a highly personalised and engaging experience, catering to the unique motivations and preferences of individual learners. Such personalisation, achieved through AI, should be widely applied in language classrooms across the UK for maximum benefit.

A Closer Look: Digital Innovation and Fandom Learners

In their work, Darvin and Norton (2015) introduce a novel model of language learning that acknowledges the transformative influence of technology and globalisation on contemporary language education. Learners today enjoy unprecedented ease in moving between various online and offline spaces, providing them with fresh opportunities for language acquisition and expressing their identities. More importantly, this shift challenges traditional notions of power dynamics in language learning, moving beyond the dichotomy of native and non-native speakers.

Darvin and Norton assert that 21st-century language learners must navigate a complex landscape of online and offline environments, with their identities and language learning investments shaped by these spaces and their underlying power relations. They propose a comprehensive model of investment that resides at the intersection of identity, capital and ideology. This model urges educators to critically examine how language learning unfolds in the digital era and to develop educational strategies that empower learners to negotiate their identities and investments in language learning.

Furthermore, the context of fandom language learners offers an intriguing case study within this framework. Particularly, Anglophone learners engaging with East Asian languages find themselves immersed in culturally and geopolitically distinctive value systems. These learners occupy unique and often less visible positions, embodying multiple identities: first language (L1) speakers, learners of the target language (Ln speakers), and fans of a specific interest group. Participation in a fandom legitimises these plural identities, such as being both Korean speakers and fandom members, which are facilitated by digital platforms.

This dynamic intersection between language learning and fandom participation provides learners with a multifaceted context for identity formation and linguistic development. The digital realm, along with innovative learning methods, motivates learners by offering them a rich and engaging space to develop their language skills while strengthening their fan identity. This fusion of language learning and fandom participation demonstrates how contemporary digital tools and approaches can profoundly influence and motivate language learners in unique and meaningful ways.

General Language Subject

I propose a general language subject as one way in which we can effectively integrate AI into UK language classrooms. Imagine a platform like Duolingo – interactive, engaging, and fun even for children. Now, imagine it being non-commercial, properly monitored, entirely free and reliable. Through careful collaboration between linguists and software developers, the general language subject will include crowd-sourced information and a range of resources to cover the UK's languages, going far beyond the European realm, on a new platform for language learning. Intended to be a fun, pseudo-immersive experience for language learners, once piloted in the UK, it can be internationally scaled and applied to other countries around the world. The often-cited problem of continuity (many children, both older and younger, can testify to the sense of 'starting from scratch' in language learning each time they move schools) can be mitigated through the general language subject, as it would safely and securely store and record the language learning progress of each individual pupil, even generating certificates to help them keep track of their level. This pseudo-immersive experience intends to make language learning both fun and relevant for our AI natives. Innovation is the key to solving many of the current problems in UK language learning classrooms, and the creation of a general language subject is one step closer to achieving this.

The general language subject represents a forward-thinking integration of AI into language education in the UK, aligning with innovative curricula like the WoLLoW (World of Languages and Languages of the World) syllabus. This subject is designed as a dynamic, non-commercial platform, similar to popular language learning apps, but it stands out by being tailored specifically to the unique multilingual landscape of the UK. It aims to offer a broad range of languages, moving beyond European languages to include those widely spoken across the UK, thus providing a pseudo-immersive learning environment that reflects the country's linguistic diversity.

Much like the WoLLoW syllabus – which is implemented in Key Stages 2 and 3 to foster an interconnected understanding of languages through a holistic educational approach – the general language subject seeks to create seamless continuity in language learning. This continuity is crucial as it addresses the common educational gap where students feel they must start anew with each educational transition. By storing and monitoring each student's progress on a secure platform, the general language subject not only makes learning more engaging and relevant for digital natives but also ensures consistent educational development. This approach not only complements the objectives of WoLLoW but also enhances them by incorporating AI to adapt and scale language learning, potentially extending its reach globally. Through collaboration between linguists, educators and technologists, the general language subject could significantly enrich and modernise language education, making it more inclusive and effective for students across the UK and beyond.

One Step Forward to Solving Social Inequality

Through AI-assisted language education, the issue of language inequality can be improved. AI innovation will help bring equity to UK language classrooms through the option of more sustainable and affordable resources available to all. This will help to make language learning more inclusive, no matter the socioeconomic background of the pupil. Li *et al.* (2023), for example, show how Chinese language learners from low-income families can improve their Chinese writing with the help of ChatGPT. Regarding heritage languages, improving and diversifying the language education landscape in the UK will also help to reduce and overcome intergenerational conflicts, fostering a warm, welcoming linguistic environment. Rather than aggravating divides, AI in language education can help bridge gaps.

Food for Thought: A New Type of Generativity?

Since 1957, Chomsky's transformational grammar theory, based on the notion that humans alone have such a level of syntactic complexity, recursion and creativity, has revolutionised the field and led to a whole branch of research known as 'generative linguistics'. However, this concept of generativity is now being challenged with the release of LLMs incorporating deep learning; ChatGPT may become the master of generations with its ever-increasing number of parameters. Perhaps we need to reconsider the terms we use and distinguish between human generativity and AI generativity. Although a distinction is proposed, the two are not mutually exclusive; rather, they can help each other in a dynamic and symbiotic relationship, where humans can accomplish great feats with the help of AI.

It is important to remember that while ChatGPT may not be most suited for primary language acquisition and should be kept away from infants, it has significant benefits in second language acquisition and foreign language education. It can also help address the current teacher problem in the UK, as limited human resources are slowing down progress that can be made in the country's language classrooms. Since the advent of generative AI, it has become the new norm to always be living, whether intentionally or not, whether consciously or not, with languages assisted and interrupted by AI. Rather than shutting AI out completely in the realm of language teaching and learning, we can work towards making an embodied AI language assistant available to mitigate many of the current problems faced in our language classrooms. The high demand for diverse languages persists to this day, and will keep persisting, as global mobility continues to increase. We must ensure that the UK does not fall behind in this area, by making the most of our already multilingual and multicultural population.

Like other countries such as South Korea, the UK needs to embrace technological advancements as a matter of urgency; we want to be pioneers, not stragglers in the realm of education. Innovation is set to revolutionise the classroom experience, as we witness a shift towards the adoption of both physical and virtual digital classrooms as the new standard. Human teachers and AI counterparts are poised to collaborate in the education of our children. The coexistence of human and AI educators looms on the horizon, and our task is to seamlessly integrate their respective strengths, paving the way for blended learning to define the future of education.

7 Collaboration Matters

Practical tips:
- **Connect with the wider community:** Encourage collaboration among students, teachers, parents and the wider community to enrich language education. This can include organising language exchange programmes or inviting parents and community members to share their linguistic backgrounds.
- **Gain a global perspective:** Adopt an inclusive and international perspective on language and culture in the classroom. This can be achieved by encouraging projects that explore different cultures and fostering an inclusive classroom environment.

Translanguaging in Everyday Talk

Translanguaging is a dynamic meaning-making process, often highly collaborative, in which one employs diverse semiotic resources across the borders of language. I often think of translanguaging as being like cooking. Even if two people are cooking the same dish, they will tailor the dish to suit their tastes. In intercultural homes, dishes often combine different cultural staples. In my home, we often eat rice and kimchi, but other side dishes can come from any of our other culinary inspirations. The food also needs to be catered to each individual's needs. My children were brought up eating kimchi from a young age, so they like to eat spicy food as much I do. However, when their English granddad or dad's family comes over, we add fewer or even no chillies. On the other hand, when their Korean grandmother comes to visit, we increase the spice. It all depends on the people and the occasion.

Just like cooking, the fluid and innovative nature of translanguaging can capture and explain the complex linguistic and cultural experiences of multilingual families and, in particular, how young children with diverse backgrounds can make sense of their multilingual world. The term was originally coined in Welsh as 'trawsieithu' by Cen Williams in the 1980s (Conteh, 2018: 445), before being translated into English as 'translanguaging' by Colin Baker, who introduced the term as a verb to capture the nature of the phenomenon as a process rather than a result. Translanguaging was then developed further by other researchers. Baker (2011: 288) defined translanguaging as the process of 'making meaning, shaping experiences, gaining understanding and knowledge through the use of two languages'. Translanguaging goes beyond code-switching, as it shows a hybridity of language use that transcends the typical features of any single language involved.

Although many assume that translanguaging practices, such as fluidly switching and incorporating different languages into one's speech, are transitional behaviours that children will eventually grow out of once they become more linguistically competent, translanguaging is far from transitional; rather, it is a useful linguistic tool that forms part of everyday language for multilingual speakers and families throughout their lives. As Cenoz and Gorter (2021) show, translanguaging is a skill that aids the development of bilingualism. It is a unique, fluid bilingual process that can make multilingual speakers' speech creative and efficient while helping them build solidarity with other multilinguals through their shared linguistic experiences. The lexicons of multilingual families' languages cannot be described using only one language, as they comprise a blend of words from languages tailor-made to each family. When a child says a word from another language in an English sentence, they have not made a mistake or failed in constructing a 'proper' English sentence. Rather, they have succeeded in conveying a nuanced meaning by fully applying their multilingual repertoire. The lens of translanguaging allows us to interpret children's use of non-English words as being creative, rather than erroneous. These behaviours are natural and pragmatically optimal. Translanguaging behaviours are not simply a stepping stone for proficiency in one language, but are in themselves a natural, productive language system. As Nakamura and Quay (2012) suggest, translanguaging is a complex interaction between the amount of input, language preferences, children's personalities, and how caregivers respond to language mixing. Our lives and languages are now connected on a global scale. As the world becomes more and more virtually interconnected, the distinctions between nation-state, ethnicity and identity will become even more blurred. As a result, the practice of translanguaging will become more common than ever before – not only for a limited population but for everyone as virtual mobility soars. Far from a sign of insufficient language proficiency, translanguaging allows children to show care and be considerate to those in their lives by accommodating others linguistically. It enriches their everyday communicative experience, allowing them to connect more deeply with relatives, friends, and beyond. Translanguaging is not a process of teaching but rather, of learning together.

Havens of Translanguaging: Home and the Community

Sometimes, we think children can adapt and learn new languages without any problems; we think that they can learn a new language as easily as a sponge absorbs water. Yet, in my previous work, I showed the contrary: how language acquisition can be overwhelming and challenging when children are not in an environment where they have the freedom to explore. The support from family and friends plays a crucial role too. Without support, children can feel anxious and daunted about language learning, just like adults (Kiaer *et al.*, 2021). Li (2011: 1234) first coined the term 'translanguaging space' to refer to 'a space for the act of translanguaging as well as a space created through translanguaging', where people with multiple linguistic and cultural repertoires feel comfortable shifting creatively between repertoires and asserting their full linguistic identity. Following Li Wei's work, which addressed translanguaging primarily in social spaces within educational spheres (such as universities or weekend Chinese schools), several studies have begun to explore further types of 'translanguaging spaces'. Hua *et al.* (2017), for instance, discuss the multimodality of translingual space in a Polish shop in London. Mazzaferro (2018) presents examples of diverse settings where translanguaging can be used in daily practice. Most recently, Kiaer *et al.* (2022) examine a range of translanguaging spaces, including 'personal', 'philosophical' and 'playful' spaces. Perhaps most pertinent to this chapter is Kiaer *et al.* (2021), which introduces the notion of 'safe translanguaging space' in a study that demonstrates how ethnic minority community centres play the role of a 'home away from home' for ethnic minority diasporic groups by providing a linguistically safe translanguaging space. The home is also a 'safe space' for bilingual families. It is a haven where translanguaging takes place in the comfort of one's own family language. Everyone in multilingual families needs this space where their languages and lives can be understood and appreciated as they are, in order to learn, to assert and to relax. For children and their parent(s) whose first language (L1) is not the dominant language of the society in which they live, this space is vital for their linguistic and psychological well-being.

Revitalising Community Centres

One type of place in which linguistic and cultural communities can be cultivated is community centres. Consider Chinese community centres, for example, where people with Chinese heritage can engage in linguistic and cultural activities that welcome and nurture their background in a communal setting. Such spaces are filled with promise; while younger generations can learn more about the language and culture, older generations can acquire and develop digital skills through intergenerational interactions. Such encounters play an important role in ensuring social cohesion as communication is not one-directional but multidirectional. Revitalising community centres is one of many actions we can take to improve the language learning landscape. Parents can even be the teachers, and through collaboration with the wider community, language learning can become an engaging, culturally enriching experience. For language to thrive and last, we must use it outside the classroom by practicing it in real life. What we should be aiming to nurture are living languages – not classroom languages. Like Belgium's thriving multilingual landscape, we want our languages to be alive. The current bottom-up structure in the UK makes this possible, as collaboration with local authorities can help with reviving community centres and implementing initiatives with local libraries, such as the Language Café run by Oxfordshire libraries (Oxfordshire County Council, n.d.). The UK is primed for autonomous language learning, meaning that a top-down approach is not always necessary to improve the language education landscape, and we should facilitate more (grand)parent–teacher–community collaboration.

More than Physical: Mobile Communities

In the current digital era, people can connect with others from around the world, with messages and call requests being sent and delivered within a matter of mere seconds. This has helped to initiate, foster and maintain relationships despite geographical boundaries. Indeed, a community includes more than just people meeting in a physical space; the online, mobile community is important too. Through social media, fans can congregate in group chats or video calls, united by their shared appreciation of a particular celebrity or show, for example. In the context of the K-wave, fans can interact on Twitter and build a community to encourage one another in their Korean language learning endeavours. Nonetheless, this does not negate nor replace the role of in-person communities. Instead, both physical and virtual spaces can and should be used to create supportive communities where language learners can share their experiences and support each other along the way.

Current Classroom Landscape: Translanguaging in Practice

My daughter, Jessie, attended a small local state primary school where most of her friends had multilingual heritages. For instance, Leila, with Indian heritage; Rosa, with Serbian heritage; Manon, with French heritage; Olivia, with Irish heritage; Vilia, with Finnish heritage; and Miki, with Japanese heritage, filled her daily interactions. These children could speak various languages, or at least understand a bit of them, thanks to one of their parents keeping them connected to their heritages and languages. While multilingual children in UK classrooms are becoming increasingly common, there remains uncertainty among them and their parents about the benefits and methods of maintaining their multilingual competence. This narrative draws inspiration from my daughter's school experience, where her classroom was a microcosm of multiculturalism. Jessie's classroom was a vibrant space filled with children from diverse heritages who, while learning in English, had all been exposed to languages other than English from birth.

Some of them could speak their parents' heritage language(s) fluently, while others had varying levels of proficiency, and a few spoke none at all. Nevertheless, the majority had heritages that extended beyond English. Jessie's friend Mimi, with a French father and Chinese mother, did not speak much English. However, in her classroom, she had companions such as Grace, whose parents were Chinese and had moved to the UK from China a few years previously. When Mimi faced communication challenges, peers like Grace came to her aid. If they were unable to help, there was Jules, Aimee's mother, who not only worked at the school as a teaching assistant but also ran a French club.

Another close friend of Jessie's in Year 1 was Lily, who hailed from China. Oxford, being home to many visiting academics, attracted families from diverse heritages. Lily and Jessie became friends, but initially, Lily's English did not improve significantly. This was because there were several Chinese children, four in Jessie's class, who often conversed in Chinese. Lily became frustrated when she could not express herself, resorting to screaming. The teacher was understandably stressed during these moments, but then a Year 5 Chinese girl stepped in to interpret for Lily. This pattern was repeated on several occasions, highlighting the rich tapestry of languages and cultures in Jessie's classroom.

In addition to the diverse group of students, I also used to bring my Chinese DPhil student to the school to help Chinese children with maths. While these students were exceptionally talented in maths, they faced language barriers as they could not understand English well. One such child was Yiming, a boy talented in maths but limited by his English language skills. Beth, my DPhil student, visited the school for three weeks and helped Yiming understand key terms that would help him in his studies. It was only after this time that Yiming's aptitude for maths was uncovered, highlighting the value of effective communication achieved through translanguaging. This initiative further enriched the classroom experience by providing targeted support for those who needed it, creating a truly inclusive and vibrant learning environment that celebrated the richness of diverse heritages and languages.

One final story involves my daughter Jessie and her friend, Valentine. Valentine's mother is Chinese, and her father is French. When she first arrived at my daughter's school, her English proficiency was almost non-existent and, as a result, she struggled to settle in. However, by sourcing different multilingual children in the school who spoke Chinese, French and English, Valentine was able to communicate with other students and teachers and form close friendships along the way. What I found particularly interesting and encouraging was the effect of such translanguaging on other pupils. For example, my daughter knew no Chinese or French before making friends with Valentine, but in doing so, she has picked up some words and phrases in these languages, using them in conversation with Valentine and others in their friendship group. This multilingual dynamic in action, which involves the blending of multiple languages to help enrich children's educational experiences, was the inspiration for this book.

Children and staff, including teachers, helped one another overcome language barriers and enriched their classroom experience by embracing and celebrating their diverse heritages and languages, creating a truly inclusive and vibrant learning environment. The removal of language barriers was not achieved through one miraculous resource but through the collaborative efforts of the entire classroom community, fostering an atmosphere of mutual support and celebration of diversity.

The Case of Australia

The Australian 'National Policy on Languages' emphasises the significance of language as a fundamental form of human communication, encompassing oral, written and non-verbal forms (Lo Bianco, 1987). It plays a central role in intellectual development and the socialisation of children, and underpins learning and concept formation. Furthermore, language contributes to personal growth, cultural enrichment and recreation. The policy recognises that language is not solely a means of communication but also serves cultural, artistic, intellectual and sociopolitical functions. It acknowledges the linguistic and non-linguistic aspects of individual, ethnic, racial and national identities and allegiances. Australia's language policy aims to make informed decisions about language-related issues, considering factors like linguistic diversity, national unity, economic needs and citizen preferences. It stresses the importance of recognising, preserving and promoting Aboriginal languages, which provide valuable insights into the nature of human language. The policy acknowledges the challenges faced in language education, including disparities in opportunities. It proposes measures such as expanding language education programmes, supporting Aboriginal language initiatives, and establishing a language testing unit. Additionally, it suggests the creation of a foundation with multicultural aims to contribute to its objectives, particularly through languages. In the realm of business and international relations, the policy calls for the training of high-level interpreters and translators in specific languages and technical fields. It recommends the establishment of a language testing unit to develop Australian language tests for various purposes.

To facilitate the implementation and further development of the national language policy, the Australian Council for the Arts convenes meetings and provides advice to the government, ensuring coherence in addressing language-related issues (Australian Government, 2023). Australia's multilingualism includes various languages spoken domestically, and there is a need to promote multilingualism while maintaining English proficiency. Interestingly, the policy does not use the term 'foreign' to classify their languages, causing us to reflect on our own use of the term in the context of a multicultural and linguistically diverse UK.

Solutions: Reciprocal, Bi-directional Learning

While there are strong models of translanguaging (such as Baker, 2011), we must be aware of the specific needs of extremely multicultural and multilingual UK classrooms. We should promote a language ecology where other languages and cultures are properly understood and appreciated, and multilingualism is increasingly accepted as the norm. However, at the same time, we must provide effective ways for children with EAL to familiarise themselves with English medium instruction (EMI). This is all the more crucial in light of the finding that nearly 9 out of every 10 primary schools in England have EAL students (Collen, 2023).

Scotland's 1+2 Language Policy

In Scotland, there has already been some success with inventive approaches to language learning at both primary and secondary school levels, particularly regarding Gaelic medium education (GME), which has seen some growth in recent years. However, evidence suggests that the quality of modern language education can vary vastly between schools. There has also been a drop in the number of pupils obtaining national qualifications in languages (Collen, 2020) – a trend that applies to the UK as a whole, not just Scotland. This is due to several factors, such as the increasing dominance of English worldwide across a variety of sectors. The Scottish government's commitment to encouraging and improving language education in Scotland is based on the belief that learning another language has positive educational, cognitive and linguistic benefits for children and young people.

The Scottish government's 1+2 language policy supports modern language provision for all school pupils from age 5 upwards. The aim of this policy is to give every child the opportunity to learn an additional language (L2) from P1 onwards and a second additional language (L3) from P5 onwards (Education Scotland, 2023). The policy was due to be fully implemented by 2020.

It is believed that introducing a first additional language (L2) from the earliest possible stages of education will expose both pupils and their parents to the benefits of language acquisition as Scotland becomes increasingly multilingual and multicultural. Schools across the country will not face any restrictions on which languages are taught to pupils, but as other European nations remain Scotland's closest neighbours, it has been recommended that European languages such as German, French, Italian and Spanish should continue to maintain an important place within the education system. The government also remains committed to Gaelic language provision, so for some pupils, Gaelic will be their L2. The policy also considers the growing number of pupils in Scotland whose L1 is not English – new arrivals. For such pupils, English will be their L2 under the 1+2 initiative.

New arrivals face many challenges when they first enter the UK's education system. A report by Her Majesty's Inspectorate of Education (HMIE) on the impact of new on local education services in Scotland explored many of these issues as well as solutions implemented by local authorities across Scotland to resolve them (RR Donnelley, 2009). Such challenges arise due to the many stresses involved in transitioning to life in a new country; they may feel isolated or may struggle to deal with trauma due to their past experiences, for example. Young children's limited experience with English also makes it difficult for them to demonstrate their knowledge and understanding of their schools' curriculum, making it difficult for teachers to accurately assess their progress. It is clear that children and young people from immigrant backgrounds have specific needs. Various legislative initiatives place some responsibility for meeting these needs on local education authorities: for example, schools are required to promote good race relations as well as maximise the potential of bilingual pupils by providing additional support if and when required.

The extent to which schools have been able to adhere to these requirements has not been consistent. Readiness to overcome common challenges varies significantly between local authorities and even individual schools under the jurisdiction of the same local authority. However, there have been many successful cases across Scotland.

Examples extracted from the report on inclusive education (RR Donnelley, 2009) follow.

Cuthbertson Primary School, Glasgow City Council

A significant number of newly arrived children attend Cuthbertson Primary School in Glasgow. At Cuthbertson, the headteacher is directly involved in welcoming newly arrived children and their families. The school collects detailed information on its new pupils, such as previous schooling, health issues, religion and family background. This information is collated and used to help the school build a programme of education that ensures that newly arrived pupils settle in and progress quickly. Their level of English is also assessed. Teachers ensure that learning activities include opportunities to practice listening and speaking. The pupils' L1s are also used to promote learning: from P1/2, children count in several languages in integrated mathematics lessons. Visual learning methods are also used to enhance language acquisition, such as the use of information and computer technology (ICT). For example, MP3 players and cameras are used in class projects. These initiatives have contributed to new arrivals at Cuthbertson settling in successfully and becoming confident individuals as they progress.

Edinburgh EAL Service and St Augustine's High School, Edinburgh

St Augustine's High School in Edinburgh has also implemented successful initiatives, particularly through its EAL service. At St Augustine's, individual support is provided to newly arrived young people. Like Cuthbertson, detailed information on pupils is gathered as soon as possible after they arrive at the school in order to develop a programme to meet their educational needs. Pupils also attend English for speakers of other languages (ESOL) classes to increase their English language proficiency as quickly as possible. They are encouraged to participate in the school's various extracurricular activities, such as football, rugby and dance; in addition, they are encouraged to learn how to play a musical instrument. Using initial assessments to develop the best programmes of support has allowed pupils at St Augustine's to integrate seamlessly into the school community, socially as well as academically.

Aberdeenshire EAL Service

Aberdeenshire EAL Service has also successfully used initial assessments to support new arrivals' social and learning needs. They have developed their own set of materials to assist local schools in identifying and assessing pupils' learning needs. Using language competence guides, staff are encouraged to assess how pupils use language in social contexts (such as when watching films, listening to music, helping out at home) as well as in learning environments. Language profiles like these help teachers accurately monitor pupils' progress in various skills – reading, listening and speaking. This approach supports staff in schools to identify which bilingual pupils require additional support, thus allocating resources effectively.

St Columbia's Primary School, Fife

St Columbia's Primary School in Fife has been successful in developing close relationships with pupils' families and including them in their children's education as well as in school life. In partnership with a local college, St Columbia's set up a family learning group for children and parents whose L1 is not English. The group was staffed by an English language tutor, but St Columbia's headteacher, as well as other members of staff, would drop by occasionally in order to build relationships with pupils and their parents. The English lessons were informal and relaxed in nature to avoid being simply an extension of the school's ordinary day classes. In addition, staff engaged with parents on general topics and provided assistance with more practical applications of language, such as using local services. This approach was successful in improving communication between the school and parents. It also provided a peer support network for pupils and their families. It worked to improve the use and understanding of English in day-to-day activities by both children and their parents and increased their engagement in the community as a whole.

Edinburgh EAL Service and St John Vianney Primary School

Similarly, St John Vianney Primary School in Edinburgh partnered with Edinburgh EAL Service to provide additional support to pupils and their parents. Staff from Edinburgh EAL Service helped the school carry out initial assessments with the parents of new arrivals; information gathered during these consultations was then used to develop tailored EAL programmes. The school also encouraged and supported parents to raise their profile in the school community and promote their unique cultures. For example, the school organised assemblies allowing parents to share their religions, languages and traditional customs with the wider school community. Migrant parents were also encouraged to participate in Scottish cultural events, such as Burns Day celebrations. The school's demonstration of its dedication to such cultural exchanges helped both pupils and their parents feel welcomed and valued. In addition, the school encourages migrant parents to serve on the parent council, ensuring their continued involvement in school life throughout the duration of their children's time at the school.

Although individual schools and local authorities have taken steps to encourage cultural diversity, exam boards have been reluctant to continue offering community languages in national curriculums. However, action has been taken to ensure that qualifications in some of these languages continue to be offered. In 2016, Nicky Morgan, former education secretary, announced that A-level qualifications will continue to be offered in languages such as Arabic, Modern Greek, Gujarati, Bengali, Japanese, Modern Hebrew, Biblical Hebrew, Punjabi, Polish, Portuguese, Turkish and Urdu (Department for Education and Morgan, 2016).

A Dynamic Atmosphere of Linguistic Pluralism

Bilingual and bilateral education is not a 'one-size-fits-all' approach. In order to make the greatest use of language resources, the local cultural and linguistic demographics must be taken into account. For this reason, rather than advocating for one fixed and rigid method of introducing bilingual education into UK schools, we propose a more flexible model that encourages teachers to use their own agency and creativity in response to the needs of their classrooms. Rather than attempting to achieve bilingualism in a set few languages, as may be the case in a Chinese international school, our focus is on encouraging an atmosphere of linguistic pluralism in which students learn openness, flexibility and respect with regard to other languages.

Gone are the days of learning languages in the solitude of your own room with earphones plugged into your MP3. Nowadays, language learning encompasses a wider variety of methods. The Learning Together Model is not about monologue building, but dialogue making. Through consistent and continued multilingual efforts achieved by means of improved (grand)parent–teacher–community collaboration, language education can be made more engaging and relevant to the lives of younger generations. By shifting the focus slightly away from developing literacy in another language, children learning through this model will attain oral competency in a more efficient manner. In the case of children with a heritage language, such an environment will also help to build their confidence and identity, which has both individual and social benefits.

Culture

Another key aspect of our Learning Together Model is the use of culture to encourage linguistic pluralism and motivate EAL and EO children to pursue language learning. This is especially relevant to primary school students who may not have the attention span or intellectual capacity to pursue formal language training at such an early age. By teaching children through culture, their language skills are immediately placed in context and become relevant to subsequent cultural activities. For example, as of 2021/2022, 45 schools in Britain are teaching Korean once or twice a week in after-school clubs (Korean Education Centre UK, n.d.). Most of the pupils do not have Korean heritage; children who speak Korean as a heritage language go to complementary weekend schools instead. These after-school clubs are very popular, and children learn language alongside culture. The classes are attended voluntarily, and many who are 'inspired' by Korean language and culture go on by themselves to learn more of the Korean language and may eventually become interested in other aspects of Korean culture such as food, martial arts, K-pop and K-drama. This is precisely what we are hoping for; it is not necessarily our aim to teach children to be fully proficient in foreign languages, but to encourage a desire to learn, a curiosity to know other languages and cultures and openness.

CLIL

An extension of this combination of linguistic and cultural education is CLIL. In their study on CLIL trials in Spain, Lasagabaster and de Zarobe (2010) note that foreign language learning in the early years does not negatively impact the learning and development of dominant languages, and they also indicate the efficacy of teaching as the key factor in the time-proficiency equation of L2 development. Bilingual immersion programmes in Spain have produced encouraging results, with students' proficiency in both L1 and L2 being deemed age-appropriate. Results from Spain suggest that immersion programmes can have equally positive results when started at a later stage; the key is that students have well-developed literacy skills in their L1 which can then be transferred to other languages (Lasagabaster & de Zarobe, 2010). As mentioned above, students who maintain both the dominant language (English) and home language tend to exhibit greater cognitive and cross-linguistic literacy skills. CLIL applies language to other skills, demonstrating its relevance and flexibility beyond a static classroom setting. The Association for Language Learning (n.d.b) has set up the Future for Languages as a Medium for Education (FLAME) initiative in the UK; however, CLIL methods are still seldom found in British classrooms.

Sustainable Teaching through Technology and Community Resources

While the suggestions above may raise concerns about funding, I propose that rather than invest financial resources in such activities, schools can use the human resources already available in the classroom and wider school community by inviting students, teachers and parents to share their own experiences and cultures. Furthermore, technology is increasingly being used in classrooms to engage students and appeal to their interests, and this can also be useful in early language learning. Concerning assessments, AI may be able to help evaluate the language level and progress of students. Not only can this aid in EAL children's integration into the classroom, but it can also provide an opportunity for EO children to explore languages and cultures beyond those with which they are familiar.

8 Towards Translanguaging Pedagogy

Practical tip:
- **Embrace multilingualism:** Develop a teaching approach that celebrates students' native languages and allows them to leverage their existing linguistic skills.

Why Now is the Time: Findings from the Bell Foundation

Moving towards a translanguaging pedagogy with the help of AI and other emerging technologies is the way forward in improving language education. Findings from the Bell Foundation (2021a) report provide us with an overview of the contemporary landscape concerning language teaching and learning in the UK and ultimately show how now is the time to enact change and make multilingual classrooms. The Bell Foundation is a charity that aims to overcome inequality in the UK through language education. In particular, they work with partners to generate and apply evidence with the goal of improving practice, policy and systems for those who use EAL in the UK.

According to the Bell Foundation's (2021a) Impact Report, highlights of the year included an 89% increase in new grant commitments, 10,518 EAL webinar views (live or recorded), the launching of four new ESOL grant partnerships to support refugees, and 51,140 downloads of EAL resources. Additionally, 2021 was the year of the COVID-19 pandemic and coincided with the arrival of new refugees from Afghanistan and Hong Kong. As a result, the UK experienced an unprecedented need for increased and improved language support. For instance, the survey found that 74% of primary school teachers and 59% of secondary school teachers observed a loss in one or more language skill areas among their EAL pupils, which was heavily impacted by school closures due to the pandemic. In response, the foundation provided necessary support to affected communities and groups with which the foundation works, as well as continuing to work to influence policy and practice. Financially, £1.754 million was invested into the foundation's charitable objects, including new grant commitments of £497,000.

In terms of resources, the foundation places a greater focus on equity, diversity and inclusion (EDI). They achieved this by improving the accessibility of their information and resources, including broadening the languages in which they are available, such as Dari, Pashto and Traditional Chinese. This was largely influenced by the linguistic needs and backgrounds of newly arriving refugees. The Bell Foundation also ran a webinar with a children's charity, I CAN, titled *Is it English as an Additional Language, a Language Disorder, or Both?* (The Bell Foundation, 2021b). This webinar and other partnered work aim to raise awareness of how to identify EAL learners who have a speech, language and communication need, and how to support them and their families.

In 2021, the foundation continued to influence UK policy through evidence and recommendations submitted to relevant government consultations and select committee inquiries. For example, the foundation submitted eight responses to government consultations in 2021. The foundation also took part in research with leading universities. In particular, they published the final report from Professor Strand at the University of Oxford, completing a five-year research programme examining the relationships between EAL, proficiency in English, and the educational achievement of EAL learners at school (Strand & Hessel, 2018), as well as two research reports from UCL IOE as part of the ESOL programme which provide key insights into the young people who use English as a second or additional language (Cook *et al.*, 2021; Hutchinson *et al.*, 2021). In addition, the foundation maintained partnerships and collaborations with a range of statutory bodies, professional organisations, key stakeholders, ESOL practitioners and more to influence national policy and practice. For instance, the foundation, in partnership with Ofqual, created an easy-to-understand guide translated into 17 languages so that schools, learners and parents could understand and utilise the guidance on the allocation of exam grades through teacher assessments and how to appeal them (The Bell Foundation, 2021a).

Given that there are over 1.6 million pupils in state-funded primary and secondary schools in England who speak EAL (over 21.2% of primary students and 17.5% of secondary students) (The Bell Foundation, 2021a), there is a clear need for additional language support and direction. The EAL programme managed and run by the foundation aims to improve the educational outcomes of disadvantaged children and young people in the UK who speak EAL, for individual, familial and wider societal benefit.

As for teacher support, the foundation's Language for Results programme intends to develop the knowledge and skills of school staff. In 2021, the programme focused on topics such as methods of supporting EAL pupils during school closures. The foundation also developed free, evidence-informed teaching materials for providers of initial teacher training (ITT), focusing on preparing student teachers to work in diverse, multilingual classrooms. Additionally, the foundation supplied free, evidence-informed and curriculum-based EAL resources to school staff. There was also the continued use and endorsement of the EAL Assessment Framework and digital tracker, offered free to schools, so that teachers can assess the English proficiency of each EAL learner, set individual targets and tailor support to the pupil.

Launched in 2020 to improve educational, social and employment outcomes for English as a second language (ESL) speakers, the foundation's ESOL programme published two research reports and submitted two consultation responses, alongside launching four new grant partnerships in 2021. The four new partnerships focused on enabling refugees to achieve their education and employment goals. One example is Refugee Education UK (REUK); by working with the foundation, REUK intended to develop and integrate new ESOL components into their educational mentoring programme to ameliorate young refugees' ESOL outcomes and contribute to the evidence in this area.

Through the Bell Foundation's 2021 Impact Report, we see a clear increase in the number of refugee children in the UK. Charities such as the Bell Foundation work closely with government, policymakers and educational practitioners to help address the needs of these persons. In particular, they strive to offer teaching and learning aid so that non-native English speakers are able to gain appropriate English language skills, which will help them to flourish academically and socially. One inclusion manager and SENCO offers the testimonial, 'The use of [translanguage] teaching and learning is a really good way to ensure an inclusive learning environment with high expectations. Thank you for showing us how easy this can be' (The Bell Foundation, 2021a: 5). Translanguaging in teaching and learning can involve making use of one's multilingual skills to help create a more welcoming and inclusive linguistic environment for speakers who do not speak the dominant language in the classroom.

However, while learning English is without doubt important in this day and age where the English language is a lingua franca, it is not the be-all and end-all of an individual's linguistic development. English matters, but perhaps not to the extent that formal public education has made it out to be. While the work of organisations like the Bell Foundation has great value and plays a vital role in better integrating the non-native English-speaking demographic into the UK, a balance must be struck so that such speakers are able to cherish their home language alongside English. Part of achieving this involves a greater shift in governmental and institutional policy, which will have a top-down effect on wider society. For instance, this will positively impact more covert and problematic ideologies, such as by combating linguistic prejudice through dismantling a hidden hierarchy of languages where English is at the top, followed by Western European languages, including French, German and Spanish. To mitigate the linguistic injustice done to languages that have been sidelined or excluded entirely from the national curriculum, much more work must be done to decolonise the curriculum. The Association for Language Learning (n.d.a) has a web page devoted to research and pedagogical intervention relating to such an issue. Particularly for the younger generation, which is becoming increasingly multicultural and multilingual as more and more children arrive from non-Anglophone nations, it is important that they belong to an environment that both welcomes their linguistic background and seeks to enhance it. In doing so, these speakers can be part of a society that accepts and appreciates their heritage language and culture, which in turn is essential for building a strong sense of self-identity and fostering a more inclusive setting.

Developing Translingual, Transcultural Competence

The current goals of language learning in the UK need to change. Rather than focusing on attaining fluency in individual languages, developing transferable translingual and transcultural competence is key. An article by Leung and Scarino (2016) emphasises the evolving nature of language education in the context of today's linguistically and culturally diverse society. The sociolinguistic realities of our pluralistic world underscore the importance of individuals becoming informed and educated learners capable of effectively navigating between languages and cultures. Leung and Scarino advocate for a shift in the goals and outcomes of language education. They argue that learners should aim to develop translingual and transcultural competence, enabling them to proficiently utilise a wide range of semiotic resources. These resources encompass not only their first language (L1) but also languages acquired formally or informally to varying degrees of mastery. Additionally, these resources constitute the accumulation and continuous development of multiple fragments of linguistic and cultural knowledge throughout the lives of individuals. The authors assert that language education should align with the multilingual character of contemporary communication. Rather than aiming solely to become native speakers, learners should strive to participate in the focal language as multilingual users. By adopting this approach, learners can fully embrace and benefit from the complex, multilingual nature of modern communication.

In summary, the goals of language learning, as proposed by Leung and Scarino (2016), need to be updated to equip learners with translingual and transcultural competence. Just as languages constantly change, so must our approach to language teaching and learning. Part of this involves diversifying the curriculum to include more relevant languages – languages that are already living and thriving in the UK – and encouraging their maintenance among heritage speakers. This shift in perspective reflects the evolving landscape of language education in our globally interconnected society, emphasising the importance of navigating between languages and cultures effectively.

Together Learning Paradigm

The Ignorant Schoolmaster by Jacques Rancière (trans. Kristin Ross, 1991) describes the story of Joseph Jacotot, a lecturer in French literature, as he teaches French to a group of Flemish students who do not speak any French. With no shared language, Jacotot looks for anything that he might have in common with his students; what he finds is a bilingual edition of the novel *Télémaque*. Left to themselves, the students learn French through repetition and recitation of the novel. The novel questions the existential necessity of the teacher and how teaching can either be enslaving or emancipating, depending on whether learning is one-directional (teacher to student) or two-directional (teacher to student and student to teacher). The story of Joseph Jacotot may not be so different from the experiences of our young children.

Although children may have shared some commonality to begin with, they are still exposed to their differences on a more fine-grained level as time goes on, particularly given the diverse, multilingual and multicultural landscape of UK classrooms. They may start with little or no understanding of their peers' language and culture, and then gradually and intuitively, they begin to learn. This is a lifelong journey that extends beyond formal schooling, requiring constant reflection and negotiation – though the classroom is one formative place for growing in this aspect. As in Rancière's book, linguistic and cultural learning should be two-directional and, crucially, sustained.

'Together learning' or 'co-learning' are terms that I coined in the book *Young Children's Foreign Language Anxiety: The Case of South Korea* (Kiaer *et al.*, 2021) to show how children and parents learn and explore their languages and cultures together. As mentioned throughout this book, the majority of languages spoken in the UK are not Western European languages. Despite this, the most common languages taught in British schools are Spanish, French and German. Arabic and Mandarin are slowly gaining popularity for economic and political reasons, but overall, the languages taught in schools are not representative of the languages in our country. The UK government rarely acknowledges the skill of multilingualism and instead urges immigrants to the UK to learn English or face the consequences. For years, there has hardly been space for anything but 'proper' or 'standard' English in our education system. Many non-Western European children growing up in the UK are not aware of the value or potential of their rich linguistic and cultural assets. When children translanguage outside of the home, they are often condemned as speaking a 'broken' language. Children produce language output that is well suited to their situation, and often translanguaging can be the most appropriate output. There should be spaces for children to translanguage, and a better understanding of translanguaging in pedagogical spaces. The border-crossing nature of translanguaging should be viewed as a nurturing practice, which helps to unite us in an efficient and thoughtful way. The Anglocentric approach of the UK education system is in dire need of an update.

Translanguaging Classrooms

In recent years, translanguaging has garnered notable attention in language education research, particularly among educators hoping to create language learning environments that decrease FLA, encourage language enjoyment, and aid in additive second language (L2) acquisition. A translanguaging classroom is the alternative to English-only classroom teaching models, and I argue that it is an ideal practice for alleviating FLA among young language learners.

In a translanguaging classroom, languages mix freely as students use their L1 repertoire to help build up their L2 semiotic repertoire. Much of the fear of bilingual education stems from misguided or misinterpreted advice from scholars in the early periods of linguistic research on bilingualism. The belief that children will learn the L2 slower and to a poorer level if they use multiple languages at the same time, alongside the assumption that bilingualism holds students back academically because they are unable to fully develop in either language, must be debunked. In various studies, researchers have shown that the variance between bilingual and monolingual children's acquisition of features of language is not statistically significant (Bergman, 1976; Grosjean, 2010; Meisel, 1989; Oller & Eilers, 2002; Pearson, 1998). Translanguaging classrooms are spaces where students are allowed to access all their previous knowledge through their native language as they learn English, enabling them to continue progressing in other subject areas while building up their English repertoire.

In addition, translanguaging allows students to access all their semiotic resources in order to engage in fuller and richer communication with their conversational counterparts. If they are forced to speak one language alone, their ability to express themselves would be restrained. In their article clarifying the concept of translanguaging, Otheguy *et al.*

(2015) assert that in a language learning classroom, translanguaging must be limited in order to assess the acquisition of specific language components. However, in a situation where a student's ability to express themselves is being tested, rather than some specific lexical or grammatical components in the target language, it is important to give students the chance to use 'all the learners' linguistic and semiotic resources' (Otheguy *et al.*, 2015: 305). In other words, in a classroom, a student should be allowed to use all the words and structures available to them in their linguistic arsenal in order to best express themselves. In the current educational methodology, multilingual students and language learners are expected to limit their expressions to a much lower percentage of their whole linguistic repertoire. This barring of access to existing knowledge can increase a student's FLA, which could dramatically decrease the success of their language acquisition. In contrast, if students are allowed to translanguage with their teacher and peers in the language learning classroom, this increases motivation, as the affective filters are lowered, FLA decreases and students gain confidence as they realise how much of their linguistic repertoire they have already developed.

Translanguaging in the classroom is a useful practice that teachers can employ to create a welcoming classroom environment. As stated in Kiaer *et al.* (2021), the United Nations Children's Fund (UNICEF) has declared that there are three dimensions to educating children that must be taken into account when ensuring that human rights are respected in educational settings: the right of access to education, the right to quality education, and the right to respect within the learning environment. In order for this right to be realised, 'education must be provided in a way that is consistent with human rights, including equal respect for every child, opportunities for meaningful participation, freedom from all forms of violence, and respect for language, culture, and religion' (UNICEF/UNESCO, 2007: 4). We affirm that this can be achieved through a translanguaging approach in the language classroom. This method of communication respects the differences in linguistic repertoire between individual students and allows all students in the language classroom to have the opportunity to participate meaningfully.

Language Sharing

The concept of a 'translanguaging classroom' may seem like a distant and idealised educational setting, but in reality, it is already happening, even in everyday life. An illustrative example comes from my own experience with my daughter, who is bilingual in Korean and English, and her friend Lara, who is bilingual in Mexican Spanish and English. What is fascinating is that Lara happens to be a K-pop fan, which has sparked a beautiful language exchange between the two. In their friendship, they seamlessly practice both Korean and Spanish. Lara engages in conversations about her favourite K-pop bands with my daughter, improving her Korean language skills in a fun and interactive way. In return, my daughter practices her Spanish by discussing various topics with Lara. This real-life scenario showcases the power of language exchange and highlights how individuals from diverse linguistic backgrounds can come together, naturally creating a 'translanguaging' environment where language boundaries blur and effective communication thrives. It is a testament to the fluidity and adaptability of language use in our interconnected world.

Case study: Chinese–English translanguaging in action

In 2017, one of my graduate students, Beth, worked at a primary school and employed translanguaging techniques, tailored in Chinese and English, in the classroom. She worked with five five-year-old Chinese pupils with varied, but all non-native, proficiencies in English. These children were identified as having varying levels of classroom anxiety and difficulty settling into the class, mostly due to their limited English language skills. On one occasion, two of the Chinese pupils who understood English the least were play fighting raucously and talking to each other when they were meant to be quiet – in this instance, when listening to a story with the class before home time. While the teacher told them off, the twins did not respond directly to the teacher, but instead started to play with each other more quietly than before. Given that the story was told in English without any visual guides, it can be easily imagined that, to these two children, listening in silence must have been quite understimulating. Oftentimes, Beth observed the teachers trying to communicate to these two pupils through mime, which they ignored. The teachers made active use of Beth to explain what was required of the children, and she received the impression that the teachers often felt exasperated over communication issues with the children. One of them sighed and told Beth, 'I wish we could have you here every day'.

Beth's role in teaching and learning involved delivering and discussing a selection of bilingual storytelling texts to the children. For example, the story of George the Giant, who gives away his clothes, was the focus of one session, which aimed at helping the children learn arithmetic. This session was held simultaneously with a class where the primary teacher taught a lesson on the same subject to the remainder of the pupils. Beth and the children sat on mats and used whiteboards and dry wipe pens along with elephant-shaped counting props to practice the mathematical concept of halving. The children's reaction to her language ability was highly positive, as they took an interest in how she could speak Chinese proficiently and even asked, 'How do you know Chinese?'. A sample of one dialogue went as follows:

Child:	Are you a 外國人? (This is better understood as 'non-Chinese' than 'foreigner' because it is applicable to me even when I [Beth] am in the UK.)
Beth:	I am British.
Child:	My mum and dad have lots of friends who speak Chinese.
Beth:	Are they 外國人?
Child:	They are Chinese.

Over the course of the sessions, Beth helped the children learn key vocabulary that would be used in their schooling and daily life. For one child in particular, it was through these sessions that Beth and the teachers discovered his aptitude for mathematics, which was initially hidden by his limited English. Beth's research observation report and later follow-up show us the great benefits of bi-directional translanguaging in teaching and learning; it connects the dots and breaks down strict boundaries of teacher–student relationships by allowing children to take the lead where appropriate. Given the curious nature of children, many of whom are eager to learn more about the world – whether they may outwardly express it or not – it is our duty as parents, researchers, educators and policymakers to nurture this spirit in welcoming, inclusive and dynamic environments.

Minimise Anxiety, Maximise Enjoyment, Mitigate Boredom

It may seem obvious, but the best way to prevent the long-term effects of anxiety on children's brains is by detecting it early. In order to do so, parents and educators should be trained in recognising signs of anxiety in their children and students. Being aware of these signals that indicate anxiety in children enables earlier diagnosis and consequently early receipt of the corresponding treatment. As emphasised in Kiaer *et al.* (2021), parents, teachers and those who care for children should be trained to notice the signs of both an anxious student and a non-anxious student. In particular, teachers working in language classrooms, or in classrooms with a large number of non-native English speakers, should be trained to quickly recognise the signs of FLA so that they can be part of the early detection system.

Concerning FLA, it is hypothesised that the trigger for such an experience in children is specific to situations, brought about by fear of negative evaluation and negative communication apprehension, which might impair one's ability to function in a foreign language. A range of treatment methods have been well established to treat anxiety through medical intervention. However, there are also interventions that can be taken on the part of the teacher or parent in order to reduce school-related anxiety so that it does not worsen to the extent that medical intervention is necessary.

Yet, we now find ourselves asking the following: Once classroom anxiety is identified, what do we do to reduce it and keep it from worsening? One answer is to increase FLE in the language classroom. As explored in more depth in Kiaer et al. (2021), FLE enables students to mentally reframe the work that is asked of them and helps them to form more positive emotions concerning these tasks, which will in turn aid in their successful completion of the given tasks regardless of any underlying anxiety. Table 8.1 includes Furner and Berman's (2003) final list of suggestions for alleviating maths-related anxiety on the left and how they could work in an early childhood language classroom on the right.

Most studies on maths and test anxiety reference increased positivity towards the topic or task as one of the best methods for alleviating anxiety; this finding can be transferred and applied to language classrooms. It also coincides with MacIntyre and Mercer (2014), MacIntyre et al. (2016) and Dewaele et al. (2019)'s emphasis on positive psychology.

To make language learning more engaging and effective, alongside reducing FLA and increasing FLE, educators should work to alleviate foreign language boredom (FLB). Younger generations are composed of AI natives, as discussed in more detail in Chapter 6. Therefore, it is imperative that our language pedagogies are developed in such a way that they remain fun and relevant for them. Pen and paper are no longer the primary tools used by this generation of children when learning languages. Instead, they rely on tablets, phones, laptops and computers. In the digital age, FLB can be mitigated by incorporating successful models of language learning found outside the traditional physical classroom, such as by borrowing gamification elements already implemented in apps like Quizlet and Duolingo. In doing so, our classrooms can become creative and lively spaces where languages can grow and flourish at the intersection of humans and AI.

Translation of Emotion: A Continuing Challenge in the AI Age

Bąk (2023) offers a compelling case study that explores the importance of language learning in an era of advanced AI translation tools like ChatGPT. It delves into the formidable challenges of achieving translation equivalence between English and Polish emotion terms, shedding light on broader implications for languages that differ significantly from each other, such as Korean and English. Bąk's investigation revealed a striking revelation: over 80% of emotion terms in both English and Polish have only partial translation equivalents. This striking statistic illustrates the intricate nature of translating nuances and emotions, a challenge that persists even in the age of advanced AI translation tools. Bąk's research underscores the vital role of language in comprehending and communicating emotions. It illuminates how language is an essential driver of our

Table 8.1 Adapting Furner and Berman's suggestions for alleviating math anxiety for application in a foreign language classroom

Furner and Berman's suggestions, taken from the National Council of Teachers of Mathematics (NCTM)	Application in an early childhood foreign language classroom
Accommodating for different learning styles	Flexible lesson plans allow for students of all learning types to learn in the way that works best for them (e.g. visual, aural, kinaesthetic, verbal, logical, social, solitary).
Creating a variety of testing environments	Similar to the first suggestion, teachers can create a variety of ways to assess their students' language acquisition. These should not all be ascribed to what is typically thought of as a test, and the students do not even need to know that they are being assessed.
Designing positive experiences in math classes	Focus on including experiences that will create positive attitudes and emotions towards both the target and home language within the classroom setting in order to cultivate FLE.
Refraining from tying self-esteem to success with math	Especially at such a young age, do not scare the children into learning the new language by making them think it is the only conduit through which they can have a successful career/life in the future.
Emphasising that everyone makes mistakes in mathematics	Perfectionism can lead to higher instances of FLA; therefore, creating an environment in which mistakes are accepted and learned from rather than denigrated is important in creating a positive, low anxiety learning environment.
Making math relevant	Task-based language teaching (TBLT) enables students to learn and use the target language in order to complete an actual activity or task. This is one way to emphasise the relevance of the language. Interactions with materials and speakers of English can also aid in showing the relevance of learning English. However, these encounters must be planned well in order to make sure a sudden encounter with a native speaker does not induce more anxiety.
Letting students have some input regarding their own evaluations	This suggestion can be directly applied to early childhood language learning classrooms. Teachers and parents can have conversations with children about what they find difficult in the topics they are learning. This, in conjunction with formal and informal assessments, should be adequate in providing educators with the information they need to determine how students are progressing and areas where they need more help.
Allowing for different social approaches to learning mathematics	Similar to the first point, varied approaches and diversifying ways in which the target language is used in interactions with classmates, teachers, family members and the outside world will facilitate more positivity and comfort in using the target language.
Emphasising the importance of original, quality thinking rather than rote manipulation of formulas	Rote learning techniques reject the higher levels of Bloom's taxonomy, ultimately creating anxious students who lack communicative competence. Teachers must therefore use more communicative teaching methods and reduce the use of rote learning methods in early childhood language classrooms.
Characterising maths as a human endeavour	This point is probably more easily achievable with language learning, as languages are inherently linked to people and cultures. However, emphasising the communicative usefulness of learning a new language for actual social interactions with other speakers of the language is important in the classroom. This will help in making English learning more of a 'human endeavour' than merely a set of grammatical rules to learn and apply to a long list of typed vocabulary words.

Source: Adapted from Kiaer *et al.* (2021).

ability to grasp the intricacies of emotions, particularly when it comes to translation. While the study examines English and Polish specifically, its implications extend far beyond these two languages. It underscores the ongoing need for improved resources and methods to enhance the translatability of emotions across languages. Thus, in a world becoming increasingly reliant on AI translation tools, language learning remains a critical skill for preserving the nuances and depth of human emotions and other 'untranslatable' concepts across cultures and languages.

The 3E Model in a Translanguaging Classroom: Creating Cross-Border Classrooms

In my previous works, I proposed the 3E model, which asserts that the key driving forces behind human language are efficiency, expressivity and empathy. In the context of UK language classrooms, working with AI and new digital technologies will help boost the efficiency aspect of human communication through tools such as LLMs. However, the expressive and empathetic goals of language cannot be fully met through AI integration alone – the human touch is still necessary. In translanguaging classrooms, both teachers and pupils are able to make full use of their linguistic repertoire, mixing languages when and where they feel appropriate to best express themselves. Moreover, through translanguaging practices, we can create a welcoming, safe space in which young people can learn to better understand each other, particularly those from different linguistic and cultural backgrounds. A modern translanguaging classroom in the UK is, by nature, cross-border; it traverses the boundaries between human and AI, teacher and student, and a range of nation-state languages, to create and nurture a sustainable, healthy living language ecology which is vital in our increasingly interconnected world.

Integrating AI into the Translanguaging Classroom

Like TBLL, smartphone applications and AI can be used to increase the amount of enjoyment that students experience in the language classroom. Since many children already like to play on smartphones and tablets, teachers can take advantage of this to promote more successful and comfortable language learning. Apps and the use of AI can help encourage children to experiment with their language without the worry of negative assessment by a teacher or a peer. This highlights the enjoyment factor of language learning, which reduces feelings of FLB and relieves much of the FLA that some students might experience through direct interaction with teachers and peers. Together, translanguaging, TBLL, and the use of technology can help create a language learning environment for young language learners that is healthy, increases FLE, and attempts to alleviate factors that might cause higher rates of FLA.

'Nucleolects'

In an era when human and AI interactions are on the rise and predicted to become the norm, it is an apt time to revisit and, where necessary, create terms that are fitting for the current situation. In the context of language and linguistics, I coined the term 'nucleolect'. 'Nucleolect' implies a language that is at the core or nucleus of an individual's communication. 'Nucleolect' and 'idiolect' both pertain to the individualisation of language but differ in key aspects. 'Nucleolect' encompasses the rapidly changing and highly personalised language driven by global mobility and AI interaction. It highlights the dynamic, ever-evolving nature of language in the modern digital age. On the other hand, 'idiolect' refers to the unique linguistic system of a particular individual, shaped by personal experiences and preferences, and tends to be relatively stable over time. According to the Oxford English Dictionary (2023), 'idiolect' is defined as 'the linguistic system of one person, differing in some details from that of all other speakers of the same dialect or language'. While both concepts emphasise individuality in language, 'nucleolect' focuses on the dynamic, globalised and technology-driven nature of linguistic evolution, while 'idiolect' emphasises the inherent uniqueness of an individual's speech patterns.

The term 'nucleolect' draws its inspiration from the nucleus, which serves as the core or central component of an atom. In this context, the nucleus symbolises the essence of individual communication. Just as atoms are constantly in motion and evolving, our language is undergoing a rapid and unprecedented transformation. Nucleolect describes the phenomenon of rapidly evolving and individualised languages in the digital age, driven by the convergence of global mobility, generative AI and LLMs. It signifies the explosive diversification and personalisation of language interactions, both among humans and between humans and AI. In today's interconnected world, language has taken on a new dimension. Traditional languages, dialects and forms of communication have always been subject to evolution, but nucleolect represents a paradigm shift in the pace and nature of linguistic transformation.

The key elements contributing to the concept of 'nucleolect' are as follows:

Global mobility

Today, people move across the globe more than ever before, encountering a rich tapestry of languages and cultures. This mobility exposes individuals to diverse linguistic influences, leading to the continual blending and reshaping of their linguistic repertoire.

Generative AI

The advent of generative AI, powered by LLMs, has revolutionised how we communicate. These AI systems not only understand human language but also generate content in a manner that mimics human expression. They adapt to individual preferences and writing styles, further fuelling linguistic diversification.

Explosive diversification

Nucleolect encapsulates the idea that as individuals engage in conversations with each other and with AI, their language evolves rapidly and diverges from standardised forms. This diversification is driven by the unique preferences of each communicator and the distinctive contexts and interactions in which they engage.

Individualisation

In the world of nucleolects, each individual's language becomes highly personalised. It adapts to their experiences, interactions and the AI with which they engage. No two individuals communicate in exactly the same way, as their linguistic repertoires become as unique as their fingerprints.

Cell-to-cell communication

This term emphasises the direct and personal nature of linguistic exchange. Language is no longer a monolithic entity; it is a dynamic, individualised form of communication akin to cells communicating within a complex organism.

The concept of nucleolect serves as a lens through which we can understand the unprecedented speed and depth of linguistic evolution in our modern world. It reminds us that language is a living, breathing entity, constantly shaped by the forces of technology, globalisation and individual expression.

A Healthy Language Ecology: Practical Steps Forward

Moving forward, we must collectively think of active ways to nurture our living languages. In an era of rapid digital and AI development, with globalisation having significant impacts on the languages and technologies involved in communication, it is even more crucial that we carefully consider how to make language teaching and learning engaging and sustainable. There are a variety of ways to help develop a healthy language ecology. However, for this to be maintained, it is important to remember that steps must be taken both inside and outside the classroom. The following are some suggested actions that parents and/or educators can take.

Start slow and relaxed

Let the child explore language in a relaxed way. All kids need this time. Begin with the language they are most comfortable with and continue from there. This familiar language becomes the base upon which other languages can be built.

Mix the languages

Encourage the child to use a mix of languages with which they feel comfortable. This approach helps children feel comfortable using a new language and sparks their curiosity to express themselves in it.

Use the language at home

This resource, based on conversations with children, introduces simple phrases in the new language into daily interactions. These phrases become a natural part of your home communication, making your child feel at ease with the new language.

Do not worry about specific phrases

This is key. You do not need to use specific phrases or expressions word for word as mentioned in textbooks. What is essential is introducing these simple expressions into everyday conversations with the child. As an encouragement and reminder, your own proficiency in the language(s) is not what matters most. The vital point is to engage with the child in the new language to boost their confidence without putting too much pressure on them.

Expose the child to the new language independently

As the child becomes more comfortable, it is a good idea to let them explore the new language on their own. They can do this by reading books, watching shows in the target language and, if possible, choosing their own language study materials.

By creating a nurturing environment that embraces multiple languages and gradually introducing the new language, you can help children construct a strong foundation upon which they can build for the rest of their lives. Focus on building their confidence and practical use of the new language first, rather than worrying too much about grammar rules.

Towards a Culture of Translanguaging

When speaking, multilinguals assess the nationality, age, gender, status, occupation, relation and various other attributes of the people/person they are conversing with, and as such they choose which language to speak, which politeness rules to adhere to, and which cultural system to follow. This is true regardless of whether the multilingual speaker is young or old. Translanguaging shapes a multilingual's life, affecting their verbal and non-verbal habits and choices in a way that is closely linked to their personal identity. It is a community-wide process, requiring active collaboration between families, educators and others, in which multilingual individuals engage for the entirety of their lifetimes.

Linguistic and cultural diversity is now at its zenith, enhanced by rapid technological advancement. As our life trajectory becomes more complex, so do our languages. My daughter Jessie has friends from all over the world, with the pupils at her school speaking a total of over 40 languages at home. Jessie has also told me that many of her friends love playing on Roblox, a metaverse platform. For children growing up in the modern era, the digital world is not unfamiliar. With even AI influencing us, we are experiencing unprecedented diversity and complexity in how we develop our language, or to be more precise, our nucleolects. Not only is the student–teacher boundary blurred, but other boundaries, such as those between languages and cultures, online and offline worlds, and verbal and non-verbal repertoires, are also being blurred. In today's world, we are actively engaged in creating our own languages by crossing these borders. The ability to fine-tune and mould languages is therefore essential. This translanguaging competence is a skill that multilingual children and families develop throughout their lives.

Be it at home, in schools, in our communities, or in the wider society, we need to help individuals recognise the value of their languages and cultures, so they can look upon themselves and others without prejudice. A more established translanguaging culture can help to foster a nuanced understanding of our multicultural societies and ultimately build a society that provides a safe space where people with different cultural and linguistic backgrounds can live. This form of culture lives in between and beyond languages and cultures as defined by the nation-state. Developing a sustainable translanguaging culture is crucial for us to move towards a more equal society, as this eliminates issues of prestige and prejudice. By nature, translanguaging sets no hierarchy among languages; all languages become equal and can be mixed in a fluid and hybrid way. Translanguaging culture provides us with the best way to negotiate our ever-evolving multicultural and multilingual world. Ultimately, it allows us to build a society that is more caring, nurturing and accepting.

While it is good to think about ways that we can improve young children's language learning environments, recommendation and implementation are not the same thing. It is important that a variety of people who influence the language education of young children be made aware of all these available methods for the improvement of young children's educational experiences. This includes, but is not limited to, government agents working in education-related departments, school administrators, teachers and parents. Those in charge of a child's institutional education should be made aware of the effectiveness of translanguaging in classrooms, alongside the dangers of FLA and FLB. Teachers need to go through a training process specifically targeted at cultivating an awareness of different pedagogical practices that encourage FLE, as well as educating them on how best to teach languages to young children of different cultural backgrounds. As parents, teachers and policymakers re-evaluate the methods used in language learning environments involving children, they will be able to create more motivated students, which will ultimately lead to more successful and sustainable language learning. Rethinking and innovating our traditional methods of teaching languages is the key to moving forward.

References

5 News (2016) Muslim women risk deportation if they don't learn English [Video]. YouTube, 19 January. https://www.youtube.com/watch?v=ZRdk-MKD2LA (Accessed 17 July 2023).

Addley, E. (2023) Pens away, laptops open – Pupils told to type, not write, GCSE exam answers. *The Guardian*, 17 October. https://www.theguardian.com/education/2023/oct/17/pens-away-laptops-open-pupils-told-to-type-not-write-gcse-exam-answers (accessed 30 October 2023).

Adolphs, S., Clark, L., Dörnyei, Z., Glover, T., Henry, A., Muir, C., Sánchez-Lozano, E. and Valstar, M. (2018) Digital innovations in L2 motivation: Harnessing the power of the Ideal L2 Self. *System* 78, 173–185. https://doi.org/10.1016/j.system.2018.07.014

Ahmadi-Azad, S., Asadollahfam, H. and Zoghi, M. (2020) Effects of teacher's personality traits on EFL learners' foreign language enjoyment. *System* 95, 1–15. https://doi.org/10.1016/j.system.2020.102369

Aistear Siolta (n.d.) Supporting children to become bilingual. Government of Ireland. https://www.aistearsiolta.ie/en/planning-and-assessing-using-aistears-themes/resources-for-sharing/supporting-children-to-become-bilingual-birth-6-years-.pdf (accessed 5 May 2023).

Alladi, S., Bak, T.H., Duggirala, V., Surampudi, B., Shailaja, M., Shukla, A.K., Chaudhuri, J.R. and Kaul, S. (2013) Bilingualism delays age at onset of dementia, independent of education and immigration status. *Neurology* 81 (22), 1938–1944. https://doi.org/10.1212/01.wnl.0000436620.33155.a4

Alliance for the Advancement of Heritage Languages (n.d.) Heritage FAQs. Heritage Languages in America. https://www.cal.org/heritage/research/faqs.html#:~:text=In%20the%20United%20States%2C%20a%20family%2C%20or%20a%20community (accessed 8 June 2023).

Alsahafi, M. (2022) When homeland remains a distant dream: Language attitudes and heritage language maintenance among Rohingya refugees in Saudi Arabia. *International Journal of Bilingual Education and Bilingualism* 25 (4), 1292–1303. https://doi.org/10.1080/13670050.2020.1754753

Amelia, R. (2016) Benefits of early second language acquisition. *Indonesian Journal of Integrated English Language Teaching* 2 (1), 19–30.

Anderson, B.R.O. (1991) *Imagined Communities: Reflections on the Origin and Spread of Nationalism*. Verso.

Appel, R. and Muysken, P. (2005) *Language Contact and Bilingualism*. Amsterdam Academic Archive.

Association for Language Learning (n.d.a) Decolonise MFL curriculum special interest groups. https://www.all-languages.org.uk/about/community/special-interest-groups/de-colonising-the-curriculum/ (accessed 20 August 2023).

Association for Language Learning (n.d.b) FLAME. https://www.all-languages.org.uk/initiatives/flame/ (accessed 21 August 2023).

Australian Bureau of Statistics (2021) Language used at home (LANP). https://www.abs.gov.au/census/guide-census-data/census-dictionary/2021/variables-topic/cultural-diversity/language-used-home-lan (accessed 12 September 2023).

Australian Bureau of Statistics (2022) Cultural diversity: Census. https://www.abs.gov.au/statistics/people/people-and-communities/cultural-diversity-census/2021 (accessed 4 August 2023).

Australian Government (2023) A new National Cultural Policy. https://www.arts.gov.au/what-we-do/new-national-cultural-policy (accessed 20 October 2023).

Ayres-Bennett, W., Hafner, M., Dufresne, E. and Yerushalmi, E. (2022) *The Economic Value to the UK of Speaking Other Languages*. RAND Europe and University of Cambridge. https://www.rand.org/content/dam/rand/pubs/research_reports/RRA1800/RRA1814-1/RAND_RRA1814-1.pdf (accessed 29 July 2023).

Babino, A. and Stewart, M.A. (2020) *Radicalizing Literacies and Languaging: A Framework toward Dismantling the Mono-Mainstream Assumption*. Palgrave Macmillan. https://doi.org/10.1007/978-3-030-56138-3

Bąk, H. (2023) Issues in the translation equivalence of basic emotion terms. *Ampersand* 11, 1–11. https://doi.org/10.1016/j.amper.2023.100128

Baker, C. (2011) *Foundations of Bilingual Education and Bilingualism* (5th edn). Multilingual Matters.

Baker, P. and Eversley, J. (eds) (2000) *Multilingual Capital: The Languages of London's Schoolchildren and Their Relevance to Economic, Social and Educational Policies*. Battlebridge Publications.

Baldwin, J.R. (2017) Intercultural communication in families. In Y.Y. Kim and K.L. McKay-Semmler (eds) *The International Encyclopedia of Intercultural Communication* (pp. 1–12). John Wiley & Sons. https://doi.org/10.1002/9781118783665.ieicc0046

Bates, E., Dale, P.S. and Thal, D. (1996) Individual differences and their implications for theories of language development. In P. Fletcher and B. MacWhinney (eds) *The Handbook of Child Language* (pp. 95–151). Blackwell Publishing. https://doi.org/10.1111/b.9780631203124.1996.00005.x

Bawden, A. (2019) Modern language teaching 'under threat from tough exams'. *The Guardian*, 11 May. https://www.theguardian.com/education/2019/may/11/modern-language-teaching-under-threat-from-tough-exams (accessed 18 August 2023).

BBC (2014) Languages across Europe: United Kingdom. *BBC*, 14 October. https://www.bbc.co.uk/languages/european_languages/countries/uk.shtml (accessed 2 November 2023).

Bergman, C.R. (1976) Interference vs. independent development in infant bilingualism. In G.D. Keller, R.V. Teschner and S. Viera (eds) *Bilingualism in the Bicentennial and Beyond* (pp. 86–95). Bilingual Press.

Berlitz Singapore (2023) The confidence-boosting effects of language learning in children. *Berlitz Singapore*, 21 July. https://berlitzsingaporeonline.com/blogs/berlitz-singapore-blog/language-learning-and-childrens-confidence (accessed 25 August 2023).

Bialystok, E. (2007) Acquisition of literacy in bilingual children: A framework for research. *Language Learning* 57 (s1), 45–77. https://doi.org/10.1111/j.1467-9922.2007.00412.x

Bialystok, E. (2011) Reshaping the mind: The benefits of bilingualism. *Canadian Journal of Experimental Psychology/Revue canadienne de psychologie expérimentale* 65 (4), 229–235. https://doi.org/10.1037/a0025406

Bialystok, E. (2018) Bilingual education for young children: Review of the effects and consequences. *International Journal of Bilingual Education and Bilingualism* 21 (6), 666–679. https://doi.org/10.1080/13670050.2016.1203859

Bialystok, E., Craik, F.I.M. and Freedman, M. (2007) Bilingualism as a protection against the onset of symptoms of dementia. *Neuropsychologia* 45 (2), 459–464. https://doi.org/10.1016/j.neuropsychologia.2006.10.009

Bielefeldt, H. and Wiener, M. (2023) *Declaration on the Rights of Persons Belonging to National or Ethnic, Religious and Linguistic Minorities*. United Nations Audiovisual Library of International Law. https://legal.un.org/avl///pdf/ha/ga_47-135/ga_47-135_e.pdf (accessed 19 October 2023).

Black Lab Films (2023) Why being bilingual is good for your brain [Video]. *BBC Ideas*, 12 October. https://www.bbc.co.uk/ideas/videos/why-being-bilingual-is-good-for-your-brain/p0gl245p (accessed 10 November 2023).

Blanco, C. (2020) Changes in Duolingo usage during the COVID-19 pandemic. *Duolingo Blog*, 8 April. https://blog.duolingo.com/changes-in-duolingo-usage-during-the-covid-19-pandemic/ (accessed 9 August 2023).

Blanco, C. (2022) 2022 Duolingo language report. *Duolingo Blog*, 6 December. https://blog.duolingo.com/2022-duolingo-language-report/ (accessed 2 September 2023).

Bloomfield, L. (1933) *Language*. Holt, Rinehart & Winston.

Blum-Kulka, S. (1997) *Dinner Talk: Cultural Patterns of Sociability and Socialization in Family Discourse* (1st edn). Lawrence Erlbaum.

Borneman, B. (2018) Serving the forgotten language communities in a time of change. *Wycliffe Today* 6 (1), 3–5. https://wycliffe.org.au/documents/wycliffe-today-feb-2018.pdf/ (accessed 21 July 2023).

Bova, A. (2021) Co-construction of argumentative discussions between parents and children during mealtime conversations. A pragma-dialectical analysis. *Learning, Culture and Social Interaction* 29, 1–15. https://doi.org/10.1016/j.lcsi.2021.100519

Boyd, J. (2023) The 20 most-retweeted tweets. *Brandwatch*, 17 May. https://www.brandwatch.com/blog/most-retweeted-tweets/ (accessed 17 July 2023)

Bradford, S. and Stevens, C. (2023) Births by parents' country of birth, England and Wales: 2022. *Office for National Statistics*, 17 August. https://www.ons.gov.uk/peoplepopulationandcommunity/birthsdeathsandmarriages/livebirths/bulletins/parentscountryofbirthenglandandwales/2022 (accessed 27 September 2023).

Brann, C.M.B. (1994) The role of sociolinguistics in national development in Nigeria. *Multilingua* 13 (4), 361–380. https://doi.org/10.1515/mult.1994.13.4.361

Briant, E. (2016) Language, empathy and reflection: Teaching journalists about the refugee crisis. *Media Education Journal* 60, 19–24.

British Academy SHAPE Observatory (2023a) GCSE entries for SHAPE subjects (England, Northern Ireland and Wales). *The British Academy*. https://www.thebritishacademy.ac.uk/policy-and-research/british-academy-shape-observatory/shape-indicators/gcse-entries-for-shape-subjects-england-northern-ireland-and-wales/ (accessed 1 December 2023).

British Academy SHAPE Observatory (2023b) Scottish National 5, higher and advanced higher entries for SHAPE subjects. *The British Academy*. https://www.thebritishacademy.ac.uk/policy-and-research/british-academy-shape-observatory/shape-indicators/scottish-national-5-higher-and-advanced-higher-entries-for-shape-subjects/ (accessed 1 December 2023).

British Council (2018) Divide growing between rich and poor for school language learning. *British Council*. https://www.britishcouncil.org/contact/press/divide-growing-between-rich-and-poor-school-language-learning (accessed 17 June 2023).

British Council (2021a) Mandarin Excellence programme successfully putting pupils 'on path to fluency', report finds. *British Council*. https://www.britishcouncil.org/about/press/mandarin-excellence-programme-successfully-putting-pupils-%E2%80%98-path-fluency%E2%80%99-report-finds (accessed 17 June 2023).

British Council (2021b) Learning languages: Motivation and influences at Year 9. *British Council*. https://www.britishcouncil.org/sites/default/files/learning_languages_-_motivation_and_influences_at_year_9.pdf. (accessed 26 August 2023).

British Council (2023a) Spanish the most popular A-level language in schools across England while German falls behind at GCSE, new report reveals. *British Council*. https://www.britishcouncil.org/about/press/spanish-most-popular-level-language-schools-across-england-while-german-falls-behind (accessed 22 July 2023).

British Council (2023b) One in four UK adults regret never learning another language. *British Council*. https://www.britishcouncil.org/about/press/one-four-uk-adults-regret-never-learning-another-language (accessed 5 July 2023).

British Council (n.d.) About the Mandarin Excellence Programme. *British Council*. https://www.britishcouncil.org/about-mandarin-excellence-programme#:~:text=There%20are%20now%20around%2010%2C000,participating%20schools%20by%20September%202024 (accessed 4 July 2023).

Brito, N. and Barr, R. (2012) Influence of bilingualism on memory generalization during infancy. *Developmental Science* 15 (6), 812–816. https://doi.org/10.1111/j.1467-7687.2012.1184.x

Brown, C.L. (2011) Maintaining heritage language: Perspectives of Korean parents. *Multicultural Education* 19 (1), 31–37.

Bryant, M. (2021) Latin to be introduced at 40 state secondaries in England. *The Guardian*, 31 July. https://www.theguardian.com/education/2021/jul/31/latin-introduced-40-state-secondaries-england (accessed 17 August 2023).

Byers-Heinlein, K. and Lew-Williams, C. (2013) Bilingualism in the early years: What the science says. *LEARNing Landscapes Journal* 7 (1), 95–112. https://doi.org/10.36510/learnland.v7i1.632

Cabinet Office (2023) Integrated Review Refresh 2023: Responding to a more contested and volatile world. Gov.uk. https://assets.publishing.service.gov.uk/media/641d72f45155a2000c6ad5d5/11857435_NS_IR_Refresh_2023_Supply_AllPages_Revision_7_WEB_PDF.pdf (accessed 17 September 2023)

Cambridge Dictionary (n.d.) Heritage language. https://dictionary.cambridge.org/dictionary/english/heritage-language?q=%2Bheritage%2Blanguage (accessed 3 August 2023)

Campbell-Cree, A. (2017) Which foreign languages will be most important for the UK post-Brexit? *British Council*. https://www.britishcouncil.org/research-insight/foreign-languages-post-brexit (accessed 22 August 2023).

Canagarajah, S. (2011) Translanguaging in the classroom: Emerging issues for research and pedagogy. *Applied Linguistics Review* 2 (2011), 1–28. https://doi.org/10.1515/9783110239331.1

Cenoz, J. (2013) Defining multilingualism. *Annual Review of Applied Linguistics* 33, 3–18. https://doi.org/10.1017/S026719051300007X

Cenoz, J. and Gorter, D. (2021) *Pedagogical Translanguaging*. Cambridge University Press. https://doi.org/10.1017/9781009029384

Cenoz, J., Hufeisen, B. and Jessner, U. (2003) Why investigate the multilingual lexicon? In J. Cenoz, B. Hufeisen and U. Jessner (eds) *The Multilingual Lexicon* (pp. 1–9). Springer. https://doi.org/10.1007/978-0-306-48367-7_1

Centre for Development of Advanced Computing (n.d.) *Multilingual Computing & Heritage Computing*. Centre for Development of Advanced Computing (C-DAC). https://www.cdac.in/index.aspx?id=mlingual_heritage

Chan, D.Y.-C. and Wu, G.-C. (2004) A study of foreign language anxiety of EFL elementary school students in Taipei County. *Journal of National Taipei Teachers College* 17 (2), 287–320.

Chang, C.B. (2016) Bilingual perceptual benefits of experience with a heritage language. *Bilingualism: Language and Cognition* 19 (4), 791–809. https://doi.org/10.1017/S1366728914000261

Chang, S.-E. and Weiss-Cowie, S. (2021) Hyper-articulation effects in Korean glides by heritage language learners. *International Journal of Bilingualism* 25 (1), 3–20. https://doi.org/10.1177/1367006920935512

Channel 4 News (2016) Muslim women on English language, integration and extremism [Video]. *YouTube*, 9 March. https://www.youtube.com/watch?v=Vg1yyFOPPEI (accessed 15 September 2023)

Chen, M. and Fang, Y. (2022) The relationship between bilingual and empathy. In A. Khalil and J.S. Zha (eds) *Proceedings of the 2022 8th International Conference on Humanities and Social Science Research (ICHSSR 2022)* (pp. 2338–2342). Atlantis Press. https://doi.org/10.2991/assehr.k.220504.423

Cho, G. (2000) The role of heritage language in social interactions and relationships: Reflections from a language minority group. *Bilingual Research Journal* 24 (4), 369–384. https://doi.org/10.1080/15235882.2000.10162773

Cho, H. and Song, K. (2022) Korean as a heritage language from transnational and translanguaging perspectives. In H. Cho and K. Song (eds) *Korean as a Heritage Language from Transnational and Translanguaging Perspectives* (pp. 1–12). Routledge. https://doi.org/10.4324/9781003227250-1

Chomsky, N. (1957) *Syntactic Structures*. Mouton.

CI Guest (2016) Thirty million words: A conversation with Dr. Dana Suskind. *Children's Institute*, 23 March. https://childinst.org/thirty-million-words-a-conversation-with-dr-dana-suskind/ (accessed 15 July 2023)

Clark, D. (2023) Pupil to teacher ratio in the United Kingdom from 2010/11 to 2018/19, by school type. *Statista*, 11 October. https://www.statista.com/statistics/282994/pupil-teacher-ratio-in-the-united-kingdom-uk-y-on-y-by-school-type/ (accessed 8 November 2023)

Clyne, M. (1991) *Community Languages: The Australian Experience*. Cambridge University Press.

Collen, I. (2020) Language trends 2020: Language teaching in primary and secondary schools in England. *British Council*. https://www.britishcouncil.org/sites/default/files/language_trends_2020_0.pdf (accessed 8 July 2023)

Collen, I. (2022) Language trends 2022: Language teaching in primary and secondary schools in England. *British Council*. https://www.britishcouncil.org/sites/default/files/language_trends_report_2022.pdf (accessed 8 July 2023)

Collen, I. (2023) Language trends 2023: Language teaching in primary and secondary schools in England. *British Council*. https://www.britishcouncil.org/sites/default/files/language_trends_england_2023.pdf (accessed 8 July 2023)

Collins Dictionary (n.d.) Community language. https://www.collinsdictionary.com/dictionary/english/community-language#google_vignette (accessed 27 July 2023)

Community Languages Australia (n.d.) Community language Australia. https://www.communitylanguagesaustralia.org.au/communitylanguageschoolsinaustralia/ (accessed 2 July 2023)

Conboy, B.T. and Kuhl, P.K. (2011) Impact of second-language experience in infancy: Brain measures of first-and second-language speech perception. *Developmental Science* 14 (2), 242–248. https://doi.org/10.1111/j.1467-7687.2010.00973.x

Conteh, J. (2018) Translanguaging. *ELT Journal* 72 (4), 445–447. https://doi.org/10.1093/elt/ccy034

Cook, L., Hutchinson, V., Cara, O., Mallows, D. and Tereshchenko, A. (2021) Policy briefing: Education and employment outcomes of young people who use English as a second or additional language. *UCL Institute of Education & The Bell Foundation*. https://www.bell-foundation.org.uk/app/uploads/2021/10/ESOL-policy-briefing-report-FV.pdf (accessed 12 September 2023)

Cook, V. (2016) Premises of multi-competence. In V. Cook and Li Wei (eds) *The Cambridge Handbook of Linguistic Multi-Competence* (pp. 1–25). Cambridge University Press. https://doi.org/10.1017/CBO9781107425965.001

Craik, F.I.M., Bialystok, E. and Freedman, M. (2010) Delaying the onset of Alzheimer disease: Bilingualism as a form of cognitive reserve. *Neurology* 75 (19), 1726–1729. https://doi.org/10.1212/WNL.0b013e3181fc2a1c

Creese, A. and Blackledge, A. (2010) Towards a sociolinguistics of superdiversity. *Zeitschrift für Erziehungswissenschaft* 13 (4), 549–572. https://doi.org/10.1007/s11618-010-0159-y

Cummins, J. (1992) Heritage language teaching in Canadian schools. *Journal of Curriculum Studies* 24 (3), 281–286. https://doi.org/10.1080/0022027920240306

Curdt-Christiansen, X.L., Li, W. and Hua, Z. (2023) Pride, prejudice and pragmatism: Family language policies in the UK. *Language Policy* 22 (4), 391–411. https://doi.org/10.1007/s10993-023-09669-0

Darvin, R. (2019) L2 motivation and investment. In M. Lamb, K. Csizér, A. Henry and S. Ryan (eds) *The Palgrave Handbook of Motivation for Language Learning* (pp. 245–264). Palgrave Macmillan. https://doi.org/10.1007/978-3-030-28380-3_12

Darvin, R. and Norton, B. (2015) Identity and a model of investment in applied linguistics. *Annual Review of Applied Linguistics* 35, 36–56. https://doi.org/10.1017/S0267190514000191

Davis, F.D. (1989) Perceived usefulness, perceived ease of use, and user acceptance of information technology. *MIS Quarterly* 13 (3), 319–340. https://doi.org/10.2307/249008

De Houwer, A. (2005) Early bilingual acquisition: Focus on morphosyntax and the separate development hypothesis. In J.F. Kroll and A.M.B. De Groot (eds) *Handbook of Bilingualism: Psycholinguistic Approaches* (pp. 30–48). Oxford University Press. https://doi.org/10.1093/oso/9780195151770.003.0003

De Houwer, A., Bornstein, M.H. and Putnick, D.L. (2014) A bilingual–monolingual comparison of young children's vocabulary size: Evidence from comprehension and production. *Applied Psycholinguistics* 35 (6), 1189–1211. https://doi.org/10.1017/S0142716412000744

De Wilde, V., Brysbaert, M. and Eyckmans, J. (2020) Learning English through out-of-school exposure. Which levels of language proficiency are attained and which types of input are important? *Bilingualism: Language and Cognition* 23 (1), 171–185. https://doi.org/10.1017/S1366728918001062

Dearing, R. and King, L. (2006) *Languages Review Consultation Report: December 2006*. Department for Education and Skills. https://webarchive.nationalarchives.gov.uk/ukgwa/20070109111215/http://www.teachernet.gov.uk/docbank/index.cfm?id=10690 (accessed 8 September 2023)

Delaney, M. (2016) Can learning languages help refugees cope? *British Council*. https://www.britishcouncil.org/voices-magazine/can-learning-languages-help-refugees-cope (accessed 14 July 2023)

Department for Business and Trade & Department for International Trade (2022, June 14) UK–Singapore Digital Economy Agreement. Gov.uk. https://www.gov.uk/government/collections/uk-singapore-digital-economy-agreement (accessed 2 September 2023)

Department for Business and Trade & Department for International Trade (2023, July 11) UK–Ukraine Digital Trade Agreement. Gov.uk. https://www.gov.uk/government/collections/uk-ukraine-digital-trade-agreement#:~:text=The%20UK%20and%20Ukraine%20have,our%20economic%20ties%20with%20Ukraine (accessed 2 September 2023)

Department for Education (2019, August 20) Guidance: English Baccalaureate (EBacc). Gov.uk. https://www.gov.uk/government/publications/english-baccalaureate-ebacc/english-baccalaureate-ebacc (accessed 29 July 2023)

Department for Education and Morgan, N. (2016, April 22) Community languages saved to ensure diverse curriculum continues. Gov.uk. https://www.gov.uk/government/news/community-languages-saved-to-ensure-diverse-curriculum-continues (accessed 26 August 2023)

Department of the Environment, Climate and Communications (2021, January 12) Official Languages Act. Gov.ie. https://www.gov.ie/en/organisation-information/e992e-official-languages-act/ (accessed 2 September 2023)

Dewaele, J.-M. and Pavelescu, L.M. (2021) The relationship between incommensurable emotions and willingness to communicate in English as a foreign language: A multiple case study. *Innovation in Language Learning and Teaching* 15 (1), 66–80. https://doi.org/10.1080/17501229.2019.1675667

Dewaele, J.-M., Chen, X., Padilla, A.M. and Lake, J. (2019) The flowering of positive psychology in foreign language teaching and acquisition research. *Frontiers in Psychology* 10, 1–13. https://doi.org/10.3389/fpsyg.2019.02128

Dietrich, S. and Hernandez, E. (2022) Nearly 68 million people spoke a language other than English at home in 2019. *United States Census Bureau*. https://www.census.gov/library/stories/2022/12/languages-we-speak-in-united-states.html (accessed 2 September 2023)

Dörnyei, Z. (2005) *The Psychology of the Language Learner: Individual Differences in Second Language Acquisition*. Routledge. https://doi.org/10.4324/9781410613349

Dörnyei, Z. (2009) The L2 motivational self system. In Z. Dörnyei and E. Ushioda (eds) *Motivation, Language Identity and the L2 Self* (pp. 9–42). Multilingual Matters. https://doi.org/10.21832/9781847691293-003

Dörnyei, Z. and Ottó, I. (1998) Motivation in action: A process model of L2 motivation. *Working Papers in Applied Linguistics* 4, 43–69.

Dörnyei, Z. and Skehan, P. (2003) Individual differences in second language learning. In C.J. Doughty and M.H. Long (eds) *The Handbook of Second Language Acquisition* (pp. 589–630). Blackwell Publishing. https://doi.org/10.1002/9780470756492.ch18.

Dörnyei, Z. and Ushioda, E. (2011) *Teaching and Researching Motivation* (2nd edn). Routledge.

Dörnyei, Z. and Kubanyiova, M. (2014) *Motivating Learners, Motivating Teachers: Building Vision in the Language Classroom*. Cambridge University Press.

Dörnyei, Z. and Al-Hoorie, A.H. (2017) The motivational foundation of learning languages other than global English: Theoretical issues and research directions. *The Modern Language Journal* 101 (3), 455–468.

Dressler, R. (2014) Exploring linguistic identity in young multilingual learners. *TESL Canada Journal* 32 (1), 42–52. https://doi.org/10.18806/tesl.v32i1.1198

Edge Early Learning (2023) The benefits of learning a second language for children. *Edge Early Learning*, 15 February. https://edgeearlylearning.com.au/the-benefits-of-learning-a-second-language-for-children/

Education Scotland (2023) A 1+2 approach to modern languages. *Education Scotland*, 11 April. https://education.gov.scot/resources/a-1-plus-2-approach-to-modern-languages/#:~:text=The%20Scottish%20Government's%20policy%2C%20Language,broad%20general%20education%20(S3) (accessed 30 September 2023)

Ehrman, M.E., Leaver, B.L. and Oxford, R.L. (2003) A brief overview of individual differences in second language learning. *System* 31 (3), 313–330. https://doi.org/10.1016/S0346-251X(03)00045-9

Ellis, E. (2016) *The Plurilingual TESOL Teacher: The Hidden Languaged Lives of TESOL Teachers and Why They Matter*. De Gruyter Mouton. https://doi.org/10.1515/9781614513421

Ellis, R. (2003) *Task-Based Language Learning and Teaching*. Oxford University Press.

Ely, C.M. (1995) Tolerance of ambiguity and the teaching of ESL. In J.M. Reid (ed.) *Learning Styles in the ESL/EFL Classroom* (pp. 87–95). Heinle & Heinle.

Evans, M., Schneider, C., Arnot, M., Fisher, L., Forbes, K., Hu, M., Liu, Y., Deniz, A., Gilevskaja, J., Maingay, S., Marciniak, K., Nevin, N., Richardson, S. and Sutton, D. (2016) *Language Development and School Achievement: Opportunities and Challenges in the Education of EAL Students*. University of Cambridge, Anglia Ruskin University, & The Bell Foundation. https://www.educ.cam.ac.uk/research/programmes/ealead/Executive_Summary.pdf (accessed 26 August 2023)

Fan, S.P., Liberman, Z., Keysar, B. and Kinzler, K.D. (2015) The exposure advantage: Early exposure to a multilingual environment promotes effective communication. *Psychological Science* 26 (7), 1090–1097. https://doi.org/10.1177/0956797615574699

Feely, A.J. and Harzing, A.-W. (2003) Language management in multinational companies. *Cross Cultural Management: An International Journal* 10 (2), 37–52. https://doi.org/10.1108/13527600310797586

Ferlazzo, L. (2023) 19 ways to use ChatGPT in your classroom. *Education Week*, 18 January. https://www.edweek.org/teaching-learning/opinion-19-ways-to-use-chatgpt-in-your-classroom/2023/01 (accessed 17 May 2023)

Fernald, A., Marchman, V.A. and Weisleder, A. (2013) SES differences in language processing skill and vocabulary are evident at 18 months. *Developmental Science* 16 (2), 234–248. https://doi.org/10.1111/desc.12019

Field, F. (2011) *Bilingualism in the USA: The Case of the Chicano-Latino Community*. John Benjamins Publishing Company. https://doi.org/10.1075/sibil.44

Florit, E., Barachetti, C., Majorano, M. and Lavelli, M. (2021) Home language activities and expressive vocabulary of toddlers from low-SES monolingual families and bilingual immigrant families. *International Journal of Environmental Research and Public Health* 18 (1), 1–18. https://doi.org/10.3390/ijerph18010296

Foreign Service Institute (n.d.) *Foreign Language Training*. U.S. Department of State. https://www.state.gov/foreign-language-training/ (accessed 2 November 2023)

Foreman-Peck, J. and Wang, Y. (2014) *The Costs to the UK of Language Deficiencies as a Barrier to UK Engagement in Exporting: A Report to UK Trade & Investment*. Cardiff Business School. https://assets.publishing.service.gov.uk/media/5a7e47c840f0b6230268a56f/Costs_to_UK_of_language_deficiencies_as_barrier_to_UK_engagement_in_exporting.pdf (accessed 4 November 2023)

Forsdick, C. (2023) The revival of language learning is key to a culturally and linguistically rich future. *The British Academy*, 26 September. https://www.thebritishacademy.ac.uk/news/the-revival-of-language-learning-is-key-to-a-culturally-and-linguistically-rich-future/ (accessed 4 October 2023)

Fox, R., Corretjer, O. and Webb, K. (2019) Benefits of foreign language learning and bilingualism: An analysis of published empirical research 2012–2019. *Foreign Language Annals* 52 (4), 699–726. https://doi.org/10.1111/flan.12424

Frenchin-Pollard, Z. and Bartlett-Imadegawa, R. (2023) K-wave hits European classrooms. *Nikkei Asia*, 14 May. https://asia.nikkei.com/Business/Business-trends/K-wave-hits-European-classrooms (accessed 17 June 2023)

Furner, J.M. and Berman, B.T. (2003) Review of research: Math anxiety: Overcoming a major obstacle to the improvement of student math performance. *Childhood Education* 79 (3), 170–174. https://doi.org/10.1080/00094056.2003.10522220

García, O. and Li, W. (2014) *Translanguaging: Language, Bilingualism and Education*. Palgrave Macmillan. https://doi.org/10.1057/9781137385765

Gardner, R.C. and Lambert, W.E. (1972) *Attitudes and Motivation in Second-Language Learning*. Newbury House Publisher.

Gayle, E. (2016) Cameron: Language classes for Muslim women can help fight extremism. *Euronews*, 18 January. https://www.euronews.com/2016/01/18/cameron-language-classes-for-muslim-women-can-help-fight-extremism (accessed 21 September 2023)

Giguere, D. and Hoff, E. (2020) Home language and societal language skills in second-generation bilingual adults. *International Journal of Bilingualism* 24 (5–6), 1071–1087. https://doi.org/10.1177/1367006920932221

González-Lloret, M. (2003) Designing task-based CALL to promote interaction: En busca de esmeraldas. *Language Learning & Technology* 7 (1), 86–104.

Goriot, C., McQueen, J.M., Unsworth, S., van Hout, R. and Broersma, M. (2020) Perception of English phonetic contrasts by Dutch children: How bilingual are early-English learners? *PloS ONE* 15 (3), 1–21. https://doi.org/10.1371/journal.pone.0229902

Gov.uk (2022, February 1) Academic year 2020/21: Key Stage 4 performance. https://explore-education-statistics.service.gov.uk/find-statistics/key-stage-4-performance-revised/2020-21 (accessed 15 October 2023)

Gov.uk (2023a, November 23) Academic year 2022/23: Schools, pupils and their characteristics. https://explore-education-statistics.service.gov.uk/find-statistics/school-pupils-and-their-characteristics (accessed 15 December 2023)

Gov.uk (2023b, August 8) English baccalaureate entry and achievement. https://www.ethnicity-facts-figures.service.gov.uk/education-skills-and-training/11-to-16-years-old/english-baccalaureate-entry-and-achievement/latest/ (accessed 17 October 2023)

Greater London Authority (2016) Mayor welcomes all to light up their senses at Diwali. *Greater London Authority*, 30 September. https://www.london.gov.uk/press-releases/mayoral/mayor-welcomes-all-to-diwali-in-trafalgar-square (accessed 17 August 2023)

Greater London Authority (n.d.) 20 facts about London's culture. https://www.london.gov.uk/programmes-strategies/arts-and-culture/vision-and-strategy/20-facts-about-london%E2%80%99s-culture#:~:text=There%20are%20over%20300%20languages,world's%20most%20popular%20music%20venue (accessed 17 August 2023)

Groba, A., De Houwer, A., Mehnert, J., Rossi, S. and Obrig, H. (2018) Bilingual and monolingual children process pragmatic cues differently when learning novel adjectives. *Bilingualism: Language and Cognition* 21 (2), 384–402. https://doi.org/10.1017/S1366728917000232

Grosjean, F. (1992) Another view of bilingualism. In R.J. Harris (ed.) *Cognitive Processing in Bilinguals* (pp. 51–62). North-Holland. https://doi.org/10.1016/S0166-4115(08)61487-9

Grosjean, F. (2010) *Bilingual: Life and Reality*. Harvard University Press. https://doi.org/10.4159/9780674056459

Grosjean, F. (2022) *The Mysteries of Bilingualism*. John Wiley & Sons.

Grosse, C.U. (2004) The competitive advantage of foreign languages and cultural knowledge. *The Modern Language Journal* 88 (3), 351–373. https://doi.org/10.1111/j.0026-7902.2004.00234.x

Haft, S.L., Gys, C.L., Bunge, S., Uchikoshi, Y. and Zhou, Q. (2022) Home language environment and executive functions in Mexican American and Chinese American preschoolers in head start. *Early Education and Development* 33 (4), 608–633. https://doi.org/10.1080/10409289.2021.1912548

Hall, T., Manning, A. and Sumption, M. (2023) Why are the latest net migration figures not a reliable guide to future trends? *The Migration Observatory*, 14 December. https://migrationobservatory.ox.ac.uk/resources/reports/why-are-the-latest-net-migration-figures-not-a-reliable-guide-to-future-trends/ (accessed 15 January 2024)

Han, Y. (2021) Understanding multilingual young adults and adolescents' digital literacies in the wilds: Implications for language and literacy classrooms. *Issues and Trends in Learning Technologies* 9 (1), 27–46. https://doi.org/10.2458/azu_itlt_v9i1_han

Hart, B. and Risley, T.R. (1995) *Meaningful Differences in the Everyday Experience of Young American Children*. Paul H. Brookes Publishing.

Hart, B. and Risley, T.R. (2003) The early catastrophe: The 30 million word gap by age 3. *American Educator* 27 (1), 4–9.

Hartshorne, J.K., Tenenbaum, J.B. and Pinker, S. (2018) A critical period for second language acquisition: Evidence from 2/3 million English speakers. *Cognition* 177, 263–277. https://doi.org/10.1016/j.cognition.2018.04.007

Hecht, E. (2023) What years are Gen X? A detailed breakdown of generation age ranges. *USA Today*, 13 December. https://www.usatoday.com/story/news/2022/09/02/what-years-gen-x-millennials-baby-boomers-gen-z/10303085002/ (accessed 2 March 2024)

HHCL Advisory Group (n.d.) Home, heritage and community languages advisory group: Vision and goals. *Association for Language Learning*. https://www.all-languages.org.uk/wp-content/uploads/2022/10/Vision-statement-for-HHCL.pdf (accessed 18 August 2023)

Higgins, C. (2023) Why am I learning Ukrainian? Because language is political for the country I've grown to love. *The Guardian*, 2 January. https://www.theguardian.com/commentisfree/2023/jan/02/learning-ukrainian-language-political-solidarity-victims-vladimir-putin (accessed 18 August 2023)

HM Revenue & Customs (2023) UK overseas trade in goods statistics July 2023: Commentary. https://www.gov.uk/government/statistics/uk-overseas-trade-in-goods-statistics-july-2023/uk-overseas-trade-in-goods-statistics-july-2023-commentary#exports-country-analysis (accessed 12 November 2023)

Hoff, E. (2013) Interpreting the early language trajectories of children from low-SES and language minority homes: Implications for closing achievement gaps. *Developmental Psychology* 49 (1), 4–14. https://doi.org/10.1037/a0027238

Hoff, E., Core, C., Place, S., Rumiche, R., Señor, M. and Parra, M. (2012) Dual language exposure and early bilingual development. *Journal of Child Language* 39 (1), 1–27. https://doi.org/10.1017/S0305000910000759

Hoff, E., Giguere, D., Quinn, J. and Lauro, J. (2018) The development of English and Spanish among children in immigrant families in the United States. *Pensamiento Educativo: Revista de Investigación Educacional Latinoamericana* 55 (2), 1–17. https://doi.org/10.7764/PEL.55.2.2018.1

Horwitz, E. (2001) Language anxiety and achievement. *Annual Review of Applied Linguistics* 21, 112–126. https://doi.org/10.1017/S0267190501000071

Howson, P. (2013) The English effect. *British Council*. https://www.britishcouncil.org/sites/default/files/english-effect-report-v2.pdf (accessed 18 September 2023)

Hu, J., Torr, J., Wei, Y. and Jiang, C. (2021) Mealtime talk as a language learning context: Australian Chinese parents' language use in interactions with their preschool-aged children at the dinner table. *Early Child Development and Care* 191 (3), 415–430. https://doi.org/10.1080/03004430.2019.1621862

Hua, Z. (2008) Duelling languages, duelling values: Codeswitching in bilingual intergenerational conflict talk in diasporic families. *Journal of Pragmatics* 40 (10), 1799–1816. https://doi.org/10.1016/j.pragma.2008.02.007

Hua, Z. (2010) Language socialization and interculturality: Address terms in intergenerational talk in Chinese diasporic families. *Language and Intercultural Communication* 10 (3), 189–205. https://doi.org/10.1080/14708470903348531

Hua, Z. and Li, W. (2016) Transnational experience, aspiration and family language policy. *Journal of Multilingual and Multicultural Development* 37 (7), 655–666. https://doi.org/10.1080/01434632.2015.1127928

Hua, Z., Li, W. and Lyons, A. (2017) Polish shop(ping) as translanguaging space. *Social Semiotics* 27 (4), 411–433. https://doi.org/10.1080/10350330.2017.1334390

Huang, H. and Liao, W. (2024) Maintaining a minor language or a heritage language? A case study of maintaining Chinese with preteenagers in Australian interlingual families. *International Journal of Bilingual Education and Bilingualism* 27 (3) 360–373. https://doi.org/10.1080/13670050.2023.2173519

Huang, T., Loerts, H. and Steinkrauss, R. (2022) The impact of second-and third-language learning on language aptitude and working memory. *International Journal of Bilingual Education and Bilingualism* 25 (2), 522–538. https://doi.org/10.1080/13670050.2019.1703894

Huang, Y. and Fang, F. (2024) 'I feel a sense of solidarity when speaking Teochew': Unpacking family language planning and sustainable development of Teochew from a multilingual perspective. *Journal of Multilingual and Multicultural Development* 45 (5), 1375–1391. https://doi.org/10.1080/01434632.2021.1974460

Hur, E., Lopez Otero, J.C. and Lee, E. (2021) Attitudes and expectations towards heritage language instruction: Evidence from Korean and Spanish in the US. *Languages* 6 (1), 1–16. https://doi.org/10.3390/languages6010014

Hutchinson, V., Tereshchenko, A., Mallows, D., Cara, O., Cook, L. and Sutton, D. (2021) *Young People, Education, Employment and ESOL*. UCL Institute of Education & The Bell Foundation. https://www.bell-foundation.org.uk/app/uploads/2021/10/UCL_Young-People-ESOL.pdf (accessed 22 September 2023)

Ibrahim, N. (2017) Developing literacy, and identities, in multiple languages. In B.V. Street and S. May (eds) *Literacies and Language Education* (3rd edn, pp. 211–224). Springer. https://doi.org/10.1007/978-3-319-02252-9_25

Ibrahim, N. (2021) Artefactual narratives of multilingual identity: Methodological and ethical considerations in researching children. In A. Pinter and K. Kuchah (eds) *Ethical and Methodological Issues in Researching Young Language Learners in School Contexts* (pp. 126–146). Multilingual Matters. https://doi.org/10.21832/9781800411432-008

ICEF Monitor (2013) Globalised economy continues to drive demand for foreign language proficiency. *ICEF Monitor*, 23 January. https://monitor.icef.com/2013/01/globalised-economy-continues-to-drive-demand-for-foreign-language-proficiency/ (accessed 12 October 2023)

IRIS Center (n.d.) What are some unique issues related to working with families of these children?: Importance of home language maintenance. https://iris.peabody.vanderbilt.edu/module/dll/cresource/q2/p03/ (accessed 13 October 2023)

Itani, S., Järlström, M. and Piekkari, R. (2015) The meaning of language skills for career mobility in the new career landscape. *Journal of World Business* 50 (2), 368–378. https://doi.org/10.1016/j.jwb.2014.08.003

Jia, G. (2008) Heritage language development, maintenance, and attrition among recent Chinese immigrants in New York City. In A.W. He and Y. Xiao (eds) *Chinese as a Heritage Language: Fostering Rooted World Citizenry* (pp. 189–203). University of Hawaii Press.

Jin, Y. and Zhang, L.J. (2021) The dimensions of foreign language classroom enjoyment and their effect on foreign language achievement. *International Journal of Bilingual Education and Bilingualism* 24 (7), 948–962. https://doi.org/10.1080/13670050.2018.1526253

Jo, A., Richardson, S. and de Jong, E.J. (2023) 'I feel really special and proud that I am bilingual': Exploring a second-generation Korean American bilingual adolescent's emotions and sense of belonging through family language policy. *International Journal of Bilingualism* 27 (2), 199–216. https://doi.org/10.1177/13670069221126272

Kamenetz, A. (2016) What's going on inside the brain of a bilingual child? *KQED*, 30 November. https://www.kqed.org/mindshift/47054/whats-going-on-inside-the-brain-of-a-bilingual-child (accessed 8 November 2023)

Kantaridou, Z., Papadopoulou, I. and Angouri, J. (2018) 'It's good to have a language under your belt': The value of foreign languages in the Greek job market. In T. Sherman and J. Nekvapil (eds) *English in Business and Commerce: Interactions and Policies* (pp. 256–275). De Gruyter Mouton. https://doi.org/10.1515/9781501506833-011

Karatsareas, P. (2018) The fragile future of the Cypriot Greek language in the UK. *British Academy Review* 33, 42–44. https://www.thebritishacademy.ac.uk/documents/377/BAR33-13-Karatsareas.pdf

Karhunen, P., Kankaanranta, A., Louhiala-Salminen, L. and Piekkari, R. (2018) Let's talk about language: A review of language-sensitive research in international management. *Journal of Management Studies* 55 (6), 980–1013. https://doi.org/10.1111/joms.12354

KBS News (2021) "I learned Korean because of BTS" /KBS 2021.10.09 [Video]. YouTube, 9 October. https://www.youtube.com/watch?v=JoV2ibY1n0Y&ab_channel=KBSNews (accessed 25 May 2023)

Kennedy, J. (2023) Privileging Māori and Chinese: Translanguaging in Chinese language teaching in Aotearoa New Zealand. In D. Wang and M. East (eds) *Teaching Chinese in the Anglophone World: Perspectives from New Zealand* (pp. 163–180). Springer. https://doi.org/10.1007/978-3-031-35475-5_11

Kiaer, J. (2017) Why is 'modern language' taken to mean 'European language'?. *OpenLearn*, 7 June. https://www.open.edu/openlearn/languages/learning-languages/why-modern-language-taken-mean-european-language (accessed 17 May 2023)

Kiaer, J. (2020) *Pragmatic Particles: Findings from Asian Languages*. Bloomsbury Publishing.

Kiaer, J. (2023a) *Multimodal Communication in Young Multilingual Children: Learning Beyond Words*. Multilingual Matters. https://doi.org/10.21832/9781800413344

Kiaer, J. (2023b) *The Future of Syntax: Asian Perspectives in an AI Age*. Bloomsbury Publishing.

Kiaer, J. (2024) *Conversing in the Metaverse: The Embodied Future of Online Communication*. Bloomsbury Academic.

Kiaer, J. (n.d.) K-pop fandom. Victoria and Albert Museum. https://www.vam.ac.uk/articles/k-pop-fandom (accessed 2 September 2023)

Kiaer, J. and Ahn, H. (2023a) *Emergence of Korean English: How Korea's Dynamic English is Born*. Routledge. https://doi.org/10.4324/9781003284956

Kiaer, J. and Ahn, H. (2023b) *Lessons from a Translingual Romance: Conflict and Cultural Innovation of Intercultural Couples*. Palgrave Macmillan. https://doi.org/10.1007/978-3-031-32921-0

Kiaer, J., Morgan-Brown, J.M. and Choi, N. (2021) *Young Children's Foreign Language Anxiety: The Case of South Korea*. Multilingual Matters. https://doi.org/10.21832/9781800411616

Kiaer, J., Kim, L., Hua, Z. and Li, W. (2022) Tomorrow? *Jayaji*! (자야지): Translation as translanguaging in interviews with the director of *Parasite*. *Translation and Translanguaging in Multilingual Contexts* 8 (3), 260–284. https://doi.org/10.1075/ttmc.00094.kia

Kieseier, T., Thoma, D., Vogelbacher, M. and Holger, H. (2022) Differential effects of metalinguistic awareness components in early foreign language acquisition of English vocabulary and grammar. *Language Awareness* 31 (4), 495–514. https://doi.org/10.1080/09658416.2022.2093888

Kim, C., Lee, S.-G. and Kang, M. (2012) I became an attractive person in the virtual world: Users' identification with virtual communities and avatars. *Computers in Human Behavior* 28 (5), 1663–1669. https://doi.org/10.1016/j.chb.2012.04.004

Kim, S.H.O., Ehrich, J. and Ficorilli, L. (2012) Perceptions of settlement well-being, language proficiency, and employment: An investigation of immigrant adult language learners in Australia. *International Journal of Intercultural Relations* 36 (1), 41–52. https://doi.org/10.1016/j.ijintrel.2010.11.010

Kim, Y. (2021) #KpopTwitter achieves new record of 6.7 billion Tweets globally in 2020. *Twitter Blog*, 4 February. https://blog.twitter.com/en_us/topics/insights/2021/kpoptwitter-achieves-new-record-of-6-billion-tweets-globally-in-2020 (accessed 25 August 2023)

Kim, Y. (2022) #KpopTwitter reaches new heights with 7.8 billion global Tweets. *Twitter Blog*, 27 January. https://blog.twitter.com/en_us/topics/insights/2022/-kpoptwitter-reaches-new-heights-with-7-8-billion-global-tweets#:~:text=With%20a%20massive%207.8%20billion,6.7%20billion%20Tweets%20in%202020 (accessed 25 August 2023)

Korean Education Centre UK. (n.d.) Korean after school clubs in UK schools. http://koreaneducentreinuk.org/en/korean-language-courses-in-uk-schools/ (accessed 1 October 2023)

Kramsch, C. (1998) *Language and Culture*. Oxford University Press.

Kuhl, P.K. (2011) Early language learning and literacy: Neuroscience implications for education. *Mind, Brain, and Education* 5 (3), 128–142. https://doi.org/10.1111%2Fj.1751-228X.2011.01121.x

Kwon, J. (2017) Immigrant mothers' beliefs and transnational strategies for their children's heritage language maintenance. *Language and Education* 31 (6), 495–508. https://doi.org/10.1080/09500782.2017.1349137

Laitin, D.D. and Ramachandran, R. (2022) Linguistic diversity, official language choice and human capital. *Journal of Development Economics* 156, 1–19. https://doi.org/10.1016/j.jdeveco.2021.102811

Lambton-Howard, D., Kiaer, J. and Kharrufa, A. (2021) 'Social media is their space': Student and teacher use and perception of features of social media in language education. *Behaviour & Information Technology* 40 (16), 1700–1715. https://doi.org/10.1080/0144929X.2020.1774653

Lanvers, U., Doughty, H. and Thompson, A.S. (2018) Brexit as linguistic symptom of Britain retreating into its shell? Brexit-induced politicization of language learning. *The Modern Language Journal* 102 (4), 775–796. https://doi.org/10.1111/modl.12515

Lanza, E. and Gomes, R.L. (2020) Family language policy: Foundations, theoretical perspectives and critical approaches. In A. Schalley and S. Eisenchlas (eds) *Handbook of Home Language Maintenance and Development: Social and Affective Factors* (pp. 153–173). De Gruyter Mouton. https://doi.org/10.1515/9781501510175-008

Lasagabaster, D. and de Zarobe, Y.R. (2010) Ways forward in CLIL: Provision issues and future planning. In D. Lasagabaster and Y.R. de Zarobe (eds) *CLIL in Spain: Implementation, Results and Teacher Training* (pp. 278–295). Cambridge Scholars Publishing.

Latukha, M., Doleeva, A., Järlström, M., Jokinen, T. and Piekkari, R. (2016) Does corporate language influence career mobility? Evidence from MNCs in Russia. *European Management Journal* 34 (4), 363–373. https://doi.org/10.1016/j.emj.2015.12.006

Laure (2023) 9 K-pop groups & the emojis widely used by their fandoms on Twitter. *Kpopmap*, 7 March. https://www.kpopmap.com/9-kpop-groups-the-emojis-widely-used-by-their-fandoms-on-twitter/ (accessed 27 September 2023)

Lee, J.S. and Suarez, D. (2009) A synthesis of the roles of heritage languages in the lives of children of immigrants: What educators need to know. In T.G. Wiley, J.S. Lee and R.W. Rumberger (eds) *The Education of Language Minority Immigrants in the United States* (pp. 136–171). Multilingual Matters. https://doi.org/10.21832/9781847692122-008

Lee, Y.-J. (2023) Korea to adopt AI textbooks for core subjects starting in 2025. *Hankyoreh*, 24 February. https://english.hani.co.kr/arti/english_edition/e_national/1081129.html#:~:text=The%20ministry%20intends%20to%20adopt,in%20high%20school%20in%202025 (accessed 19 April 2023)

Lenneberg, E.H. (1967) *Biological Foundations of Language*. Wiley.

Leonard, D., Vitrella, A. and Yang, K. (2020) Power, politics, and preservation of heritage languages. *Education Evolving & Coalition of Asian American Leaders*. https://www.educationevolving.org/files/Heritage-Languages-Paper.pdf (accessed 1 September 2023)

Leung, C. and Scarino, A. (2016) Reconceptualizing the nature of goals and outcomes in language/s education. *The Modern Language Journal* 100 (S1), 81–95. https://doi.org/10.1111/modl.12300

Li, W. (2011) Moment analysis and translanguaging space: Discursive construction of identities by multilingual Chinese youth in Britain. *Journal of Pragmatics* 43 (5), 1222–1235. https://doi.org/10.1016/j.pragma.2010.07.035

Li, W. (2018) Translanguaging as a practical theory of language. *Applied Linguistics* 39 (1), 9–30. https://doi.org/10.1093/applin/amx039

Li, W. (2021) 'Community' or 'modern' languages? Isn't it time for change? *Talking Humanities*, 7 December. https://talkinghumanities.blogs.sas.ac.uk/2021/12/07/community-or-modern-languages-isnt-it-time-for-change/ (accessed 19 July 2023)

Li, W. and Hua, Z. (2013) Diaspora: Multilingual and intercultural communication across time and space. *AILA Review* 26 (1), 42–56. https://doi.org/10.1075/aila.26.04wei

Li, W.L. (1982) The language shift of Chinese-Americans. *International Journal of the Sociology of Language* 1982 (38), 109–124. https://doi.org/10.1515/ijsl.1982.38.109

Li, X., Li, B. and Cho, S.-J. (2023) Empowering Chinese language learners from low-income families to improve their Chinese writing with ChatGPT's assistance after-school. *Languages* 8 (4), 1–16. https://doi.org/10.3390/languages8040238

Little, S. (2023) 'Half of who you are': Parent and child reflections on the emotional experiences of reversing familial language shift. *International Journal of Bilingualism* 27 (2), 217–231. https://doi.org/10.1177/13670069221125705

Lo Bianco, J. (1987) *National Policy on Languages*. Australian Government Publishing Service. https://www.multiculturalaustralia.edu.au/doc/lobianco_2.pdf (accessed 20 June 2023)

Lo Bianco, J. (2014) A cerebration of language diversity, language policy, and politics in education. *Review of Research in Education* 38 (1), 312–331. https://doi.org/10.3102/0091732X13511050

Long, R. and Danechi, S. (2022, September 7) Language teaching in schools (England). House of Commons Library. https://researchbriefings.files.parliament.uk/documents/CBP-7388/CBP-7388.pdf (Accessed 15 July 2023)

Lu, Z. and Liu, M. (2011) Foreign language anxiety and strategy use: A study with Chinese undergraduate EFL learners. *Journal of Language Teaching and Research* 2 (6), 1298–1305. https://doi.org/10.4304/jltr.2.6.1298-1305

Luo, R., Pace, A., Levine, D., Iglesias, A., de Villiers, J., Golinkoff, R.M., Wilson, M.S. and Hirsh-Pasek, K. (2021) Home literacy environment and existing knowledge mediate the link between socioeconomic status and language learning skills in dual language learners. *Early Childhood Research Quarterly* 55, 1–14. https://doi.org/10.1016/j.ecresq.2020.10.007

MacIntyre, P.D. and Mercer, S. (2014) Introducing positive psychology to SLA. *Studies in Second Language Learning and Teaching* 4 (2), 153–172.

MacIntyre, P.D., Gregersen, T. and Mercer, S. (eds) (2016) *Positive Psychology in SLA*. Multilingual Matters. https://doi.org/10.21832/9781783095360

MacIntyre, P.D., Baker, S.C. and Sparling, H. (2017) Heritage passions, heritage convictions, and the rooted L2 self: Music and Gaelic language learning in Cape Breton, Nova Scotia. *The Modern Language Journal* 101 (3), 501–516. https://doi.org/10.1111/modl.12417

Mak, E., Vanni, N.N., Yang, X., Lara, M., Zhou, Q. and Uchikoshi, Y. (2023) Parental perceptions of bilingualism and home language vocabulary: Young bilingual children from low-income immigrant Mexican American and Chinese American families. *Frontiers in Psychology* 14, 1–10. https://doi.org/10.3389/fpsyg.2023.1059298

Mandela, N.R. (1995) *Long Walk to Freedom: The Autobiography of Nelson Mandela*. Macdonald Purnell.

Marini, A. and Fabbro, F. (2007) Psycholinguistic models of speech production in bilingualism and multilingualism. In A. Ardila and E. Ramos (eds) *Speech and Language Disorders in Bilinguals* (pp. 47–67). Nova Science Publishers.

Marsden, E., Hawkes, R., Earnshaw, L., Hobson, V. and NCELP Team (2023) *Evaluation Report March 2023*. National Centre for Excellence for Language Pedagogy, University of York, and Department of Education. https://eprints.whiterose.ac.uk/200637/1/NCELP_Final_Report_9_April_2023.pdf (accessed 2 September 2023)

Mårtensson, J., Eriksson, J., Bodammer, N.C., Lindgren, M., Johansson, M., Nyberg, L. and Lövdén, M. (2012) Growth of language-related brain areas after foreign language learning. *NeuroImage* 63 (1), 240–244. https://doi.org/10.1016/j.neuroimage.2012.06.043

Mason, R. and Sherwood, H. (2016) Cameron 'stigmatising Muslim women' with English language policy. *The Guardian*, 18 January. https://www.theguardian.com/politics/2016/jan/18/david-cameron-stigmatising-muslim-women-learn-english-language-policy (accessed 22 June 2023)

Mazzaferro, G. (2018) Translanguaging as everyday practice: An introduction. In G. Mazzaferro (ed.) *Translanguaging as Everyday Practice* (pp. 1–12). Springer. https://doi.org/10.1007/978-3-319-94851-5_1

McArthur, T., Lam-McArthur, J. and Fontaine, L. (2018) (eds) *The Oxford Companion to the English Language* (2nd edn). Oxford University Press. https://www.oxfordreference.com/display/10.1093/acref/9780199661282.001.0001/acref-9780199661282-e-809?rskey=9ar9qX&result=881

McCabe, A. (2014) Silencing the mother tongue makes it harder for bilingual children to learn English. *Child & Family Blog*, September. https://childandfamilyblog.com/bilingual-children/ (accessed 13 August 2023)

Meisel, J.M. (1989) Early differentiation of languages in bilingual children. In K. Hyltenstam and L.K. Obler (eds) *Bilingualism across the Lifespan: Aspects of Acquisition, Maturity and Loss* (pp. 13–40). Cambridge University Press. https://doi.org/10.1017/CBO9780511611780.003

Melzi, G., Prishker, N., Kawas, V. and Huancacuri, J. (2022) Multilingual parenting in the United States: Language, culture and emotion. In A. Stavans and U. Jessner (eds) *The Cambridge Handbook of Childhood Multilingualism* (pp. 515–536). Cambridge University Press. https://doi.org/10.1017/9781108669771.028

Menacker, T. (2001) *Community Language Resources: A Handbook for Teachers*. National Foreign Language Resource Center.

Merriam-Webster. (n.d.) Transculturation. https://www.merriam-webster.com/dictionary/transculturation (accessed 1 July 2023)

Mieszkowska, K., Łuniewska, M., Kołak, J., Kacprzak, A., Wodniecka, Z. and Haman, E. (2017) Home language will not take care of itself: Vocabulary knowledge in trilingual children in the United Kingdom. *Frontiers in Psychology* 8, 1–11. https://doi.org/10.3389/fpsyg.2017.01358

Mills, J. (2001) Being bilingual: Perspectives of third generation Asian children on language, culture and identity. *International Journal of Bilingual Education and Bilingualism* 4 (6), 383–402. https://doi.org/10.1080/13670050108667739

Ministry of Business, Innovation and Employment (n.d.a) Language groups. https://www.mbie.govt.nz/cross-government-functions/language-assistance-services/face-to-face-interpreting-service/language-groups/ (accessed 12 October 2023)

Ministry of Business, Innovation and Employment (n.d.b) List of community languages. https://www.mbie.govt.nz/cross-government-functions/language-assistance-services/face-to-face-interpreting-service/list-of-community-languages/ (accessed 12 October 2023)

Ministry of Business, Innovation and Employment (n.d.c) 2M language services. https://www.mbie.govt.nz/cross-government-functions/language-assistance-services/face-to-face-interpreting-service/providers/2m-language-services/ (accessed 12 October 2023)

Ministry of Foreign Affairs and Korea Foundation (2023) 2022 지구촌 한류현황 1 [Global Hallyu Status 2022]. https://overseas.mofa.go.kr/viewer/skin/doc.html?fn=20230410114909764.pdf&rs=/viewer/result/202409 (accessed 8 July 2023)

Montanari, S. and Quay, S. (eds) (2019) *Multidisciplinary Perspectives on Multilingualism: The Fundamentals*. De Gruyter Mouton. https://doi.org/10.1515/9781501507984

Morales, J., Calvo, A. and Bialystok, E. (2013) Working memory development in monolingual and bilingual children. *Journal of Experimental Child Psychology* 114 (2), 187–202. https://doi.org/10.1016/j.jecp.2012.09.002

Muradás-Taylor, B. (2023) Undergraduate language programmes in England: A widening participation crisis. *Arts and Humanities in Higher Education* 22 (3), 322–342. https://doi.org/10.1177/14740222231156812

Nakamura, J. and Quay, S. (2012) The impact of caregivers' interrogative styles in English and Japanese on early bilingual development. *International Journal of Bilingual Education and Bilingualism* 15 (4), 417–434. https://doi.org/10.1080/13670050.2012.665827

NALDIC (2011) What are community languages? https://www.naldic.org.uk/Resources/NALDIC/Initial%20Teacher%20Education/Documents/Whatarecommunitylanguages.pdf (accessed 29 October 2023)

National Hangeul Museum (2021) '방탄 때문에 한글 배웠다': 방탄소년단의 영향력, 한글문화 전파에 날개를 달다 ['I learned Korean because of BTS': BTS's influence gives wings to the spread of Hangeul culture]. *National Hangeul Museum Newsletter* 90. https://www.hangeul.go.kr/webzine/202102/sub3_3.html (accessed 30 October 2023)

Nicolay, A.-C. and Poncelet, M. (2013) Cognitive advantage in children enrolled in a second-language immersion elementary school program for three years. *Bilingualism: Language and Cognition* 16 (3), 597–607. https://doi.org/10.1017/S1366728912000375

Norton, B. (2013) *Identity and Language Learning: Extending the Conversation* (2nd edn). Multilingual Matters. https://doi.org/10.21832/9781783090563

Oakes, L. (2013) Foreign language learning in a 'monoglot culture': Motivational variables amongst students of French and Spanish at an English university. *System* 41 (1), 178–191. https://doi.org/10.1016/j.system.2013.01.019

Office for National Statistics (2017) Holidays in the 1990s and now. https://www.ons.gov.uk/peoplepopulationandcommunity/leisureandtourism/articles/holidaysinthe1990sandnow/2017-08-07 (accessed 6 November 2023)

Office for National Statistics (n.d.) Census maps. https://www.ons.gov.uk/census/maps/ (accessed 5 November 2023)

Ofsted (2021) Research and analysis: Research review series: Languages. Gov.uk. https://www.gov.uk/government/publications/curriculum-research-review-series-languages/curriculum-research-review-series-languages (accessed 12 November 2023)

Oksaar, E. (1983) Multilingualism and multiculturalism from the linguist's point of view. In T. Husén and S. Opper (eds) *Multicultural and Multilingual Education in Immigrant Countries* (pp. 17–36). Pergamon Press.

Oller, D.K. and Eilers, R.E. (eds) (2002) *Language and Literacy in Bilingual Children*. Multilingual Matters. https://doi.org/10.21832/9781853595721

Otheguy, R., García, O. and Reid, W. (2015) Clarifying translanguaging and deconstructing named languages: A perspective from linguistics. *Applied Linguistics Review* 6 (3), 281–307. https://doi.org/10.1515/applirev-2015-0014

Our SG Fund (n.d.) 1st Kristang language festival. Our SG. https://www.sg/oursingaporefund/project-showcase/kristang-language-fest (accessed 6 October 2023)

Oxford CLIL (2018) The benefits of learning a second language early. *Oxford CLIL*, 7 February. https://www.oxfordclil.es/the-benefits-of-learning-a-second-language-early/ (accessed 1 July 2023)

Oxfordshire County Council (n.d.) Language learning in the library. https://www.oxfordshire.gov.uk/residents/leisure-and-culture/libraries/library/language-learning#:~:text=Language%20Caf%C3%A9%20is%20run%20by,and%20listening%20in%20other%20languages (accessed 6 July 2023)

Oxford English Dictionary (2023, July) Idiolect. https://doi.org/10.1093/OED/7112683157 (accessed 8 August 2023)

Papadopoulou, D., Rinker, T., Bosch, J., Di Pisa, G., Foppolo, F., Olioumtsevits, K. and Marinis, T. (2022) *How to Support Language and Literacy Development in Heritage, Majority and Foreign Language Classrooms*. The Multilingual Mind. https://doi.org/10.48787/kops/352-2-dgc9sc4q6iz97 (accessed 28 October 2023)

Park, J.S.-Y. (2011) The promise of English: Linguistic capital and the neoliberal worker in the South Korean job market. *International Journal of Bilingual Education and Bilingualism* 14 (4), 443–455. https://doi.org/10.1080/13670050.2011.573067

Park, S.M. and Sarkar, M. (2007) Parents' attitudes toward heritage language maintenance for their children and their efforts to help their children maintain the heritage language: A case study of Korean-Canadian immigrants. *Language, Culture and Curriculum* 20 (3), 223–235. https://doi.org/10.2167/lcc337.0

Patel, S. (2023) How heritage language education promotes cultural competence. *KidsLipi*, 24 February. https://kidslipi.com/cultural-competence-heritage-language/#:~:text=Learning%20about%20a%20culture%20through,in%20conversations%20about%20global%20issues (accessed 25 October 2023)

Pavelescu, L.M. and Petrić, B. (2018) Love and enjoyment in context: Four case studies of adolescent EFL learners. *Studies in Second Language Learning and Teaching* 8 (1), 73–101. https://doi.org/10.14746/ssllt.2018.8.1.4

Pearson, B.Z. (1998) Assessing lexical development in bilingual babies and toddlers. *International Journal of Bilingualism* 2 (3), 347–372. https://doi.org/10.1177/136700699800200305

Peltokorpi, V. (2023) The "language" of career success: The effects of English language competence on local employees' career outcomes in foreign subsidiaries. *Journal of International Business Studies* 54 (2), 258–284. https://doi.org/10.1057/s41267-022-00544-4

Perkins, S.C., Finegood, E.D. and Swain, J.E. (2013) Poverty and language development: Roles of parenting and stress. *Innovations in Clinical Neuroscience* 10 (4), 10–19.

Pew Research Center (2015) The whys and hows of generations research. *Pew Research Center*, 3 September. https://www.pewresearch.org/politics/2015/09/03/the-whys-and-hows-of-generations-research/ (accessed 7 June 2023)

Pikhart, M. and Klimova, B. (2020) Maintaining and supporting seniors' wellbeing through foreign language learning: Psycholinguistics of second language acquisition in older age. *International Journal of Environmental Research and Public Health* 17 (21), 1–15. https://doi.org/10.3390/ijerph17218038

Portes, A. and Schauffler, R. (1994) Language and the second generation: Bilingualism yesterday and today. *International Migration Review* 28 (4), 640–661. https://doi.org/10.1177/019791839402800402

Potter-Collins, A. (2013) Language in England and Wales: 2011. *Office for National Statistics*, 4 March. https://www.ons.gov.uk/peoplepopulationandcommunity/culturalidentity/language/articles/languageinenglandandwales/2013-03-04#:~:text=In%20the%202011%20Census%2C%2092.3,main%20language%20other%20than%20English (accessed 12 June 2023)

Prensky, M. (2001) Digital natives, digital immigrants Part 1. *On the Horizon* 9 (5), 1–6. https://doi.org/10.1108/10748120110424816

Prevoo, M.J.L., Malda, M., Mesman, J. and van IJzendoorn, M.H. (2016) Within- and cross-language relations between oral language proficiency and school outcomes in bilingual children with an immigrant background: A meta-analytical study. *Review of Educational Research* 86 (1), 237–276. https://doi.org/10.3102/0034654315584685

Raising Children Network (2023) Multilingual and bilingual children: Questions and answers. *Raising Children Network*, 3 November. https://raisingchildren.net.au/babies/connecting-communicating/bilingualism-multilingualism/bilingualism#:~:text=Also%2C%20if%20your%20child%20grows,who%20speak%20their%20heritage%20language (accessed 15 December 2023)

Rancière, J. (1991) *The Ignorant Schoolmaster: Five Lessons in Intellectual Emancipation* (trans. K. Ross). Stanford University Press.

Refugee Council (2017) Leeds school children welcome Syrian refugees. *Refugee Council*, 22 May. https://www.refugeecouncil.org.uk/latest/news/4928_leeds_school_children_welcome_syrian_refugees (accessed 12 August 2023)

Ripollés, P., Marco-Pallarés, J., Hielscher, U., Mestres-Missé, A., Tempelmann, C., Heinze, H.-J., Rodríguez-Fornells, A. and Noesselt, T. (2014) The role of reward in word learning and its implications for language acquisition. *Current Biology* 24 (21), 2606–2611. https://doi.org/10.1016/j.cub.2014.09.044

Rodina, Y., Bogoyavlenskaya, A., Mitrofanova, N. and Westergaard, M. (2023) Russian heritage language development in narrative contexts: Evidence from pre-and primary-school children in Norway, Germany, and the UK. *Frontiers in Psychology* 14, 1–11. https://doi.org/10.3389/fpsyg.2023.1101995

Romeo, R.R., Uchida, L. and Christodoulou, J.A. (2022) Socioeconomic status and reading outcomes: Neurobiological and behavioral correlates. *New Directions for Child and Adolescent Development* 2022 (183–184), 57–70. https://doi.org/10.1002/cad.20475

Roskams, M. (2022) International migration, England and Wales: Census 2021. *Office for National Statistics*, 2 November. https://www.ons.gov.uk/peoplepopulationandcommunity/populationandmigration/internationalmigration/bulletins/internationalmigrationenglandandwales/census2021#:~:text=Out%20of%20the%2059.6%20million,were%20born%20outside%20the%20UK (accessed 8 July 2023)

RR Donnelley (2009) *Count Us In: A Sense of Belonging: Meeting the Needs of Children and Young People Newly Arrived in Scotland*. HM Inspectorate of Education. https://www.naldic.org.uk/Resources/NALDIC/Teaching%20and%20Learning/cuimnnus_tcm4-618947.pdf (accessed 13 May 2023)

Rubino, A. (2015) Performing identities in intergenerational conflict talk: A study of a Sicilian-Australian family. In D.N. Djenar, A. Mahboob and K. Cruickshank (eds) *Language and Identity across Modes of Communication* (pp. 125–152). De Gruyter Mouton. https://doi.org/10.1515/9781614513599.125

Sabzalieva, E. and Valentini, A. (2023) *ChatGPT and Artificial Intelligence in Higher Education: Quick Start Guide*. UNESCO. https://unesdoc.unesco.org/ark:/48223/pf0000385146 (accessed 17 June 2023)

Savage, M. (2020) BTS launch lessons to help their fans learn Korean. *BBC News*, 23 March. https://www.bbc.co.uk/news/entertainment-arts-52007842 (accessed 25 June 2023)

Sayer, P. and Ban, R. (2013) What students learn besides language: The non-linguistic benefits of studying English as a foreign language in primary school. *MEXTESOL Journal* 37 (3), 1–17.

Schroedler, T. (2018) *The Value of Foreign Language Learning: A Study on Linguistic Capital and the Economic Value of Language Skills*. Springer. https://doi.org/10.1007/978-3-658-19736-0

Schwab, J.F. and Lew-Williams, C. (2016) Language learning, socioeconomic status, and child-directed speech. *Wiley Interdisciplinary Reviews: Cognitive Science* 7 (4), 264–275. https://doi.org/10.1002/wcs.1393

Sharma, S. (2021) K-craze: Korean dramas and culture are taking India by storm. *Aljazeera*, 15 September. https://www.aljazeera.com/economy/2021/9/15/k-craze-korean-dramas-and-culture-are-taking-india-by-storm (accessed 22 November 2023)

Siegal, M., Surian, L., Matsuo, A., Geraci, A., Iozzi, L., Okumura, Y. and Itakura, S. (2010) Bilingualism accentuates children's conversational understanding. *PloS ONE* 5 (2), 1–8. https://doi.org/10.1371/journal.pone.0009004

Singh, L. (2018) Commentary: The benefits of bilingualism go beyond knowing two languages. *CNA*, 25 February. https://www.channelnewsasia.com/singapore/commentary-bilingualism-mother-tongue-language-benefits-836736 (accessed 15 November 2023)

Singh, N.K. (2013) *Multilingual Trends in a Globalized World: Prospects and Challenges*. Cambridge Scholars Publishing.

Siow, S., Gillen, N.A., Lepădatu, I. and Plunkett, K. (2023) Double it up: Vocabulary size comparisons between UK bilingual and monolingual toddlers. *Infancy* 28 (6), 1030–1051. https://doi.org/10.1111/infa.12562

Skehan, P. (1991) Individual differences in second language learning. *Studies in Second Language Acquisition* 13 (2), 275–298. https://doi.org/10.1017/S0272263100009979

Skehan, P. (1998) Task-based instruction. *Annual Review of Applied Linguistics* 18, 268–286. https://doi.org/10.1017/S0267190500003585

Skehan, P. (2003) Task-based instruction. *Language Teaching* 36 (1), 1–14. https://doi.org/10.1017/S026144480200188X

Skrabut, S. (2023) 80 ways to use ChatGPT in the classroom: Using AI to enhance teaching and learning. https://www.kuraaiwi.nz/uploads/1/1/8/4/118489667/80_ways_to_use_chatgpt_in_akomanga754863.pdf (accessed 2 June 2023)

Skutnabb-Kangas, T. and McCarty, T.L. (2008) Key concepts in bilingual education: Ideological, historical, epistemological, and empirical foundations. In J. Cummins and N. Hornberger (eds) *Encyclopedia of Language and Education: Bilingual Education* (2nd edn, vol. 5, pp. 3–17). Springer.

Smith, B. (2009) Task-based learning in the computer-mediated communicative ESL/EFL classroom. *CALL-EJ Online* 11 (1), 45-59.

Smolicz, J.J. and Secombe, M.J. (2003) Assimilation or pluralism? Changing policies for minority languages education in Australia. *Language Policy* 2 (1), 3–25. https://doi.org/10.1023/A:1022981528774

Song, K. (2016) "Okay, I will say in Korean and then in American": Translanguaging practices in bilingual homes. *Journal of Early Childhood Literacy* 16 (1), 84–106. https://doi.org/10.1177/1468798414566705

Spence, C. (2022) How learning a new language changes your brain. *Cambridge University – World of Better Learning*, 29 April. https://www.cambridge.org/elt/blog/2022/04/29/learning-language-changes-your-brain/ (accessed 30 October 2023)

Spolsky, B. (2009) *Language Management*. Cambridge University Press.

St Joseph's Institution International (n.d.) St Joseph's Institution International High School, Singapore: Language policy. https://resources.finalsite.net/images/v1620373715/sjiinternationalcomsg/nyhsnuvz2vjvufig4s5k/SJIInternationalHSLanguagePolicy2020revision7May2021.pdf (accessed 6 July 2023)

Staff Writer (2019) These are the most-spoken languages in South Africa in 2019. *BusinessTech*, 1 June. https://businesstech.co.za/news/business/319760/these-are-the-most-spoken-languages-in-south-africa-in-2019/ (accessed 19 November 2023)

Statistics Canada (2022) Increasing diversity of languages, other than English or French, spoken at home. https://www150.statcan.gc.ca/n1/pub/11-627-m/11-627-m2022051-eng.htm (accessed 19 November 2023)

Stavans, A. and Ashkenazi, M. (2022) Heritage language maintenance and management across three generations: The case of Spanish-speakers in Israel. *International Journal of Bilingual Education and Bilingualism* 25 (3), 963–983. https://doi.org/10.1080/13670050.2020.1731416

Strand, S. and Hessel, A. (2018) *English as an Additional Language, Proficiency in English and Pupils' Educational Achievement: An Analysis of Local Authority Data*. University of Oxford, Unbound & The Bell Foundation. https://www.bell-foundation.org.uk/app/uploads/2018/10/EAL-PIE-and-Educational-Achievement-Report-2018-FV.pdf (accessed 8 July 2023)

Sun, H., Tan, J. and Chen, W. (2023) COVID-19 and bilingual children's home language environment: Digital media, socioeconomic status, and language status. *Frontiers in Psychology* 14, 1–9. https://doi.org/10.3389/fpsyg.2023.1115108

Sun, Y. (2022) The impact of second-language acquisition on cognitive development. In Y. Chen, M.T. Anthony and Y. Ke (eds) *Proceedings of the 2022 2nd International Conference on Modern Educational Technology and Social Sciences (ICMETSS 2022)* (pp. 809–816). Atlantis Press. https://doi.org/10.2991/978-2-494069-45-9_98

Sundara, M., Ward, N., Conboy, B. and Kuhl, P.K. (2020) Exposure to a second language in infancy alters speech production. *Bilingualism: Language and Cognition* 23 (5), 978–991. https://doi.org/10.1017/S1366728919000853

Sutton, K. (2021) Why first and second language skills are a benefit to learners and society. *Cambridge University – News and Insights*, 21 April. https://www.cambridge.org/news-and-insights/blogs/first-and-second-language-skills-are-a-benefit-to-learners-and-society (accessed 2 November 2023)

Swanson, M.R., Donovan, K., Paterson, S., Wolff, J.J., Parish-Morris, J., Meera, S.S., Watson, L.R., Estes, A.M., Marrus, N., Elison, J.T., Shen, M.D., McNeilly, H.B., MacIntyre, L., Zwaigenbaum, L., St. John, T., Botteron, K., Dager, S., Piven, J. and IBIS Network (2019) Early language exposure supports later language skills in infants with and without autism. *Autism Research* 12 (12), 1784–1795. https://doi.org/10.1002/aur.2163

Szubko-Sitarek, W. (2015) *Multilingual Lexical Recognition in the Mental Lexicon of Third Language Users*. Springer Berlin. https://doi.org/10.1007/978-3-642-32194-8

Taylor, F. (2013) *Multilingual Britain*. Cumberland Lodge. https://www.academia.edu/3538682/Multilingual_Britain (accessed 19 November 2023)

The Bell Foundation (2021a) Impact Report 2021: Creating opportunity, changing lives and overcoming disadvantage through language education. https://www.bell-foundation.org.uk/app/uploads/2022/12/Impact-Report-2021-FV.pdf (accessed 5 June 2023)

The Bell Foundation (2021b) Is it English as an Additional Language, a language disorder, or both? (Webinar) [Video]. YouTube, 23 September. https://www.youtube.com/watch?v=L0nK4l4VmE8 (accessed 1 December 2023)

The British Academy (2022) Academics top 'trust' list in British Academy poll. *The British Academy*, 17 June. https://www.thebritishacademy.ac.uk/news/academics-top-trust-list-in-british-academy-poll/ (accessed 14 July 2023)

The British Academy (2023) Encourage students to futureproof themselves by choosing a mix of arts and science subjects, teachers and parents urged. *The British Academy*, 17 August. https://www.thebritishacademy.ac.uk/news/encourage-students-to-futureproof-themselves-by-choosing-a-mix-of-arts-and-science-subjects-teachers-and-parents-urged/ (accessed 27 August 2023)

The British Academy and University Council of Modern Languages (2022) Languages learning in higher education: Granular trends: Analysis of UCAS data on undergraduate courses in the UK, 2012–2021. *The British Academy*. https://www.thebritishacademy.ac.uk/documents/4437/Languages-learning-in-higher-education-November_2022_vf.pdf (accessed 16 June 2023)

The Guardian (2015) 2015 Living languages: A special report on language learning. *The Guardian & The British Academy*. https://static.guim.co.uk/ni/1428923743291/BritAcFINAL_living language.pdf (accessed 8 June 2023)

The Languages Gateway. (n.d.) The UK's portal for languages *The Languages Gateway*. https://www.thelanguagesgateway.uk/ (accessed 2 July 2023)

The Office of Ethnic Affairs (n.d.) *Language and Integration in New Zealand*. Ministry for Ethnic Communities. https://www.ethniccommunities.govt.nz/assets/Resources/7d40a0074e/LanguageandIntegrationinNZ.pdf (accessed 1 December 2023)

Thomas, J. (1992) Metalinguistic awareness in second-and third-language learning. *Advances in Psychology* 83, 531–545. https://doi.org/10.1016/S0166-4115(08)61515-0

Thompson, A.S. and Vásquez, C. (2015) Exploring motivational profiles through language learning narratives. *The Modern Language Journal* 99 (1), 158–174. https://doi.org/10.1111/modl.12187

Tinsley, T. and Doležal, N. (2018) *Language Trends 2018: Language Teaching in Primary and Secondary Schools in England*. British Council. https://www.britishcouncil.org/sites/default/files/language_trends_2018_report.pdf (accessed 29 November 2023)

Tovar-García, E.D. and Podmazin, E. (2018) The impact of socioeconomic status and population size on the use of the Tatar language at home. *Intercultural Education* 29 (1), 122–138. https://doi.org/10.1080/14675986.2017.1404740

Triebold, C. (2020) The importance of maintaining native language. *Forbes & Fifth*. https://www.forbes5.pitt.edu/article/importance-maintaining-native-language (accessed 25 August 2023)

Trifonas, P.P. and Aravossitas, T. (eds) (2018) *Handbook of Research and Practice in Heritage Language Education*. Springer. https://doi.org/10.1007/978-3-319-44694-3

Tunçel, H. (2015) The relationship between self-confidence and learning Turkish as a foreign language. *Educational Research and Reviews* 10 (18), 2575–2589.

UNICEF/UNESCO (2007) *A Human Rights-Based Approach to Education for All: Framework for the Realization of Children's Right to Education and Rights Within Education*. UNICEF/UNESCO. https://unesdoc.unesco.org/ark:/48223/pf0000154861 (accessed 11 November 2023)

United States Census Bureau (2015) Detailed languages spoken at home and ability to speak English for the population 5 years and over: 2009–2013. https://www.census.gov/data/tables/2013/demo/2009-2013-lang-tables.html (accessed 5 December 2023)

University College London (2023) UCL to lead new national consortium for languages education. *UCL News*, 3 March. https://www.ucl.ac.uk/news/2023/mar/ucl-lead-new-national-consortium-languages-education (accessed 27 May 2023)

Ushioda, E. (2009) A person-in-context relational view of emergent motivation, self and identity. In Z. Dörnyei and E. Ushioda (eds) *Motivation, Language Identity and the L2 Self* (pp. 215–228). Multilingual Matters. https://doi.org/10.21832/9781847691293-012

Ushioda, E. (2012) Christian faith, motivation, and L2 learning: Personal, social, and research perspectives. In M.S. Wong, C. Kristjánsson and Z. Dörnyei (eds) *Christian Faith and English Language Teaching and Learning: Research on the Interrelationship of Religion and ELT* (pp. 223–229). Routledge.

Valdés, G. (2000) The teaching of heritage languages: An introduction for Slavic-teaching professionals. In O. Kagan and B. Rifkin (eds) *The Learning and Teaching of Slavic Languages and Cultures* (pp. 375–403). Slavica.

Vertovec, S. (2006) *The Emergence of Super-Diversity in Britain*. COMPAS. https://www.compas.ox.ac.uk/wp-content/uploads/WP-2006-025-Vertovec_Super-Diversity_Britain.pdf (accessed 13 June 2023)

Waddington, B. (2022) Language, England and Wales: Census 2021. *Office for National Statistics*, 29 November. https://www.ons.gov.uk/peoplepopulationandcommunity/culturalidentity/language/bulletins/languageenglandandwales/census2021 (accessed 19 December 2023)

Wang, H. (2010) 澳大利亚语言政策研究 [*A Study on Language Policy in Australia*]. China Social Science Press.

Wang, J., Wen, W., Sim, L., Li, X., Yan, J. and Kim, S.Y. (2022) Family environment, heritage language profiles, and socioemotional well-being of Mexican-origin adolescents with first generation immigrant parents. *Journal of Youth and Adolescence* 51 (6), 1196–1209. https://doi.org/10.1007/s10964-022-01594-5

Wang, Y., Tetteh, V.W. and Dube, S. (2023) Parental emotionality and power relations in heritage language maintenance: Experiences of Chinese and African immigrant families in Australia. *Frontiers in Psychology* 14, 1–14. https://doi.org/10.3389/fpsyg.2023.1076418

Ward, L. (2014) Community languages not supported in UK education system, survey suggests. *The Guardian*, 28 November. https://www.theguardian.com/education/2014/nov/28/community-languages-uk-young-attitudes (accessed 19 November 2023)

Weale, S. (2023) Italian and Polish GCSEs to go digital in 2026, says England's largest exam board. *The Guardian*, 17 October. https://www.theguardian.com/education/2023/oct/17/italian-polish-gcse-digital-in-2026-exam-board-aqa (accessed 8 December 2023)

Webb, D. (2023a, November 24) Progress on UK free trade agreement negotiations. House of Commons Library. https://commonslibrary.parliament.uk/research-briefings/cbp-9314/#:~:text=The%20agreement%20with%20Australia%20was,trade%20bloc%20of%2011%20countries (accessed 15 December 2023)

Webb, D. (2023b, November 17) The Comprehensive and Progressive Agreement for Trans-Pacific Partnership (CPTPP). House of Commons Library. https://commonslibrary.parliament.uk/research-briefings/cbp-9121/ (accessed 12 December 2023)

Weekly, R. (2020) Attitudes, beliefs and responsibility for heritage language maintenance in the UK. *Current Issues in Language Planning* 21 (1), 45–66. https://doi.org/10.1080/14664208.2018.1554324

Wenger, E. (1998) *Communities of Practice: Learning, Meaning, and Identity*. Cambridge University Press.

WIDA (2014) *WIDA Focus On: The Early Years: Dual Language Learners*. Wisconsin Center for Education Research. https://wida.wisc.edu/sites/default/files/resource/FocusOn-EarlyYears.pdf (accessed 27 September 2023)

Willett, J. (1995) Becoming first graders in an L2: An ethnographic study of L2 socialization. *TESOL Quarterly* 29 (3), 473–503. https://doi.org/10.2307/3588072

Wittgenstein, L. (1922) *Tractatus Logico-Philosophicus*. Routledge & Kegan Paul.

Wong, V. (2021) Bilingualism: Key benefits of helping your child to maintain their heritage language. *Banter Speech & Language*, 7 December. https://www.banterspeech.com.au/bilingualism-key-benefits-of-helping-your-child-to-maintain-their-heritage-language/ (accessed 29 September 2023)

Xiong, T. and Yuan, Z.-M. (2018) "It was because I could speak English that I got the job": Neoliberal discourse in a Chinese English textbook series. *Journal of Language, Identity & Education* 17 (2), 103–117. https://doi.org/10.1080/15348458.2017.1407655

Yao, J.H. (2020) Mom, talk to me in my mother tongue: Socioeconomic status and heritage language maintenance of East and South Asian Canadian community. *Canadian Language Museum Blog*, 4 June. https://langmusecad.wordpress.com/2020/06/04/mom-talk-to-me-in-my-mother-tongue-socioeconomic-status-and-heritage-language-maintenance-of-east-and-south-asian-canadian-community/#:~:text=Sociolinguists%20consider%20socioeconomic%20status%20an,with%20the%20children's%20language%20development (accessed 19 August 2023)

Yu, S.-C. (2015) The relationships among heritage language proficiency, ethnic identity, and self-esteem. *FIRE: Forum for International Research in Education* 2 (2), 57–71. https://doi.org/10.18275/fire201502021039

Zabell, S. (2021) "Squid Game" could inspire a new wave of Korean language learners. *Duolingo Blog*, 4 October. https://blog.duolingo.com/squid-game-could-inspire-a-new-wave-of-korean-language-learners/ (accessed 29 November 2023)

Zepeda, M. and Rodriguez, J.L. (2014) Bilingual development in early childhood: Research and policy implications for Mexican American children. In Y.M. Caldera and E. Lindsey (eds) *Mexican American Children and Families: Multidisciplinary Perspectives* (pp. 122–134). Routledge.

Zhang, D. (2012) Co-ethnic network, social class, and heritage language maintenance among Chinese immigrant families. *Journal of Language, Identity & Education* 11 (3), 200–223. https://doi.org/10.1080/15348458.2012.686408

Index

3E model 150

Aberdeenshire 135
academic development
　–benefits of early second language learning 49–50
　–home, heritage and community language learning 73
accents 47
adaptive learning 122
Adolphs, S. 85
after-school clubs 137
Ahn, H. 80, 90
AI 108–26
　–AI natives 37, 43, 44, 109, 111–12, 118, 121
　–AI tutor bots 115
　–AI-driven teaching 43
　–assessment 110, 113–14, 116, 118–21
　–changing the linguistic landscape 7
　–fandoms 90
　–generative AI 110, 119, 151–2
　–innovation 18–19
　–insufficient on its own 150
　–nucleolects 151, 154
　–in the translanguaging classroom 150
　–translation 148–9
A-levels
　–falling enrollments in modern languages 10, 58
　–heritage learners 10, 69, 136
　–non-European languages 136
　–Spanish 56, 74
　–statistics on uptake 10, 30, 34, 58
　–UK language learning trends 30
　–use of term 'community language' 67

Al-Hoorie, A.H. 85
Anderson, B.R.O. 88
Ango-Eurocentric ideology 144 *see also* Eurocentrism; Western European language bias
anxiety *see* FLA (foreign language anxiety)
app-based learning 18, 56, 108, 150
　see also Duolingo
appropriation of multilingual discourses 70–1
Arabic
　–as heritage language in the UK 69
　–in schools 10–11
　–trade/commerce 61
　–in UK 32
Asian languages
　–Asian cultural differences 106
　–Australia 33
　–in Australia 80
　–pragmatics 71
　–prevalence of 33–4
　–in schools 10, 15, 32, 33
　–in universities 66–7
assessment
　–AI 110, 113–14, 116, 118–21
　–digital exams 37, 118
　–EAL Assessment Framework 141
　–FLA (foreign language anxiety) 98
assimilation 26, 27, 41
Association for Language Learning 138, 142
attitude/motivation test batteries 82
Australia
　–Asian languages 33
　–'community language' as term 68

178

–'home language' as term 68, 69
–language policies 51, 80, 132–3
–migration 51
–neutral use of term 'languages' 67
–use of term 'languages' 67
authentic communication 88, 122
autocorrect 111
Ayres-Bennett, W. 59–60, 61

Bąk, H. 148–9
Baker, C. 128
Baker, P. 39
balanced multilingualism 21
Baldwin, J.R. 78–9
Bell Foundation 139–42
belonging 74–5, 84, 88
Bengali 32, 105–6
bilingual signage 27
bilingual texts 146–7
bilingualism, definition of 20–1
biliteracy 50
birth statistics of multilingual children in UK 28
Blackledge, A. 22
Bloomfield, L. 21
Blum-Kulka, S. 103
boredom 112, 148 *see also* FLB (foreign language boredom)
Brexit
    –diversification of post-Brexit language education 57–9
    –impact on language learning 40
    –importance of Arabic and Chinese 11
    –rethinking multilingualism post-Brexit 7
    –trade/commerce 59
    –universities 31–2
British Academy 10, 11
British Academy and University Council of Modern Languages 6, 29
British Council 11, 13, 25, 36, 38, 42, 45, 56, 58, 69
BTS 90, 92–3
Burman, B.T. 148, 149

Cambridge Dictionary 69
Cameron, David 42
Canada 33–4, 68
Canagarajah, S. 23
Cantonese *see* Chinese
career mobility 54–6
casual fluency 13
categorising languages 67
CEFR (Common European Framework of Reference for Languages) 120
cell-to-cell communication 152
Cenoz, J. 21, 128
census data 6, 32, 39–40
Chan, D.Y.-C. 96, 97
ChatGPT 110–14, 117–18, 120, 125–6, 148
China 53, 60
Chinese
    –Chinese-English translanguaging 146–7
    –heritage learners 72
    –intergenerational connections 79
    –MEP (Mandarin Excellence Programme) 13
    –popularity of 56
    –in schools 10–11, 131
    –in universities 29, 30–1
Chomsky, N. 22, 23, 125
CLIL (content and language integrated learning) 36–7, 138
co-creation/co-production 28, 77–8, 80
code-mixing 66, 91 *see also* translanguaging
code-switching 79, 128
cognitive benefits
    –of early second language learning 48–9
    –FLE (foreign language enjoyment) 99
    –home, heritage and community language learning 72
co-learning 80, 143
Collins Dictionary 67
colonialism 15
communicative language learning 87
communities of practice 88, 90
community and home, concepts of 74–5
community centres 129–30
'community language' as term 67–8
community languages 65–80

Community Languages Australia 68
community support for heritage learners 18, 129–30
community-belonging as motivation 84
computer-mediated communication 93
confidence 50
contextual information 23, 122
continuity between key stages 37–8, 74, 124
Cook, V. 87
COVID-19 3, 11, 31–2, 74, 92, 109, 111, 139
CPD (continuous professional development) 35
CPTPP (Comprehensive and Progressive Agreement for Trans-Pacific Partnership) 57, 59
Creese, A. 22
critical period for language acquisition 47, 56
critical thinking 63
cross-cultural communication skills 41
cultural events 18, 94
culture
 –building a translanguaging culture 154
 –cultural assimilation 26, 27, 41
 –cultural capital 87
 –cultural competence 62
 –cultural creative approaches 58
 –cultural deficits 6
 –cultural events 17, 136
 –cultural identity 18
 –cultural integration 26–7
 –cultural preservation 11
 –culture and language linkages 77–8
 –Learning Together Model 137
Cummins, J. 68
Curdt-Christiansen, X.L. 75–7
curricula 33, 37, 38, 124, 141
Cuthbertson Primary School, Glasgow City Council 134–5

DALL E 108
Danechi, S. 32
Darvin, R. 87, 123
Davis, Fred 117
de Zarobe, Y.R. 138
Dearing Report 5, 6, 12

deep learning methodologies 108
deficit perspectives 6, 41
degrees in languages 6, 29
dementia 48–9
Dewaele, J.-M. 93, 148
diaspora 79, 105, 129
dictionaries 108
digital communities 130
digital exams 37, 118
digital innovation 108–26
digital learning tools 148 *see also* AI; app-based learning
digital motivation 85
digital natives 88, 111, 119, 125
digital trade 59
disconnection 36–7
discourse communities 77
discrimination 15, 62–3, 67, 69–70
disorders of language 121, 140
diversity 5, 10, 28, 40, 46, 57–9, 71, 140
Doležal, N. 32, 34, 35
Dörnyei, Z. 83–4, 85, 95
Duolingo 8, 11, 16, 92, 108, 148

EAL (English as an Additional Language) 25, 74, 133, 134–6, 137, 139, 140, 141
early language learning 34, 47, 48–9
EBacc (English Baccalaureate) 32, 35, 58
economics 11, 58, 59–62
Edinburgh EAL Service 135, 136
education policies 33
efficiency, expressivity and empathy (3E) model 150
EFL (English as a Foreign Language) 6
ELF (English as a lingua franca) 6, 13, 40, 54, 57, 60, 91, 141
Ely, C.M. 95
EMI (English medium instruction) 133
emojis 90–1, 111
emotions
 –benefits of early second language learning 49–50
 –emotional motivations for learning 93–4
 –emotional resilience 73
 –FLE (foreign language enjoyment) 99
 –heritage language loss 77

–home, heritage and community language learning 73
–language of emotion 66
–language of the heart 46–7
–translanguaging 148–50
empathy 2, 4, 22, 42, 50–2, 56, 63, 73, 94, 150
employment
  –career mobility 54–6
  –effects of linguistic discrimination 15
  –heritage learners 73
  –importance of Arabic and Chinese 11
  –instrumental motivation 82
  –job market competitiveness 52–4, 60
English
  –in Australia 80
  –English language classes 25
  –heritage language parents shifting to 76
  –instrumental motivation 87
  –on the internet 91
  –job market competitiveness 52–4, 55–6
  –love of 93
  –motivations to learn 84–5
  –as pinnacle of implied hierarchy 67
  –trade/commerce 60–1
English-is-enough concept 5, 6, 42
equity, diversity and inclusion 140
errors, attitudes towards 96
ESL (English as a Second Language) 141
ESOL (English for speakers of other languages) 135, 139, 141
EU (European Union) 53 *see also* Brexit
Eurocentrism
  –changing the linguistic landscape 6
  –changing the linguistic landscape 7
  –versus diversity 14–18
  –heritage learners 67
  –ideology 70–1
  –translanguaging pedagogy 142, 143–4
  –UK language education 32, 33
  –universities 29
European Commission 54
evening classes 56

Eversley, J. 39
exams *see* assessment
exchange visits 58
explosive diversification 152
extracurricular education 58, 137
extremism 42, 63

Fabbro, F. 21
family intercultural communication 79 *see also* intergenerational connections
family learning groups 136
fandoms 84–5, 89–90, 123–4
'first language' as term 69
FLA (foreign language anxiety) 81, 95–7, 102–3, 143–50, 154
FLAME (Future for Languages as a Medium for Education) 138
FLB (foreign language boredom) 44, 148, 150, 154
FLE (foreign language enjoyment) 81, 99–100, 148
FLP (family language policies) 70, 75–7
fluency
  –FLA (foreign language anxiety) 97
  –goals other than 56–7, 66, 71
  –rethinking 12–14
'foreign' languages as a term 67, 133 *see also* MFL (modern foreign languages)
Foreign Service Institute (US) 12–13
Foreman-Peck, J. 58
Forsdick, C. 12
French
  –Canada 33
  –GCSEs 9
  –Key Stage 3 74
  –primary schools 134
  –returns on investment in language education 61–2
  –in UK 9, 32, 56
  –universities 30
funding for language education 76, 138, 139
Furner, J.M. 148, 149
Future Academics 36
'future self' 83–4

Gaelic 133
gamification 37, 45, 90, 114, 122
García, O. 101
Gardner, Robert 81, 83
GCSEs
   –digital exams 37, 118
   –falling enrollments in modern languages 6, 9–12, 58
   –greater diversity of languages 10, 34–5
   –heritage learners 32, 34–5, 69
   –Spanish 30, 56
   –statistics on uptake 34
   –time required to achieve proficiency 13
   –UK language learning trends 30
   –use of term 'community language' 67
GDP 58, 61
Gen Alpha 43, 109, 111–12, 114, 119, 120
Gen Z 43–4, 90, 111–12, 114, 119
general language subject 124–5
generative AI 110, 119, 151–2
generativity 125–6
German 9, 30, 56, 74, 134
gesture 24, 106
Gibb, Nick 58
global citizenship 63
Global South languages 7
globalisation
   –economic benefits of multilingualism 53, 57, 59
   –home and community languages 66, 67, 71
   –intercultural competence 73
   –and the need for multilingualism 24
   –superdigital worlds 88
   –teaching of Arabic and Chinese in schools 11
   –translanguaging 104, 151
GME (Gaelic medium education) 133
goal setting 83
Gomes, R.L. 70
Google Translate 7, 24
Gorter, D. 128
GPTZero 117
'gravity model of trade' 60
Grosse, C.U. 54
Gujarati 32

Hallyu 92
Hampshire Services 69
Hart, Betty 101
heart, language of the 46–7
heritage languages/heritage learners
   –AI 125
   –benefits of continued learning 58
   –consequences of distance from 100
   –'heritage language' as term 69
   –implication of hierarchy of languages 67
   –motivation to learn languages 104–5
   –myth that learning heritage languages harms English learning 70
   –preservation/maintenance 16–17
   –as a 'problem' to be solved 42
   –revitalisation of 57–8
   –SES (socioeconomic status) 16–18
   –stopping learning 76
   –teaching of 71–2
   –in UK 11
   –use in public 76
   –value of teaching and learning 100–1
HHCL (Home, Heritage and Community Languages) Advisory Group 69
hierarchy of languages, implied 67, 142, 143
HMIE (Her Majesty's Inspectorate of Education) 134
home, concepts of 74–5
'home language' as term 67, 68–9
home language policies *see* FLP (family language policies)
Horwitz, E. 95
House of Commons report 32
Hua, Z. 79, 105, 129
Huang, H. 105
human capital effects 60, 61
human rights 43, 145

I CAN 140
ICEF Monitor 20
ideal self 84, 85
identity
   –building a culture of 153–5
   –code-switching 79

–complex 87
–cultural identity 18
–fans 90, 92
–heritage learners 72, 73
–language maintenance 104–5
–new identities 88
–positive 103
ideolects 151
Ignorant Schoolmaster (Rancière) 143
imagined communities 88
immersion 7, 47, 90, 123, 124, 138
inclusion 26, 28, 62–3, 140
Indian languages 15
individual differences in language learning 109, 121–3, 152
individual differences in language motivations 94–101
inequality 45, 53, 125
informal language learning 18
innovation 28, 44, 123–4
instant feedback 122
instrumental motivation 82, 87
integration as goal 26, 82
integrative motives 82
interactivity 123
intercultural awareness 11, 19
intercultural communication 90
intercultural competence 51–2, 54, 56, 57, 62, 73, 78, 106–7
intercultural couples 66, 78
intercultural families 78–80, 101, 103, 104–5
interest in topics 93
intergenerational connections 73, 78–80, 94, 100, 102, 105, 130
interpreting 131
investment theory 90
Ireland 68, 69
Italian 30, 56, 134
Itani, S. 55
ITT (initial teacher training) 141

Japanese 29, 72
Jo, A. 102
job market competitiveness 52–4, 73

Kantaridou, Z. 54
Karhunen, P. 54

K-dramas 16, 90, 92
Kennedy, J. 22
Key Stage 1 34, 38
Key Stage 2 34, 38, 124
Key Stage 3 34, 38, 61, 124
Key Stage 4 61
Kiaer, J. 44, 80, 90, 94, 103, 104, 105, 110, 120, 129, 143, 145, 147, 148, 149
Kim, C. 85
Kim, S.H.O. 51
Klimova, B. 50–1
Korean
–fandoms 84–5, 89–90, 123–4
–FL learning in Asia 91–2
–as heritage language 105
–KFL (Korean as a foreign language) 58
–'language of solidarity' 104
–motivations for learning 91–2
–politeness 23
–popular culture 89–93
–after-school clubs 137
–surging interest in 16
–teaching as heritage languages 72
K-pop 16, 89–93, 145–6
Kramsch, C. 77
Kubanyiova, M. 85
K-wave 90–1

L2MSS (L2 motivational self system) 83–4, 86
Lambert, W. 81
Lambton-Howard, D. 88
Language Café 130
language disorders 121, 140
Language for Results programme 141
language hubs 36, 58
language learning abilities 56
language maintenance 104–5
'language of solidarity' 104
language policies 6, 40, 58, 75, 80, 132–6, 140, 154
language profiles 135
Languages Gateway 116
Lanza, E. 70
Lasagabaster, D. 138
Latin 36

Latukha, M. 55
learner-led/learner-owned social media spaces 88
Learning Together Model 137
Lenneberg, Eric 47
LEP (Latin Excellence Programme) 36
'less widely spoken' languages 32
Leung, C. 142–3
Li, X. 125
Liao, W. 105
Liégeois, F. 48
lifelong learning 143
'Limits of my Language' 65–6
LingoDeer 8
linguistic capital 53
linguistic development
 –early language learning 49
 –home, heritage and community language learning 72
linguistic diversity in the UK 5, 10, 57–9, 71
linguistic justice 7, 85
linguistic minorities 43
linguistic multi-competence 87
linguistic pluralism 136–7
linguistic repertoires
 –benefits of expanding 6
 –emotional language 66
 –and fluency 21
 –language as complex, amalgamated entity 22
 –nucleolects 151
 –personalised 152
 –translanguaging 22–4, 102
 –translanguaging classrooms 144–5
 –translanguaging spaces 129
 –vocabulary size 49
listening comprehension 97
literacy 44, 50, 73, 97
Liu, M. 95
Living Languages Report 36
LLMs (large language models) 2, 7, 113, 116, 151
Lo Bianco, J. 68, 86, 87, 132
London 5, 28, 31, 39, 41, 56
Long, R. 32
loss of heritage languages 5, 77
love 93–4
low socioeconomic status 16–18, 58
Lu, Z. 95

MacIntyre, P.D. 84, 148
Mandarin 11, 30–1, 36, 61 see also Chinese; MEP (Mandarin Excellence Programme)
mandatory language learning 34
Mandela, Nelson 46, 64
marginalisation 51–2, 62
Marini, A. 21
Mazzaferro, G. 129
McArthur, T. 66
McCarty, T.L. 21
mealtime talk 103
media 96
memory 48, 72, 119
Menacker, T. 68
mental health 51
mentalese 104
MEP (Mandarin Excellence Programme) 13, 31, 36, 37, 61
Mercer, S. 148
metalinguistic awareness 49–50, 72
metaverse 111, 120, 154
MFL (modern foreign languages) 6, 7, 9–12, 33, 66
MFL Hub 35
migration 20, 75
Millennials 45, 90
Mills, J. 70
minority community languages 67
MNCs (multinational corporations) 54, 56
mobile communities 130, 151
monolingual norms 6, 86
monolingual students 27, 28, 41, 138
Montanari, S. 70
Morgan, Nicky 136
'mother tongue' as term 69, 103
motivation theory 81–3
multiculturalism 6, 11, 25, 54
multilingual justice 42–3
multilingualism
 –Ango-Eurocentric ideology 70–1
 –benefits of 6

–critical reflections on 6
–defining multilingualism in UK education 20–2
–definitions of 20–2, 66
–family pro-multilingual ideologies 75–6
–levels of proficiency in various languages 21
–as national asset 5–6, 57–9
–for new arrivals 9
–as norm 20
–reciprocal, bi-directional learning 133
–rethinking post-Brexit 7
–in UK classrooms 130–2
–in the US 13
multiliteracy 50, 73
multimodality 88, 129
mutual acculturation 26, 27

Nakamura, J. 128
NALDIC 68
National Curriculum 34, 37, 38, 136
National Foreign Language Resource Centre 68
national languages 67
nationalism 67
native-like proficiency 21, 47, 66, 142
NCELP (National Centre for Excellence for Language Pedagogy) 35
neuroscience 47, 50, 101
neutral use of term 'languages' 67
new arrivals to the UK 9, 57–8, 134–6, 139, 141
New Zealand 68
non-verbal communication 62, 80, 91, 106
Norton, B. 87, 88, 123
nucleolects 151–2

Oakes, L. 86
Office for National Statistics 39
Ofqual 140
Ofsted 34, 35, 38
online resources 108, 114
Otheguy, R. 144–5
'othering' 76, 77

Ottó, I. 83
'ought-to' self 84
Oxford Companion to the English Language 66
Oxford English Dictionary 151

parents *see also* FLP (family language policies); intergenerational connections
–low prioritisation of heritage languages 17–18
–parent-child communication 103
–role in heritage language preservation 17
Park, J.S.-Y. 52
partial fluency, benefits of 14
passivity 105–6
Pavelescu, L.M. 93
pedagogical approaches 96, 139–55
Peltokorpi, V. 55
personal space 80
personalised learning 89, 94, 109–10, 121–3, 152
person-in-context relational model 84
Petrić, B. 93
Pew Research Centre 45
phonetic skills 72
Pikhart, M. 50–1
Pinker, Steven 22
plagiarism detection tools 110, 117
play, exclusion from 26
pleasure 50 *see also* FLE (foreign language enjoyment)
Polish 32, 69
politeness 23, 106
Portuguese 30, 32
positive psychology 148
post-colonialism 70
power relations 87, 123
pragmatics 7, 23, 49, 71, 106
prejudices 62–3, 67, 75, 76, 77, 142, 154
Prensky, M. 111
prestige 67, 75, 154
pride in multilingualism 75, 76, 77
primary schools 74, 102–3, 133–5, 137, 140 *see also* Key Stage 1; Key Stage 2

private schools 35, 74
process-orientated model of motivation 83
proficiency
 —assessment 120
 —concerns over damaging English by teaching heritage languages 28–9
 —FLA (foreign language anxiety) 97
 —and fluency 12
 —goals other than fluency 56–7, 66, 71
 —myth that learning heritage languages harms English learning 70
 —related to employment advantages 55, 60
 —trade/commerce 61
 —translanguaging 22
psycholinguistics 36
psychology
 —benefits of early second language learning 48–9
 —job market competitiveness 55
 —of language learning 81–107
Punjabi 32

Quay, S. 70, 128

raciolinguistics 75
radicalisation 62, 63
Rancière, Jacques 143
reciprocal, bi-directional learning 133
Reddit 91
refugee children 25–7, 52, 141
Refugee Education UK 141
religion/faith based motivations 86
research banks 58
resilience 73, 74, 95, 100
resources *see also* linguistic repertoires
 —AI 18–19
 —English learning materials in China 53
 —low socioeconomic environments 17
 —online resources 108, 114
 —semiotic resources 22, 102, 127, 142, 144–5
respect 106
returns on investment in language education 61–2
reward system in brain 50

risk-taking and exploration 99–100
Risley, Todd R. 101
Roblox 111, 154
Romanian 32
RR Donnelly 134
Rubino, A. 79
rubrics 110, 113, 116

Sabzalieva, E. 113
safe talk, safe space 103
Scarino, A. 142–3
Scotland
 —1+2 language policy 133–6
 —Chinese 31
 —Highers 10, 31
secondary schools 74, 102–3, 140 *see also* Key Stage 4
self-esteem 50, 73, 149
self-study 108
semiotic resources 22, 102, 127, 142, 144–5
separation between distinct 'languages' 22, 67
SES (socioeconomic status)
 —AI 125
 —inequality 45
 —language learning in low SES 16–17
 —motivations to learn languages 42
 —uptake of MFL 35, 58
 —word gap 101
SHAPE Indicators 10
sign languages 68
silence 106
Singapore 68, 80
Skutnabb-Kangas, T. 21
soboksobok 92
social capital 55, 87
social inclusion 26
social media 78, 88–90, 92, 130
social mobility 75
sociocultural contexts 75
socio-educational models 82
sociolinguistics 42, 142
solidarity 72, 73, 94, 103–5
South Africa 46, 68, 69
South Korea 52–3, 119
Spanish
 —common goal of learning 56
 —GCSEs 30, 56

–Key Stage 3 74
–A-levels 56, 74
–primary schools 134
–returns on investment in language education 61–2
–in schools 9, 10, 11–12
–in UK 32
–universities 30
speaking/oral production 97, 115
spelling 111
Spolsky, B. 54, 75
Squid Game 92
St Augustine's High School, Edinburgh 135
St Columbia's Primary School, Fife 135–6
St John Vianney Primary School 136
St Joseph's Institution International 68–9
St Mary's School, Leeds 27
'standard' languages 144
stereotypes 62–3, 67, 75 *see also* prejudices
stigma 17, 41, 68, 70, 75
superdigital worlds 71, 88
superdiversity 71, 86
Suskind, D. 101
Szubko-Sitarek, W. 21

Taiwan 96–7
TAM (Technology Acceptance Model) 117–18
TBLL (task-based language learning) 36–7, 58
teachers
 –AI 112, 113–14, 115–17
 –CPD (continuous professional development) 35
 –FLE (foreign language enjoyment) 100
 –ITT (initial teacher training) 141
 –learner-teacher relationship 93
 –limitations of human 114–15
 –role in recognising FLA 97
 –support for 141
 –teacher shortages 43, 114–15
terms of address 105
textbooks 53, 119

Thirty Million Words 101
Thompson, A.S. 85–6
time available to parents for language education 17
time required to achieve proficiency 12–13
Tinsley, T. 32, 34, 35
TOEFL (Test of English as a Foreign Language) 120
Together Learning paradigm 143
tolerance, promotion of 63
trade/commerce 11, 59, 60
transcultural competence 142–3
transculturation 78
translanguaging
 –AI 150
 –for bridge-building 101–2
 –building a culture of 153–5
 –cross-border classrooms 150
 –in current classroom practice 130–2
 –in the definition of multilingualism 21–2
 –in everyday talk 127–8
 –at home 127–8, 129
 –intergenerational connections 80
 –is not 'broken' language 102, 144
 –pedagogy 102, 139–55
 –pragmatics 71
 –in schools 102–3
 –translanguaging competence 22–4, 154
 –translanguaging spaces 103, 129, 144–5, 150
 –translingual competence 142–3
translation 7, 24, 148–9
transnational migration flows 20
travel to home countries 77
Tune In, Talk More and Take Turns 101
Turkish 69
tutor bots 115
Twitter (X) 90, 91
two-track systems 44–5

UCL IOE (University College London Institute of Education) 36, 140
UK language learning trends 29, 74
Ukrainian 94
UNESCO 69, 145

UNICEF 145
United Nations' Declaration on the Rights of Persons Belonging to National or Ethnic, Religious, and Linguistic Minorities 43
universities
  –Asian languages 66
  –falling enrollments in modern languages 6
  –MFL departments 66
  –modern language course enrollments 6, 29, 34
  –trend towards dual-subject courses 31
untranslatability 66, 150
Urdu 10, 32, 69, 71–2, 105–6
US
  –Asian languages 34
  –'community language' as term 68
  –language proficiency 12–13
Ushioda, E. 84, 85, 86

Valentini, A, 113
Vásquez, C. 85–6
ventral striatum 50
Vertovec, S. 86

virtual learning 7, 111, 123
vocabulary size 49

Wales 39
Wang, Y. 58
weekend schools 104, 137
Wei, L. 22, 48, 67, 79, 101, 103, 105, 129
well-being 50–1
Welsh 32, 39, 127
Wenger, E. 88
Western European language bias 6, 7, 14–18, 33, 69–70, 142, 143
Weverse 92
Williams, C. 127
Wittgenstein, Ludwig 65–6
WoLLoW (World of Languages and Languages of the World) syllabus 124
word gap 101
Wu, G.-C. 96, 97

X (Twitter) 90, 91
Xiong, T. 53

YouGov 11
YouTube 93
Yuan, Z.-M. 53

For Product Safety Concerns and Information please contact our EU Authorised Representative:

Easy Access System Europe

Mustamäe tee 50

10621 Tallinn

Estonia

gpsr.requests@easproject.com

www.ingramcontent.com/pod-product-compliance
Lightning Source LLC
Chambersburg PA
CBHW071421160426
43195CB00013B/1769